CONSTRUCTING INTERNATIONAL RELATIONS IN THE ARAB WORLD

FRED H. LAWSON

Constructing International Relations in the Arab World

STANFORD UNIVERSITY PRESS
STANFORD, CALIFORNIA 2006

Stanford University Press
Stanford, California

Printed in the United States of America on acid-free, archival-quality paper

Library of Congress Cataloging-in-Publication Data
Lawson, Fred Haley, 1952–
Constructing international relations in the Arab world / Fred H. Lawson.
p. cm.
Includes bibliographical references and index.
ISBN 0-8047-5372-5 (cloth : alk. paper)
1. Arab countries — Politics and government — 20th century. 2. Arab countries — Foreign relations — 20th century. I. Title.
DS62.8.L39 2006
327.0917'4927 — dc22 2006008305

Typeset by BookMatters in 10/14 Janson

Original Printing 2006

Last figure below indicates year of this printing:
15 14 13 12 11 10 09 08 07 06

To Professor Iliya F. Harik
teacher, mentor, colleague

Contents

Preface

All too often the Arab world is written off as a region where the normal rules do not apply. This attitude produces one of two equally deleterious consequences for academic inquiry. The most common result is that students of political science simply ignore events, trends, and developments in the Arab countries. Theoretical debates in international relations and comparative politics go on without taking into account any empirical evidence drawn from the Arab world. Textbooks include no cases from this part of the globe, either by original design or, as in two cases with which I am familiar, after deciding in the end not to include a chapter on a pivotal Arab case that had been explicitly commissioned for the collection. One of the reasons that Stephen Walt's pathbreaking study of the dynamics of international alliance formation caused such a sensation, it seems to me, was that it treated inter-Arab diplomacy as an ordinary regional system. It is disappointing, albeit it par for the course, that Walt's book remains unique in this respect.

More rarely, the Arab world is incorporated into mainstream debates or textbooks, but is presented as the antithesis of whatever outcome or pattern is under investigation. Because so much current work in political science concerns liberal democracy (why it appears, what institutional forms it takes, what impact it has on international disputes, and so on), this state of affairs might be understandable. But to paraphrase a Brian Barry remark about the prisoner's dilemma, there is more to social science than liberal democracy. Once a wider range of research topics comes back into fashion in academia, we can only trust that scholars will at last give up the presumption that there is little to learn from Arab experience.

One great benefit of having spent the last two decades working at a small college, pretty much by myself, is that I have been inoculated against (or able to avoid contracting) whatever bug it is that blocks the cross-fertilization of political science and Arab studies. It is particularly gratifying to find that the immunity can be passed on to successor generations. When they sit down and think about it, undergraduates find it possible to apply concepts from the broader fields of international relations and comparative politics to Arab cases. And they turn out to be equally adept at explaining things that happen in the Arab world in terms of concepts they wrestle with in their other classes. It is this spirit of intellectual inventiveness and curiosity, unblinkered by conventional prejudices, that gives me hope for the future.

When I have at last stuck my head out into the wider world, I have been most fortunate to discover colleagues willing to offer stimulation and encouragement. Laurie Brand first pointed out that a set of overlapping conference papers contained the seeds of a book. It is thanks to a suggestion from her that this material has taken the shape of a unified monograph. When my enthusiasm for the project was flagging, Edward Ingram revived my spirits—as he has done on two other occasions over the course of my career—by accepting much of the material on Syria as an article that appeared in the September 2000 issue of *The International History Review*. I appreciate not only his initial support but also his permission to reprint large parts of that article here. Stephen Krasner let me borrow a batch of unpublished essays that played a key role in focusing my thoughts concerning the elusive topic of sovereignty. It was also his advice that I aim high in looking for a publisher. I am delighted that it is his own university's press that took the bait.

William Ochsenwald convinced me that a comparative study of Westphalian sovereignty in the Arab world required a North African case; Julia Clancy-Smith persuaded me that the case should be Tunisia. Paul Lalor, Edmund Burke III, Laurence Michalak, and Amy Aisen made it possible for me to obtain access to scarce publications on Tunisian history. John Taylor of the U.S. National Archives first introduced me to the wonders of Record Group 226, when the modern military records section was still located in a cramped upstairs office in the old building on Pennsylvania Avenue. A succession of quick trips to the new facility in College Park could only have been productive thanks to the efficiency and good humor that he and his coworkers have shown me over many years.

Roger Haydon, James Gelvin, and an anonymous reader for Stanford University Press made exceptionally constructive comments on the draft manuscript. I might well have spent another five years trying to deal with all the points raised by these early critics, except that Kate Wahl pushed me to meet a quick deadline. For this I am exceedingly grateful.

This whole project originated in a paper prepared for a December 1998 conference that marked the reopening of the Center for Arab and Middle East Studies at the American University of Beirut. Over lunch in the AUB faculty dining room, I learned that my invitation to participate in that remarkable event had come at the recommendation of my undergraduate teacher at Indiana University. It is out of deep appreciation that I dedicate this book to him, with the hope that it approaches the high standard that he always expected of his students and consistently exemplifies in his own scholarship.

CONSTRUCTING INTERNATIONAL RELATIONS IN THE ARAB WORLD

INTRODUCTION

Origins of States-systems

Three broad dynamics generated the states-system that took shape in the Middle East during the first half of the twentieth century: (1) the end of the imperial institutions of governance that had structured regional politics over the previous 600 years; (2) the rise of local nationalist movements in Cairo, Tunis, Baghdad, Damascus, and other major urban centers; and (3) the appearance of narrowly self-interested, territorially bounded, mutually antagonistic states. Existing scholarship most often conflates these three dynamics. Thus Alan Taylor observes that "after World War I all of the post-Ottoman societies of the Middle East and North Africa were confronted with the enormous task of reconstructing themselves as successor nation-states. The nation-building process required the termination of foreign controls, the conceptualization of national identities, and the establishment of modern national institutions capable of maintaining the internal and external viability of the new sovereign entities."[1] Similarly, Michael Barnett asserts that "World War I, the Arab revolt against the Ottoman Empire, the death of the Ottoman Empire, and the perception that the region was being assailed by European imperialism through the mandate system and by Jewish immigration to Palestine caused the region's inhabitants to reconsider their political identity and what sorts of political arrangements would be most meaningful and desirable."[2] Such formulations fail to recognize that the end of empire, the rise of nationalism, and the emergence of sovereign states represent separate trends that must be kept analytically distinct, because they are generated by quite different factors and processes.

Moreover, imperial collapse, the growth of nationalism, and the development of external sovereignty exhibit disparate historical trajectories. In fact, it is precisely the lack of congruence between the rise of local nationalist movements and the emergence of self-interested, territorially bounded states that has convinced many scholars that nationalism and sovereignty are inherently incompatible in the Arab world, and that the underlying tension between these two principles generates an inordinate amount of conflict in regional affairs.[3] Intellectual and social historians have identified several distinct incarnations of Arab nationalist thought, beginning as early as the 1840s. Elements of external sovereignty can be discerned even earlier, and became more pronounced during the first third of the nineteenth century when provincial rulers like Muhammad 'Ali in Cairo, Da'ud Pasha in Baghdad, and Ahmad Bey in Tunis carried out extensive state-building projects—even as they continued to recognize the suzerainty of the Ottoman sultan. It is therefore imperative to resist the temptation to conflate these three distinct processes into a single analytical account, despite the fact that they tend to reinforce one another as time goes by.

End of Empire

There can be no question that the dismantling of the Ottoman Empire contributed profoundly to the formation of the contemporary Middle Eastern states-system. Relations among the largely autonomous governors-general (*walis*) of Cairo, Tunis, Baghdad, and Damascus exhibited varying degrees of rivalry and collaboration throughout the nineteenth century.[4] But so long as local rulers remained subject to the higher authority—however loose—of the sultan in Istanbul, such interactions constituted a states-system only in a metaphorical sense. In the first place, widely shared principles and practices of Ottoman statecraft constituted an underlying institutional and discursive order that effectively limited the degree of uncertainty among actors, and thereby precluded the emergence of a fundamentally anarchic regional arena.[5] Second, successive provincial governors almost never put down roots in the territories under their command. On the contrary, walis who managed to acquire power and prestige by serving in one provincial capital regularly moved on to other, more august posts elsewhere. Third, local rulers were seldom if ever accorded formal diplomatic recognition by the great powers of Europe, whose governments tended instead to take steps to suppress strategic initiatives undertaken by ambitious walis in the name of preserving the diplomatic status and territorial integrity of the empire.[6]

So it was only after the Ottoman order disintegrated that it became possible for an anarchic international arena to take shape in the sultan's former domains. Existing scholarship connects the dissolution of empires to the emergence of states-systems in a number of different ways. Perhaps the most influential line of argument explains the rise of anarchic international orders in terms of the costs and benefits associated with any attempt to revive imperial structures of governance. Hendrik Spruyt, for instance, asserts that regional arenas made up of self-interested, mutually antagonistic states are likely to take shape whenever the former imperial core lacks the capacity to reassert its control over the former periphery.[7] David Lake adds that anarchic states-systems can be expected to arise from the ashes of empire whenever (1) the gains that might be derived from economies of scale are insufficient to justify efforts by the former core to reconstitute the empire, (2) opportunity costs make it too expensive for the states that emerge in the former periphery to abandon their newfound autonomy, and (3) the "governance costs" associated with imposing central control over a resurrected imperial system prove to be exorbitant.[8] By contrast, Alexander Motyl finds no compelling reason to assume that the high cost of restoring the empire will necessarily generate an anarchic regional order. Four ubiquitous factors can even improve the chances that some new form of imperial governance will arise even after the old empire has collapsed: a comparatively strong state in the former imperial core, an extensive set of residual ties between the former core and the newly autonomous periphery, a distribution of material resources that favors the former core in its dealings with the periphery, and shared borders between the former core and the new peripheral polities.[9]

A widely accepted alternative explanation for the emergence of anarchic states-systems out of collapsed imperial orders emphasizes the legacy of antagonism and mistrust that permeates relations between the former center and the former provinces in the postimperial era. On this view, leaders and populations in the newly autonomous polities that had previously been subordinate to the empire share a strong predisposition to see their former overlords as untrustworthy, if not actually threatening, long after the empire comes to an end. In the case of the Soviet Union, for example, deep-seated misgivings about the possibility of resurgent imperialism on the part of the Russian Federation lingered in Ukraine, Georgia, and Uzbekistan, despite the willingness of the new leadership in Moscow to establish the headquarters of the Commonwealth of Independent States in Minsk, the capital of Belarus, rather than in the Russian capital.[10] Such attitudes tend to be reinforced whenever different regions of the old empire are characterized by administrative and economic inequalities, which heighten the level of animosity not only between the former core and successor states in the periphery but also among the successor states themselves.[11] Furthermore, new states in the former periphery often construct widely divergent combinations of ethnic and civic components of nationhood. The tensions and resentments associated with such constitutional divergences contribute significantly to the consolidation of postimperial systems that consist of narrowly self-interested, mutually antagonistic states.

Two significant difficulties — one conceptual and the other empirical — confront anyone who tries to use the extensive literature on the end of empire to explain the emergence of the contemporary Middle Eastern states-system. On the conceptual side, one would have to come up with a way to demonstrate that the most dynamic of the Ottoman Empire's many successor states — the Turkish Republic led by Mustafa Kemal (Ataturk) — necessarily lacked the capacity or willingness to restore an imperial structure of governance, without falling into the trap of pointing to the appearance of a regional order made up of self-interested, mutually antagonistic states as proof that the costs of doing so were too great. As Charles Tilly remarks, "in the absence of well-established a priori measures for transaction costs and returns from empire, a cost-benefit formulation introduces into any explanation the usual circularity of such reasoning."[12]

On the empirical side, the disintegration of the Ottoman Empire prompted heightened, and more direct, intervention in the Middle East by the great powers of Europe, culminating in the establishment of novel forms of imperial governance under the auspices of the League of Nations.[13]

Nevertheless, nationalist leaderships in Cairo, Tunis, 'Amman, Baghdad, Damascus, and elsewhere in the Arab world gradually adopted postures of rivalry and antagonism in their dealings with one another, and did so in ways that did not necessarily coincide with the line that separated French-dominated from British-dominated mandatory states. The dissolution of the Ottoman Empire therefore provided the opportunity for an anarchic states-system to take shape in the Middle East, but did not directly produce this distinctive kind of regional order.

Rise of Local Nationalisms

Scholarship on the birth and evolution of nationalism in the Arab world is voluminous and shows no sign of diminishing, either in quantity or in theoretical sophistication. Conventional studies concentrate on the social background and political activities of discontented elites and secret societies in the Arab provinces of the Ottoman Empire during the late nineteenth and early twentieth centuries.[14] Revisionist writing highlights the intense conflicts that erupted immediately after the First World War between liberal leaderships and an assortment of popular movements whose adherents championed more radical conceptions of the nation.[15] Other innovative work explores reciprocal interactions between the growth of Arab and Turkish nationalisms on one hand and the transformation of Ottoman political institutions on the other during the final decades of the imperial era.[16]

How the coming of nationalism interacts with the emergence and consolidation of anarchic states-systems remains an undertheorized and rarely explored area of inquiry in the literature on international relations.[17] Even writings that might be expected to shed light on the topic generally fail to do so. In *Nationalism and the International System*, for example, F. H. Hinsley traces the origins of the modern international order not to the appearance of nations but rather to the appearance of new kinds of disputes among the dynastic states of eighteenth-century Europe.[18] James Mayall asserts that even during the age of nationalism, "the world of power politics remains intact; indeed arguably the major impact of nationalism has been to reinforce the tradition of hard-line realism, and to weaken the version in which the ineradicable egotism of the separate state was at least softened by a residual solidarity amongst states."[19] Similarly, Anthony Smith assumes that "the modern Western state, and the interstate system which it spawned, preceded the formation of the first European nations and, in fact, helped to create them." Consequently, the primary analytical issue "is to spell out some of the broader implications of demanding or possessing a national homeland within a pre-existing system of territorial states; and, in particular, to show how the drive for 'national congruence,' or co-existensiveness between state, nation and territory encompassed, has exacerbated interstate relations and threatens to destabilise them and remould them to a new pattern."[20] None of these influential texts poses the crucial question of how the coming of nationalism itself contributed to the construction or transformation of the European states-system.[21]

Nationalism's impact on the development of international relations has been addressed more explicitly, and in exhaustive detail, by Rodney Hall. For Hall, the rise of "national-sovereign" states in Europe during the course of the nineteenth century transformed the basic structure of world politics, primarily by revising the notions of strategic interest that propelled state policy and secondarily by altering the dominant forms of diplomatic, military, and legal practice. Thus "the structure of state interests of the [national-sovereign] Second Empire of Napoleon III, and that of Bismarck's [territorial-sovereign] Prussia emerge as distinctly different conceptions, derived from distinctly different notions of the nature of sovereign identity."[22] Innovative conceptions of strategic interest were particularly salient during the "new imperialism" of the 1870s and 1880s.[23]

With regard to the character of interstate interaction, the coming of nationalism turned out to be profoundly destabilizing. "The emergence of French national-sovereignty," Hall claims, "altered the rules of international engagement in asserting that the popular will overturned territorial[-]sovereign legal rights, treaties, and juridical bases for international claims. This increased uncertainties, elevated disputes over interests into disputes over principles, and enhanced the potential for international conflict."[24] As nation-states became more prevalent throughout Europe, the level of animosity and rivalry on the continent jumped: "Extraterritorial expressions of allegiance to a people with shared language, culture, or history — or simply a shared vision of social and political organization — became potential bases for the advancement of irridentist [sic] territorial claims, or conflictual secessionist movements." In addition, "territorial-sovereign legal claims were delegitimated and peaceful resolution of disputes became more difficult in the absence of consensual knowledge regarding systemic legitimating principles."[25] In short, the consolidation of discrete national communities heightened the level of mistrust and antagonism that characterized relations among the territorial-sovereign states of Europe, exacerbating the problems and dangers inherent in the anarchic regional order. This trend reached a peak in the unprecedented degree of international belligerence that accompanied the outbreak of the First World War.[26]

Daniele Conversi spells out the link between the rise of nationalism and the emergence of self-interested, mutually antagonistic states much more concisely. The construction of any national community, he argues, "is both a process of border maintenance and creation."[27] Like all other kinds of social identity, nationalism grows out of the "intense interaction between groups."[28] More specifically, "opposition is . . . the crucible of ethnic and national identity. According to [Vittorio] Lanternari, 'there is always a contradiction in the definition of a group, because it is a group (that is, it has a group identity) only in relation to other groups.'"[29] This implies that in the process of constructing a national identity, subtle differences between the prospective nation and outsiders tend to get exaggerated, while even the most glaring distinctions among members of the prospective national community are almost always minimized or ignored. As a result, innovative boundaries form that separate the nation from surrounding peoples, and these borders are no less concrete for being the product of political imagination and social mobilization.

Boundaries with the outside world become particularly sensitive and prone to conflict, Conversi contends, whenever the prospective nation is so heterogeneous that nationalizing elites find themselves unable to "touch some chord [that will allow] their message [to] reverberate amongst the people." In other words, "if the [national] group to be mobilized is too fragmented and assimilated to retain some shared hyphen, social categorization can always be enforced by stimulating borders and opposition, rather than contents and uniqueness."[30] Resorting to violence against neighboring groups represents the last resort of nationalist leaders who can come up with no other effective bonds that might unify and demarcate their own constituents. Nevertheless, Conversi is careful to distinguish the usual means whereby elites mobilize national communities from such exceptional tactics as provoking outright confrontation or deliberately antagonizing others. Such extreme measures only come into play in those rare instances "when the [underlying] ethnic culture is weak and ill-defined [and] the whole group is to be opposed to the out-group."[31]

More ambitiously, Henry Nau sets out to explain why some states-systems exhibit high levels of danger and conflict, whereas others evidence a substantial degree of peace and orderliness. Nau proposes that any given region can be categorized according to (1) the extent to which it consists of countries that generally converge with one another with regard to (a) their domestic political cultures and ideologies ("internal identity") and (b) the values and norms that govern their mutual interactions ("external identity"); and (2) whether it is made up of states that are equal or unequal in power. Nau hypothesizes that whenever a states-system consists of countries that are similar in identity and unequal in power, weaker states will accept the dominance of stronger ones, generating a hierarchical international order.[32] If the system is made up of countries that are different in identity and unequal in power, the strong will impose order on the weak, producing a hegemonic or imperial order. States-systems consisting of polities that are characterized by similar identities and equal power tend to evolve into security communities.[33] By contrast, systems made up of countries with divergent identities and equal power tend to become competitive and conflictful, that is, exhibit the features associated with an anarchic arena.

These diverse perspectives illustrate the importance of analyzing the connection between nationalism and anarchic international orders. Nevertheless, any attempt to explain the emergence of the contemporary Middle Eastern states-system in terms of the rise of nationalist movements confronts three major obstacles. First, the Arab world harbored two very different conceptions of nationalism during the course of the twentieth century. On one hand, a great deal of intellectual debate, cultural creativity, and political action has been predicated on the idea of the Arab nation as a comprehensive entity made up of all native speakers of the Arabic language, a trait that serves as a marker for people who claim descent from the original tribes of the Arabian peninsula. This notion can be traced to the writings of the late nineteenth-century scholar 'Abd al-Rahman al-Kawakibi, and it informed the thinking and activism of such later luminaries as Najib 'Azuri, 'Abd al-Ghani al-'Uraisi, Farah Antun, and Sati' al-Husri.[34] Because it emphasizes the common features of Arabs as a race or kin group (*qawm*), this form of nationalism is most often designated by the term *qawmiyyah*.[35] It dominated Arab political discourse in the early 1900s and returned to prominence in the early 1950s, but provided a touchstone for elites and the general public alike throughout the twentieth century. The ideals inherent in the notion of qawmiyyah provided the impetus for the League of Arab States, the regional organization set up in March 1945 to promote Arab unity in the face of persistent European interference and growing Zionist militancy in Palestine.[36]

On the other hand, much political thought and practice in the contemporary Arab world has been rooted in the very different idea that the inhabitants of each particular country or homeland (*watan*) share a basic national identity, which may or may not be congruent with that of any other Arab country. This essentially territorial concept of the nation, usually referred to as *wataniyyah*, has been a pervasive feature of regional affairs since at least the middle of the nineteenth century.[37] The rise of wataniyyah appears on its face to be much easier to connect to the emergence of a regional order made up of self-interested, territorially bounded states than would the dynamics associated with qawmiyyah. The trick is to link wataniyyah to the anarchic Middle Eastern states-system without constructing an argument that is either circular or teleological.

Second, one must be sure not to conflate qawmiyyah with the closely related notion of Pan-Arabism. Doing so makes it impossible to distinguish the political, economic, and cultural dynamics that determine collective identity formation from a loose package of strategic and diplomatic initiatives aimed at promoting closer diplomatic and strategic cooperation, and on rare occasions even political integration, among Arab states. A clear illustration of the problem can be found in the otherwise insightful surveys of the development of Egyptian nationalism that have been produced by Israel Gershoni and James Jankowski. In the first of these overviews, Gershoni asserts that Egyptian nationalism remained solidly rooted in a sense of the country's historical, cultural, and geographical distinctiveness during the first three decades of the twentieth century. Broader conceptions of the nation are assumed to be precursors of a Pan-Arab foreign policy program that began to coalesce in the mid-1930s. Gershoni claims, for instance, that "the first concrete signs of the supra-Egyptian concepts of identity can already be found even in the nationalist teachings of Mustafa Kamil and his successors in the 'National Party' (al-hizb al-watani)."[38] These seeds germinated in the wake of the 1936 Anglo-Egyptian Treaty, when the new ruler, King Faruq, "fostered — openly and secretly — Pan-Islamic and Pan-Arab trends; he saw Egypt as the chosen leader of all Muslims and all Arabs; and he drew to his court politicians who supported these ideas."[39] In addition, "the Pan-Arab and Pan-Islamic activities of the Egyptian King and the group of politicians close to the Royal Palace were dependent to some extent on the support of extra-parliamentary organizations led by the Pan-Islam-oriented 'Young Men's Muslim Association' (jam'iyyat al-shubban al-muslimin), and the 'Muslim Brothers' (al-ikhwan al-muslimun), on the one hand, and the radical nationalist 'Pan-Egyptian,' semi-fascist 'Young Egypt Party' (hizb misr al-fatah), on the other."[40] It was this heterogeneous collection of actors that pushed the country into playing a more active role in inter-Arab affairs during the 1940s.

Gershoni and Jankowski proffer a more nuanced version of this same story in their collaborative work. They point out in *Egypt, Islam and the Arabs: The Search for Egyptian Nationhood, 1900–1930* that a multifaceted national movement existed inside the country at the beginning of the twentieth century, but claim that "of the three nationalist orientations—Ottoman-Islamic, local Egyptian, or Arab—that vied for the allegiance of Egyptians in the 'liberal age,' the third was by far the weakest in the period prior to World War I."[41] Events during and immediately after the war catapulted the local, "territorial" orientation into the forefront of the nationalist movement, enabling its proponents to set the parameters that dictated the narrowly self-interested character of Egypt's relations with the outside world during the 1920s. Then, in *Redefining the Egyptian Nation 1930–1945*, Gershoni and Jankowski argue that "it was the conjunction of the disillusionment and alienation of the 1930s, the emergence of a new generation different in both social composition and intellectual perspective from its predecessor, and the increasing integration of Egypt with the surrounding Arab world which together laid the foundations for supra-Egyptian nationalism" in the years leading up to the Second World War .[42] The new orientation had several components—including a fascination with the East; the rise of an "Egyptian Islamic nationalism [which] was an attempt to build a religiously based alternative to supplant the territorial nationalism which had gained ascendancy in Egypt in the 1920s";[43] and, most important, a distinctive conception of Arab nationalism that envisaged the political and economic unity of the Arab world. The last of these currents eventually prevailed, thanks largely to the fact that "only Egyptian Arab nationalism gave tangible expression to the sense of Egyptian hegemony and mission found in all forms of supra-Egyptianism."[44] What is most problematic about this account is not its conceptual and methodological shortcomings,[45] but rather its consistent conflation of qawmiyyah and Pan-Arabism. Equating these two notions leads Gershoni and Jankowski not only to ignore broader conceptions of the Arab nation that lay at the heart of Egyptian politics in the period before the First World War, but also to confuse the government's subsequent efforts to promote greater cooperation among Arab states with a long-abandoned vision of an integrated regional order completely devoid of self-interested, territorially bounded polities.

Third, although it is easy to assert that qawmiyyah and wataniyyah are inherently contradictory, and have therefore generated deep-seated conflicts across the Arab world, it is considerably more difficult to spell out just how one or the other (or a specific combination of the two) has shaped the particular pattern of state interaction that one finds at any given moment. Several prominent scholars have claimed that foreign policies driven by qawmiyyah tended to predominate during the 1950s and 1960s, only to be superseded by a wataniyyah-based states-system in the 1970s.[46] But this view obscures pivotal episodes in which purportedly qawmiyyah-oriented leaderships engaged in distinctly self-interested actions throughout the era of Arab nationalism,[47] while at the same time ignoring the continued influence of qawmiyyah after 1980.[48] Presenting such incongruities as "a series of dialogues concerning the relationship between identity, norms and regional order" merely sidesteps the most important analytical issues.[49] More insightful are the few studies that chart recurrent alternations between qawmiyyah and wataniyyah on the part of particular Arab states, although they end up advancing fundamentally contradictory explanations for why such shifts have occurred.[50]

Emergence of Westphalian Sovereignty

Until the Second World War, nationalist leaderships in most parts of the Arab world acted on the basis of a presumption that the existing state institutions were inherently illegitimate. This posture reflected the fact that, with very few exceptions, governmental apparatuses in the region had been created or transformed in such a way as to advance the interests and ideologies of the European powers that seized control of the region during the nineteenth century.[51] Consequently, as a primary component of the escalating struggle for independence, Arab nationalists tended throughout the 1920s and 1930s to call for the replacement of local states with new kinds of governance structures that would transcend the "artificial" administrative boundaries that outside powers had imposed on the region.[52]

By the late 1940s, however, nationalist leaders in most Arab countries had begun to act in accordance with the defining principles of what Stephen Krasner calls "Westphalian sovereignty": They came to recognize the territorial boundaries of one another's domains, and to reject as inherently illegitimate any attempt by surrounding leaderships to interfere in the internal affairs of their respective polities. As Krasner points out, "Westphalian sovereignty is violated when external actors influence or determine domestic authority structures."[53] Furthermore, the leadership of each Arab country started to restrain itself with regard to how much territory it claimed the right to govern. In other words, nationalist leaders consciously and deliberately restricted their political ambitions to specific geographical zones, and stopped trying, or even claiming, to exercise authority over the Arab world as a whole. At the same time, and largely as a result of adopting a less expansive conception of national interest, they assumed a posture of intrinsic rivalry toward one another. Taken together, by the early 1950s these dynamics led to the consolidation of an anarchic regional order, that is, an international arena composed of narrowly self-interested, territorially bounded, mutually antagonistic states.[54] Adversarial relations between Egypt and Iraq, for instance, congealed into a protracted cold war for leadership of the Arab world, which became more pronounced in the months leading up to the conclusion of the Baghdad Pact in 1955.[55] Less powerful states acted no differently. Saudi Arabia, for instance, clashed repeatedly the Trucial States, Oman, and Yemen over a variety of territorial and dynastic issues during the course of the decade.[56]

Nonetheless, Arab leaders adopted postures congruent with Westphalian sovereignty at different times and by divergent routes. It is thus misleading to portray the appearance of the anarchic Middle Eastern states-system as a singular transition or uniform process.[57] Whereas countries as diverse as Egypt, Tunisia, and Saudi Arabia took on key attributes of Westphalian sovereignty comparatively early, others—most notably Jordan and Iraq—did not do so until much later. This implies that no one date marks the emergence of a regional order made up of self-interested, territorially bounded, mutually antagonistic polities—certainly not the formation of the League of

Arab States in 1945. Nationalist leaderships acted according to the dictates of the narrowly conceived, short-run interests of their respective countries prior to the birth of this regional organization, and they continued to pursue such interests even as they routinely affirmed their allegiance to the multilateralist principles most commonly associated with the Arab League.[58]

The emergence of Westphalian sovereignty therefore played a pivotal role in the construction of the contemporary Middle Eastern states-system. Yet it is not at all clear just what circumstances produce regional orders in which this peculiar form of interstate interaction prevails. Krasner's path-breaking analysis elaborates the various incongruities and contradictions that arise among four distinct types of sovereignty, without ever addressing the crucial question of why any particular one of them takes shape in the first place. With regard to Westphalian sovereignty, Krasner observes that "the Westphalian model has never become highly institutionalized even though it has been long-lasting because none of the mechanisms for embedding [political institutions] that have been suggested by either sociological or actor-oriented theories is applicable. The Westphalian model is [therefore] not an equilibrium outcome."[59] He sidesteps the matter of causation just as deftly in later work: In the conclusion to a volume of case studies that surveys the conceptual and practical problems associated with sovereignty in the contemporary world, for instance, Krasner remarks simply that "prevailing rules [such as Westphalian sovereignty] make it easier to do some things and harder to do others. But they are not determinative. New rules can be invented. And new rules can work, especially if they are the product of an equilibrium outcome arrived at through voluntary decisions rather than coercion."[60]

Other contributions to the massive corpus of academic writing on the topic prove no more helpful on this score. In an extensive overview of the principles and practices associated with external sovereignty, Michael Fowler and Julie Bunck deal with the matter in a brief section that poses the pertinent question, only to dismiss it: "How, then, is sovereign status conferred? The answer is that the international community determines sovereign statehood through an untidy political process that scholars have occasionally noted but have rarely studied."[61] Friedrich Kratochwil sets out to analyze successive "shifts in the functions of boundaries" in world politics, as the first step toward formulating "a better understanding of the origins and evolution of the present territorial state system."[62] But the discussion quickly bogs down in a detailed excursus of various ways in which interstate boundaries have operated throughout history. Conceptual implications that might shed light on the origins of a regional order that consists of self-interested, mutually antagonistic states remain too abstract to guide empirical inquiry: "When contacts increase and political and economic interdependencies are recognized," Kratochwil hypothesizes, "a differentiation arises between inter-system and system-environment relations. Exchanges between systems (states[!]) are increasingly regulated by normative structures, even in cases of interstate violence. Thus, a 'negative community'—one not united by a common purpose or a vision of the good life, but only by common practices and the mutual recognition of rights—comes into existence."[63] The editors of a more recent collection of papers on the topic prove equally enigmatic: "The practice of granting or withholding sovereign recognition participates [sic] in the social construction of territories, populations, and authority claims. This point," Thomas Biersteker and Cynthia Weber assert, "is key to our understanding of the relationship between the components of state sovereignty and understandings of change."[64] Just one essay in the volume directly addresses the question of "why has the trend generally been toward wider acceptance of the sovereign territorial ideal, at least through the end of the nineteenth century," but the answer is framed in terms of the presumed efficiencies that can be achieved by organizing world politics in this fashion, which in turn "come about through a complex set of circumstances."[65]

An ingenious perspective on the origins of Westphalian sovereignty in western Europe is presented by Benno Teschke. In a nutshell, Teschke claims that "the Westphalian system was characterized by distinctly non-modern relations between dynastic and other pre-modern political communities that were rooted in pre-capitalist social property relations."[66] Thus interactions among the dynastic polities of the sixteenth and seventeenth centuries grew out of the peculiar forms of class struggle that structured the economies of the precapitalist era. Such interactions differed markedly from those that came to predominate beginning in the eighteenth century. What explains the change is the sudden appearance of a powerful capitalist economy on the British Isles. Once this unprecedented political-economic entity took shape, "British foreign policy was no longer conducted exclusively on the basis of dynastic interests as formulated in *Kabinettpolitik*, but increasingly on the basis of the 'national interest' as formulated by the propertied classes self-organized in Parliament."[67] Britain's newfound national interest no longer required the annexation of territory in Europe at the end of wars, although it did somehow encourage large-scale land acquisition in Asia. Consequently, "the new idea was to stop fighting once the weaker allied partner had recovered, rather than to eliminate the common enemy."[68] Inspired by Britain's remarkable success in war making, other European powers gradually adopted not only capitalist forms of property but balance-of-power statecraft as well. Yet they refused to abandon "the principle of multiple politically constituted territories that was a legacy of pre-capitalist territory-formation."[69] As a result, Westphalian sovereignty became the norm across the continent by the middle of the nineteenth century. Even though Teschke's argument ends up reading very much like a just-so story, it is nevertheless an exceedingly clever one.[70]

Perhaps the most incisive analysis of the origins of Westphalian sovereignty to date is that of Daniel Philpott, who meticulously traces the doctrinal and philosophical roots of legitimate external autonomy and mutual recognition among the states of early modern Europe. Philpott's argument is admirably straightforward: "Religious ideas . . . are at the root of modern international relations. The Reformation was not Westphalia's sole cause; long-term material trends contributed, too. But if ideas did not act alone, they were yet indispensable: no Reformation, no Westphalia."[71] "More precisely," he continues, "were it not for the Reformation, persistently medieval features of Europe — the substantive powers of the Holy Roman Empire and its emperor, the formidable temporal powers of the church, religious uniformity, truncations of the sovereign powers of secular rulers, Spain's control of the Netherlands — would not have disappeared when they did, to make way for the system of sovereign states."[72] Instead, those polities that experienced a profound societal crisis due to widespread popular acceptance of the religious doctrines championed by Martin Luther took up arms to promote or defend the principle of external sovereignty; the major Roman Catholic powers of the age did not.

Two major problems undermine the utility of Philpott's argument as an explanation for the emergence of Westphalian sovereignty in the Arab world. First, his analysis presumes that key components of the Westphalian order coalesced in more or less complete form in the mid-seventeenth century, that is, at the time of the famous treaties of Münster and Osnabrück. This is almost certainly a distortion of the historical record, because it compresses complex developments that worked themselves out over the course of more than two centuries into no more than a generation or two.[73] More to the point, the argument is hard to square with F. H. Hinsley's crucial observation that a states-system consisting of self-interested, territorially bounded states coalesced in Europe only at the conclusion of the Napoleonic wars.[74] Second, the centrality of the Protestant Reformation in Philpott's account makes it difficult to apply the theory to the Islamic world, where relations between spiritual and temporal authority have been much more subtle and fluid than they are in most branches of Christianity. In fact, prominent critics of Islam charge that the political, cultural, and even economic backwardness that countries with predominantly Muslim populations have experienced can be traced directly to the absence of an Islamic Reformation.[75] Without wishing to join this particular debate, which appears to the non-specialist to be riddled with distortions and exaggerations on all sides, it nonetheless seems clear that doctrines, beliefs, and practices that are bound up so tightly with one specific religion are likely to be extremely hard to transfer to others.

In short, we seem to be stalled at the threshold of the ambitious research program regarding external sovereignty that Janice Thomson envisaged a decade ago.[76] There continues to be a lack of consensus regarding which specific actors are capable of, or responsible for, generating the basic components of Westphalian sovereignty. Few if any compelling alternative explanations exist for why states-systems characterized by self-interested, territorially bounded polities take shape at some historical moments rather than others, or in some parts of the world but not elsewhere. And the scholarship that does explicitly address these questions focuses almost exclusively on ideas and beliefs, rather than investigating the material conditions that make it possible for potential norms to take root and flourish.[77]

Such conceptual issues animate the reexamination of the emergence of Westphalian sovereignty in the Middle East that is offered here. Chapter One surveys the divergent historical trajectories whereby five major Arab countries adopted postures congruent with this distinctive form of interstate interaction: Egypt and Tunisia, where the transition took place comparatively early; Jordan and Iraq, where it occurred quite late; and Syria, where the shift happened in between. Chapter Two explores an influential set of concepts that has been proposed by historical sociologists, to see whether or not these concepts can account for the divergent paths these five states took. Chapter Three assesses a promising alternative approach drawn from the field of international relations. Chapter Four then builds on earlier arguments to formulate a novel explanation, which links the coming of Westphalian sovereignty to the timing and character of political struggles inside each of the five countries. Explaining the variation that one observes in the turn to Westphalian sovereignty across the Arab world not only elucidates a basic source of rivalry and conflict in the contemporary Middle East but also underscores the pivotal role that domestic politics plays in constructing foundational international institutions.

CHAPTER ONE

Westphalian Sovereignty Comes to the Arab World

Westphalian sovereignty emerged in the contemporary Arab world in a gradual, yet discontinuous, fashion. Some nationalist leaderships championed the strategic interests of their respective countries immediately after the First World War, whereas others remained committed to the goal of establishing an amalgamated political entity into the early 1950s. In some cases, the shift to a foreign policy predicated on the existence of self-interested, territorially bounded states took place even before the country concerned gained formal independence, and well before it won effective autonomy from its imperial overlords. Other nationalist leaders continued to pursue strategic and diplomatic programs oriented toward setting up an integrated regional polity long after their countries became independent not only de jure but also de facto. Consequently, the turn to Westphalian sovereignty in the Middle East is connected only tangentially to the winning of national independence.

Egypt and Tunisia represent important cases in which the leadership of the local nationalist movement adopted crucial components of Westphalian sovereignty comparatively early on. Even before they had gained de jure independence from Britain and France, respectively, Egyptian and Tunisian nationalists started to carry out foreign policies that reflected the exclusive interests of their own individual countries. The leaderships of Jordan and Iraq, by contrast, persisted in advocating the formation of a unified Arab political entity long after these two countries had secured de facto independence from Britain. Syria falls between the two extremes: nationalist leaders in Damascus shifted from what might loosely be called a multilateralist posture to one predicated on narrow self-interest during the early 1940s. Before setting out to explain the variation that is evident in these five cases, it will be useful to survey the divergent paths by which these five leaderships came to adopt foreign policy orientations congruent with the tenets of Westphalian sovereignty.

Egypt's Early Turn

Nationalist leaders exerted little direct influence over Egypt's external affairs from 1882, when British troops seized control of the country, to the outbreak of the First World War. British advisers orchestrated the most important aspects of relations with surrounding states from behind the scenes, while the country's nominal ruler, the Khedive 'Abbas II, pursued the chimera of revivifying the Ottoman Empire by snatching for himself the venerable title of Successor to the Prophet (*khalifah*) from the sultan in Istanbul. To this end, 'Abbas covertly patronized the publication and distribution of a succession of tracts and periodicals that championed Egypt's role as political, cultural, and religious leader of the western half of the Muslim world.[1] This strategy complemented a succession of complex diplomatic intrigues, whereby the khedive jockeyed continuously with the Ottoman ruler, Sultan 'Abdulhamid II, to seize the initiative in dealing with the great powers of Europe.[2]

Egypt's most important nationalist organization during the first decade of the twentieth century, the National Party (al-Hizb al-Watani) led by Mustafa Kamil, espoused an intricate foreign policy that combined tactical cooperation with Britain's primary European rivals on one hand and strategic collaboration with the Ottoman Empire on the other.[3] The presumption that Egypt shared fundamental strategic interests with the world's preeminent

Islamic power led the party's newspaper *al-Liwa* to print a series of articles that castigated the ruler of Kuwait, Shaikh Mubarak Al Sabah, for engaging in diplomatic activities that contributed to the fragmentation of Ottoman Iraq. At the same time, the newspaper applauded the decision to build the Hijaz railway, a project that promised to enhance Ottoman control over the two holy cities of Mecca and al-Madinah.[4] In 1905, *al-Liwa* ran what one British official called "a series of violent Pan-Islamic articles," in response to concerted efforts by Russia and Austria-Hungary to force the Ottoman government to cede authority over the fiscal administration of Macedonia to the International Finance Commission.[5]

It would be too simplistic to say that al-Hizb al-Watani advocated the reintegration of Egypt into the Ottoman Empire. Closer to the mark is Dennis Walker's observation that the nationalist leadership harbored a pervasive "sense of international Muslim community [that], while awarding the central role to Turkey, instead envisaged a far wider association than the Ottoman political community that had once united Egypt and Turkey in one state."[6] In any case, the party's underlying vision is hard to reconcile with the principles of Westphalian sovereignty. Walker notes that "al-Hizb al-Watani's commitment to Egypt's political entity was not nationalism of the exclusive total Western type dividing humanity up into atomistic nation-state units with freedom to fluidly alter associations formed with other nation units as change of interest decrees. [Mustafa] Kamil's Egyptian nation could not gain the singleness of commitment exacted by the European nation because al-Hizb al-Watani's thought imposed a plurality of political communities, the pan-Islamic as well as the nation."[7] Party leaders in fact consistently argued against those who asserted that Arab interests conflicted with those of the empire as a whole, and on occasion branded as a traitor anyone who advocated Arab independence.[8]

Consequently, the nationalist leadership in Cairo found itself ill-prepared to deal with security challenges that emanated from Istanbul. One such episode occurred in January 1906, when the British Frontier Administration Officer for the Sinai peninsula, Jennings Bramly, received orders to set up a permanent border post at Umm Rashrash, adjacent to the port of al-'Aqaba.[9] The Ottoman military commander in the district quickly demanded that the new outpost be dismantled, and ordered his troops to occupy the nearby fishing village of Taba. Bramly pulled his small force out of Umm Rashrash, but returned a week later with reinforcements from Egypt. Hesitant to engage the entrenched Turkish garrison in combat, he ordered his troops to take up positions on an island facing Taba harbor. Over the next two months, British and Ottoman units sparred with one another, not only along the northern shores of the Gulf of ʿAqaba but also in the area around Rafah on the Mediterranean coast. Then, at the beginning of May, British officials threatened to undertake "stiff measures" against the Ottoman authorities unless they accepted a broad reconfiguration of Sinai boundaries that would accord Egypt control over both Taba in the east and Rafah in the west.[10] Unable to rally Britain's European rivals to the defense of the empire, the sultan backed down and recognized the revised border. What is most remarkable about this incident is the fact that the leaders of the National Party firmly opposed British policy, and openly expressed sympathy for the actions and interests of the Ottoman government. In the wake of the incident, the party once again enjoined its adherents to "strive to strengthen the relations of cordiality, the bonds and the integral connection between Egypt and the Sublime [Ottoman] State."[11]

Pro-Ottomanism continued to guide the nationalists' foreign policy after the death of Mustafa Kamil in 1908. The new leader of al-Hizb al-Watani, Muhammad Farid, advocated forging closer links to the empire following the coup d'etat that brought the Committee of Union and Progress (CUP) to power in Istanbul that July.[12] When, for instance, a group of Egyptian students based in London asked for his advice regarding whether one of their manifestos should call for the "total" independence of their home country, Farid urged them to omit the adjective in question, lest it alienate the CUP.[13] Leading figures of al-Hizb al-Watani lobbied the new regime in Istanbul to authorize Egypt to send delegates to the resurrected Ottoman parliament, and Farid journeyed to the Ottoman capital on two different occasions in 1909 to show his enthusiasm for the reinstatement of a constitutional order.[14] He publicly congratulated those Egyptian military officers who took up positions in the reorganized imperial armed forces and wrote a series of articles praising the administrative and cultural reforms the CUP introduced. Two years later, Farid published a scathing critique of what he called "the Arab unity movement," charging that it represented nothing more than a British plot to undermine the integrity of the Ottoman realm.[15]

On a more practical level, officials in Cairo imposed a comprehensive ban on imports from Austria-Hungary in the fall of 1908, after the CUP government in Istanbul announced that it intended to impose a boycott against

Austrian products.[16] A year later, Egyptian military personnel collaborated with Turkish officers in an unsuccessful plot to supplant French advisers in the armed forces of Morocco.[17] Shaikh ʿAli Yusif captured the general mood in nationalist circles in January 1911, when he wrote in *al-Muʿayyad* that "Pan-Islam is to the Muslim the only bond, the only social union, to which he should give all his heart and his soul and his brains before all other considerations or social bonds. Muslims have never been in such need of a pan-Islamic union as they are today, when they are without a recognized country or home but are scattered under different skies and flags, living in poverty and humiliation among immigrants who eat the Muslims' bread."[18] Influential figures in Cairo quickly rallied to the Ottoman cause during the 1911–12 war with Italy for control of Libya: Prime Minister Muhammad Saʿid denounced as traitors all those who argued that the conflict offered an opportunity for Egypt to assert its independence from the empire, while Prince ʿUmar Tusun led a public campaign to raise funds to finance the imperial war effort.[19] The popular committees that sprang up throughout the country collected large quantities of food and medical supplies for Ottoman units operating in Libya, and even helped volunteers to cross the western desert to take part in the fighting. Activists of al-Hizb al-Watani played a key role in coordinating these committees' activities.

June 1911 saw the appearance in Cairo of a secret society committed to liberating the whole of North Africa from European rule. Edmund Burke observes that "the initial reports did not name the group, but indications were that it included prominent Egyptian nationalist leaders and was supported by the khedive himself."[20] By the summer of 1912, this movement had evolved into a formal association, al-Ittihad al-Maghribi (Maghreb United), with close ties to a number of influential activists, including ʿAli Yusif and Ahmad Sharaʿi.[21] At the same time, al-Hizb al-Watani's leaders sharply criticized British plans to renovate the decaying fortifications that commanded the entrance to the port at Alexandria, on the grounds that the project would effectively sever Egypt's few remaining ties to Istanbul.[22] That fall, nationalist groups once again spearheaded a public campaign to collect provisions for Ottoman troops fighting in the Balkans.[23]

During the opening weeks of the First World War, senior government officials joined al-Hizb al-Watani nationalists in reaffirming their loyalty to the Ottoman Empire. The khedive, just before he was summarily deposed in December 1914, promulgated a decree that directed the Egyptian people to do everything in their power to further imperial interests.[24] Prominent members of the royal family continued to harbor pronounced pro-Ottoman sympathies even after the deposition, as did a large segment of public opinion.[25] On the day that Prince Husain Kamil succeeded 'Abbas as ruler and assumed the new title of sultan, "in the Cairo Mosques the prayer for the Moslem Khalifa [i.e., the Ottoman head of state] was repeated three times in succession and each time response was general and loud, whereas that to the prayers for the Sultan of Egypt was feeble or inaudible."[26] In addition, a senior British adviser, Ronald Storrs, notes in his memoirs that "the harims, composed largely of Turkesses, are on the whole against us and imagine [the CUP minister of war] Enver as a pan-Islamic Superman in shining armour, ready and waiting to take away their reproach."[27] Meanwhile, in Istanbul, Muhammad Farid persuaded the shaikh al-Islam — the empire's senior religious scholar — to issue a *fatwa* that condemned Husain Kamil to death, on the grounds that he had "violated the authority of the Ottoman Caliphate over the Egyptian province, which was an integral part of the Ottoman Sultanate."[28] At the same time, the well-known nationalist journalist Shaikh 'Abd al-'Aziz Shawish was actively engaged in rallying assistance for the imperial war effort among the inhabitants of al-Hijaz.[29]

Concerted efforts to stamp out pro-Ottoman sentiment complemented British measures to suppress nationalist agitation throughout the war. Outspoken members of al-Hizb al-Watani, including Muhammad Farid, 'Abd al-'Aziz Shawish, 'Abd al-Malik Hamza, and Ahmad Tahir, found themselves banished for the duration of hostilities; almost all of these individuals gravitated to the Ottoman court. In their absence, a smaller organization, the Party of the Nation (Hizb al-Ummah) led by Ahmad Lutfi al-Sayyid, gained adherents in nationalist circles. This party advocated tactical cooperation with the British in return for a firm guarantee of Egypt's independence once the war came to a end.[30] More crucially, the party's newspaper *al-Jaridah* persistently remonstrated against the continuation of de jure Ottoman suzerainty over Egypt. As Ottoman fortunes on the battlefield faltered after 1915, even staunch pro-Ottomanists like Muhammad Farid began to assume a posture approximating the one adopted by Hizb al-Ummah.[31] Yet Storrs observes that the news of Sharif al-Husain bin 'Ali's capture of Mecca and Jiddah in June 1916 prompted Cairo's "Anglophobes, including nationalists, Khedivists, Turcophils, and Germanophils, [to throw] discredit upon the Sharif by representing him as a rebel against the Khalifa and the servile instrument of the English."[32] The director of the Arab Intelligence Bureau noted in July 1917 that "those members of the [royal] family of Mohammad Ali who have shown any aptitude or capacity for rulership have also displayed those pro-Turkish and Anglophobe sentiments which are common to the bulk of the Pasha class, however skilfully they may conceal them when dealing with high British officials."[33] British officers continued until the very last months of the war to report that a majority of Egyptians exhibited pro-Ottoman leanings.[34]

Growing commitment to principles of Westphalian sovereignty became evident among government officials and nationalists alike in the aftermath of the First World War. At the time of the November 1918 armistice, the new sultan, Ahmad Fuad, remarked to the British high commissioner in Cairo that he expected Egypt before long to become a constitutional monarchy, with an elected parliament and a council of ministers.[35] This conversation set the stage for the momentous 13 November meeting between the high commissioner and a trio of prominent nationalists, in which the latter intended formally to inquire what Britain's plans for the future of the country might be. In the heat of the moment, 'Abd al-'Aziz Fahmi unexpectedly asserted that he and his colleagues had come to demand Egypt's "complete independence."[36] A second member of the trio, Sa'd Zaghlul, subsequently headed the main Egyptian delegation to the 1919 Paris peace conference, where he reiterated the call for "full national independence for Egypt" in numerous speeches and official memoranda.[37] When delegates from Syria, Lebanon, and Transjordan invited Zaghlul to join them in forming a united front to push for the independence of the Arab world as a whole, he pointedly replied that "Our problem is an Egyptian problem and not an Arab problem."[38] More significantly, the team of al-Hizb al-Watani activists that also took part in the proceedings abandoned all vestiges of the party's longstanding allegiance to the Ottoman Empire, and submitted a statement to the conference that explicitly advocated complete independence for Egypt and the Sudan.[39]

Zaghlul's allies and supporters formed the core of the most powerful postwar nationalist party (known as the Wafd), whose leadership affirmed not only Egypt's right to self-determination and independence from Britain, but also its total autonomy from the Ottoman Empire. The founding manifesto of the party, issued in late November 1918, proclaimed that the country's ties to the empire had been abolished in December 1914, when the British authorities had declared Egypt to be a protectorate and elevated Husain Kamil to the post of sultan.[40] Negotiations between the Wafd and the British from mid-1919 to mid-1920 resulted in a provisional agreement according to whose terms Egypt would permit British forces to provide security for the Suez Canal and other vital lines of communication and protect the prerogatives of foreign nationals residing in the country, while Britain "will recognise the independence of Egypt as a constitutional monarchy with representative institutions" and relinquish control over the country's foreign affairs.[41] When senior Egyptian officials fell over one another in their haste to associate themselves with the draft agreement, Zaghlul quickly upped the ante. Claiming that the Egyptian people would reject out of hand any arrangement that circumscribed the government's right to administer all of the inhabitants and facilities situated within Egypt's territorial boundaries, he refused to recommend that the proposal be submitted for ratification.[42] Meanwhile, in early November, Isma'il Sidqi wrote a commentary for the influential newspaper *al-Ahram* in which he castigated British officials for failing to protect Egypt's western frontiers against persistent encroachments by Italian forces based in Cyrenaica.[43]

Two more years of intense bargaining ensued, culminating in a unilateral declaration whereby Britain relinquished all responsibility for governing the country. A key provision of the document, which was published on 22 February 1922, was that the Egyptian foreign ministry be reestablished and Egyptian diplomats once again be posted to foreign capitals.[44] The declaration set in motion a complicated political and diplomatic process that led in April 1923 to the promulgation of a formal constitution, whose terms stipulated that "Egypt is a sovereign state, free and independent."[45] Westphalian sovereignty thus became the basis for the Egyptian leadership's posture toward the outside world as early as 1919, almost four years before the country gained de jure independence.[46]

Tunisia's Early Turn

With the establishment of the Protectorate in June 1883, French officials gained full authority over Tunisia's internal and external affairs. Nevertheless, prominent opponents of European rule carried out a sort of pro-Ottoman foreign policy in the aftermath of the French occupation.

Several influential advisers to the former governor-general (*bey*) of Tunis, most notably Muhammad al-ʿArabi Zarruq, hastily decamped to the court of Sultan ʿAbdulhamid II in Istanbul. Others, including Muhammad bin al-Tayyib al-Naifar, remained in the country but seriously "considered asking help from the Ottoman Empire in order to have removed this hateful occupation by force or by political solution, because they believed that Tunisia was one of the kingdoms of the Ottoman Empire."[47] Still others, among them Salim Bu Hajib and Muhammad al-Sanusi, forged close ties to the Cairo-based reformers Jamal al-Din al-Afghani and Muhammad ʿAbduh, who had begun openly advocating the creation of a worldwide Muslim union to combat the spread of European imperialism.[48] Muhammad al-Sanusi actively promoted the ideas and activities of the shadowy Paris-based, Pan-Islamist organization al-ʿUrwa al-Wuthqa following his return from an extended trip to Cairo in 1882–83, and then orchestrated an enthusiastic welcome to Tunis for Muhammad ʿAbduh a year later.[49]

Popular demonstrations against the Protectorate erupted in the wake of ʿAbduh's visit, prompting the authorities to arrest several of the most outspoken critics of French administration. Nicola Ziadeh observes that this incident set the stage for "the appearance, within a few years, of an organized body of reformers and patriots whose main activities were directed toward reforms within the frame of revived Islam."[50] Such activists may have provided the nucleus for a local "secret society called al-jamʿiya al-ʿuthmaniya, which was formed during the mid-1880s in order to undermine the French occupation by strengthening Tunisian-Ottoman relations."[51] Ziadeh connects the appearance of these "reformers and patriots" to a group known as al-Hadirah, after the weekly publication that was issued under its auspices and edited by ʿAli Bu Shushah. The journal, which began publication in August 1888, announced that its primary objective was to protect "the interests of indigenous Tunisians that had been guaranteed by the establishment of the Protectorate," as well as "to strengthen the ties between Tunisia and the Pan-Islamic movement."[52] Besides printing articles that advocated wide-ranging administrative reform, improvements in education, and the protection of religious endowments (*awqaf* or *habus*), *al-Hadirah* published extensive reports on the domestic and foreign affairs of the Ottoman Empire. Its editors openly praised the restoration of the Ottoman constitution in 1908, a move that laid the legal foundation for a reintegration of Tunisia into the sultan's domain.[53]

In December 1896, the group affiliated with *al-Hadirah* transformed itself into an organized society, called al-Jama'iyyah al-Khalduniyyah, whose program celebrated the accomplishments of Islamic civilization in Tunisia and demanded the implementation of comprehensive reforms in the organizational structure and curriculum of the country's system of postsecondary education.[54] The new society's initial hegemony within the reform camp was challenged in 1901 by the return to Tunis of 'Abd al-'Aziz al-Tha'alibi, another associate of Muhammad 'Abduh in Cairo. In their writings and speeches, al-Tha'alibi, Muhammad al-Ja'ibi and other prominent critics of French rule consistently emphasized the historical and cultural distinctiveness of Tunisia, while pursuing what Ziadeh calls an overall "policy" of "Pan-Islamism."[55] Muhammad al-Fadil bin 'Ashur remarks that during the first years of the twentieth century, the members of al-Tha'alibi's circle believed that "Tunisia is nothing but a part of the Islamic Eastern Structure, which has gone through periods of glory and misfortune, exactly in the same way other countries have gone through them."[56]

Such ideas coalesced in 1907 with the appearance of the newspaper *Le Tunisien*, edited by 'Ali Bash Hanba. The paper urged the Arab inhabitants of Tunisia to struggle against the Protectorate to regain their legitimate "rights," which the French had usurped.[57] However, the paper argued, Tunisians were not yet capable of governing themselves. It was therefore necessary for the country to remain attached to a larger political entity, at least for the time being.[58] This theme was elaborated in a lengthy editorial by Bash Hanba that appeared in 1910: "Every Muslim is a supporter of Muslim union, and the Tunisians, to a man, are partisans of this policy and are attached to Pan-Ottomanism, which is a consequence of such an idea and a magnificent manifestation of it. If our modern education has given us a new mentality, we have, all the same, as Muslims reserved our strong loyalty to our brethren in every country. The Turks and Egyptians inspire us with feeling as much as our nearer neighbors in Algeria or the peoples in further Asia."[59] Sympathies like these blossomed into widespread popular support for the resistance to Italy's 1911–12 military campaign in Libya.[60] Shortly after the outbreak of the Libyan war, al-Tha'alibi founded a new Arabic-language newspaper, *World of the Muslims* (*'Alam al-Muslimin*), while Bash Hanba set up an explicitly pro-Tripolitanian journal called *Islamic Unity* (*al-Ittihad al-Islami*), whose very title indicated "a definite orientation of his movement towards Pan-Islamism."[61]

Overt anti-French activity in Tunisia was forcibly suppressed in the spring of 1912, when leading critics of the Protectorate were either incarcerated or sent into exile. Several senior religious figures subsequently gathered in the Ottoman capital and set up the Committee for the Independence of Tunisia and Algeria, reportedly patterned on Egypt's al-Hizb al-Watani.[62] 'Ali Bash Hanba also ended up in Istanbul, where he became a founding member of the CUP-sponsored Pan-Islamic League, as well as the head of the imperial war ministry's Central Office for the Islamic Movement.[63] In addition, he authored a series of newspaper articles that implored the Ottoman authorities "to regain possession of Tripolitania, Tunisia and Algeria and extend their sovereignty to Morocco."[64] His brother Muhammad Bash Hanba took up residence in Switzerland, and in May 1916 started to publish the influential journal *La Revue du Maghreb*, which demanded an end to injustice and exploitation throughout North Africa and appealed to all Muslims living in the region to rally to the kaliphah under the banner of Islamic unity.[65] At the end of that same year, a collection of Tunisian exiles residing in Berlin organized a committee to work for the "united independence" (*independence integral*) of Algeria and Tunisia, under the broad auspices of the Caliphate.[66] The committee tended to envisage the post-Protectorate order as one in which "each of the member countries would maintain their [sic] own political and cultural identity. This model [the group's leader, Salih al-Sharif al-Tunisi] compared with the German Empire, in which as he saw it, each of the constituent kingdoms and counties conducted its independent policies."[67]

As the First World War drew to a close, prominent opponents of French rule began to articulate more explicitly a demand for independence. In January 1918, *La Revue du Maghreb* printed a revised manifesto, which called on the international community to permit the people of Algeria and Tunisia, generally referred to as "*le peuple algéro-tunisien*," to determine their own future by holding a general referendum.[68] A year later, a group of activists dispatched a telegram to U.S. President Woodrow Wilson, entreating him to throw his support behind Algeria and Tunisia in their efforts to join the League of Nations; a second memorandum issued in February 1919 reiterated this request.[69] At the same time, the newly formed Comité Algéro-Tunisien published an open letter to the Paris peace conference that demanded "complete independence" for the two countries.[70] Yet the main thrust of the nationalist program continued to be the reinstatement of Tunisia's 1861 constitution. This objective served as the touchstone of an overtly political organization that emerged in early 1920, Hizb al-Hurr al-Dusturi al-Tunisi, commonly known as the Destour Party. In fact, the party's original platform scrupulously avoided calling for Tunisian independence from France.[71]

More important, the Destour Party initially adopted a foreign policy posture that equated the interests of Tunisia with those of the broader Islamic world. Activists rallied outside the Grand Mosque in Tunis in March 1920 to protest the British army's occupation of Istanbul, the capital of the Ottoman Empire. Over the next two years, Tunisian nationalists also supported the Turkish nationalist movement led by Mustafa Kemal (Ataturk) in its struggle against foreign enemies. Odile Moreau relates that "when Kemalist victories were reported [in Tunis], Turkish flags were flown over houses, prayers were said in mosques and processions, bearing flower-bedecked portraits of Mustafa Kemal, marched through the streets."[72] In early 1923, a group of younger Destourians formed a Committee for the Caliphate to work for the reinvigoration of that institution, which was coming under increasing assault from Turkish nationalists. French agents reported that "this Committee for the Caliphate is in contact with similar bodies in Egypt, and has become at the same time a centre for pan-Islamic activity."[73] The Destour leadership sent a cable to congratulate Mustafa Kemal and his colleagues on the occasion of the signing of the Treaty of Lausanne in July 1923, and a delegation of Tunisian notables led by al-Thaʿalibi and Jilali Ben Ramdan traveled to Istanbul for a planned Islamic congress to welcome the Kemalists to the city in the fall of 1923.[74] The Turkish Grand National Assembly's unexpected decision in March 1924 to abolish the Caliphate forced the Destour to reconsider its position vis-à-vis the Turkish nationalist movement. The act sparked a mass demonstration around the Grand Mosque in Tunis, and prominent figures in the party expressed sympathy for the former Ottoman sultan's efforts to win back the title of khalifah.[75]

Nevertheless, local nationalists started to narrow their conception of Tunisian interests in the years after the First World War to focus on matters of concern to Tunisia proper, as distinct from issues that faced the broader Islamic community. This trend accelerated following the defeat of the Ottoman Empire and the British occupation of Istanbul.[76] It was reinforced by news reports concerning the activities being undertaken by Egyptian nationalists to win independence from Britain, at least until the Resident General in Tunis succeeded in interdicting all press dispatches emanating from Cairo.[77] The overall tenor of the nationalist project during the immediate postwar period is evident in an anecdote related by the Moroccan writer ʿAlal al-Fasi: al-Thaʿalibi invited the respected Tunisian intellectual Muhya al-Din al-Qalibi to join the Destour Party, only to be rebuffed with the reply that al-Qalibi was "'prepared to work with you, but you are demanding mere constitutional reforms while I stand for the independence of Tunisia; I cannot therefore give my oath of loyalty to the party unless its aim is also for independence.' Sheikh al-Thaʿalibi smiled and replied: 'My son, this is a policy which my colleagues had accepted as a tactical move. For my part, I would have preferred the forthright and unequivocal attitude you have mentioned. However, do not give your oath except for independence, because it is the aim of all of us.'"[78] The calculated ambiguity that characterized the Destour's political program during this period can be discerned in its formal greeting to the bey at the public ceremony marking the end of Ramadan in June 1920: "the Tunisian nation has come to ask its beloved Prince to recognize the full rights and freedoms belonging to it."[79]

Nationalist leaders continued to refrain from explicitly calling for Tunisian independence during the early 1920s. In January 1921, a delegation of Destour Party notables presented the Resident General with yet another petition that demanded the immediate restoration of the constitution, pointing out that "the word 'constitution' evokes a bundle of administrative and social measures, in fact a political regime, whose essential elements are absolutely incompatible with the principle of the Protectorate."[80] Vacillation within the nationalist leadership is reflected in the sudden appearance three months later of the Reform Party organized by a group of dissident Destourians, whose platform proposed a fundamental modification of the Protectorate "in the direction of British-style 'dominions.'"[81] Meanwhile, followers of the late Shaikh Salih Sharif stepped up their campaign to abolish both the beylicate and the Protectorate.[82] The spread of such sentiments prompted French diplomats to inform their superiors in Paris in the spring of 1922 that the nationalist movement "is openly talking about independence today."[83]

There is good reason to accept the envoys' assessment. Among the specific demands that Bey Muhammad al-Nasir raised on behalf of the nationalists just prior to his abdication in April of that year was for Tunisian soldiers to serve only under their own flag.[84] On the other hand, many influential members of the Destour Party remained convinced that the most effective way to ensure Tunisia's economic, social, and political progress was to maintain some kind of association with other countries, perhaps even with France.[85] Groups of activists based in Vienna and Naples continued to work for "l'indépendance du peuple algéro-tunisien" during 1922–23.[86] As late as 1931, al-Tha'alibi attended the Pan-Islamic conference in Jerusalem as a representative of all the lands of North Africa.[87] It seems safe to conclude, though, that a posture congruent with the principles of Westphalian sovereignty triumphed in nationalist circles during the course of 1924: the Destour's newspaper *al-Thawwab* explicitly called for Tunisian independence that spring, and over the ensuing months party members rallied to the cause of establishing an autonomous polity that would be devoted to promoting the exclusive interests of the country's indigenous Muslim population. As the year came to a close, a delegation of prominent Destourians once again petitioned the French authorities to recognize the legitimate rights of the Tunisian nation, this time emphasizing the demand for full national autonomy.[88]

Jordan's Late Adoption

Throughout the 1920s and 1930s, nationalist leaders in 'Amman undertook a string of initiatives aimed at replacing the collection of Arab states that had been set up during the Mandate era with a unified Arab political entity. Walid Kazziha claims that from the very beginning, Amir 'Abdullah bin al-Husain and his allies considered the amirate of Transjordan to be little more than a way station along the road to a more extensive polity: 'Abdullah, Kazziha argues, "agreed to act as temporary head of the administration of the new Emirate in the hope that he would later on acquire the Syrian throne."[89] Following the death of Iraq's King Faisal bin al-Husain in September 1933, the Transjordanian ruler launched a campaign to convince Syrian nationalists to agree to set up a unified political entity; this effort culminated in an April 1936 telegram to the leaders of the National Bloc in Damascus, in which 'Abdullah urged the Bloc to recognize him as king of Syria.[90] The campaign was revived in 1937, when France balked at implementing the terms of the 1936 treaty, and again in 1938–39, after key figures of the 1925 Syrian revolt were at last released from confinement and the Turkish Republic signaled a willingness to acquiesce in the unification of Transjordan and Syria.[91]

During 1940–41, the leadership in ʿAmman repeatedly petitioned British military commanders to authorize it to play a greater role in shaping Syrian affairs.[92] Transjordan's Legislative Council adopted a resolution in July 1941, stating that "Syria, in view of its geographic position and natural resources, cannot survive, particularly from an economic point of view, except if united;"[93] Amir ʿAbdullah publicly reaffirmed his intention to pursue unity with Syria that November.[94] When the British Eighth Army finally succeeded in driving the German Afrika Korps out of Egypt in the fall of 1942, ʿAbdullah wrote directly to Prime Minister Winston Churchill to propose the "complete union" of Transjordan, Syria, Palestine, and Lebanon, as well as "a cultural union between greater Syria and Iraq."[95] Such entreaties set the stage for the publication of a March 1943 manifesto that demanded the immediate formation of a United Syrian State with ʿAbdullah as its ruler.[96] A month later, the amir issued a call for Syrian nationalists "from the Gulf of ʿAqaba to the Mediterranean and the Upper Euphrates" to gather in the Transjordanian capital to discuss "the proper form of government in Bilad al-Sham [geographical Syria]."[97] On the other hand, the leadership in ʿAmman joined the National Bloc in Damascus in denouncing the Iraqi government's Fertile Crescent Unity project, albeit for reasons having more to do with intra-Hashemite rivalry than any lack of sympathy for the notion of regional unification.[98]

As soon as Syria and Lebanon gained de jure independence in July 1943, ʿAbdullah issued a proclamation to the people of Syria, Lebanon, and Palestine, reminding them that the entire region "with its natural boundaries is one fatherland united by bonds of nationalism, geography and history." It was now incumbent on the people of geographical Syria, the document continued, to take immediate steps to "prevent the disruption of our own true home, our one fatherland and our one family."[99] This pronouncement was followed by a personal letter from ʿAbdullah to the Syrian nationalist Faris al-Khuri, in which the amir observed that "Free France has promised the country [i.e., Syria] its independence and its sovereignty. . . . When this was proclaimed, Transjordan expressed its desire to be annexed to Syria or to annex Syria to it. I approved this for the sake of unity and the security of the homeland. I do not know what the future form of government will be, whether it will be a republic or monarchial, and this is a sacrifice on my part."[100] Transjordanian officials took pains throughout the summer of 1943 to impress upon both Iraq's Nuri al-Saʿid and Egypt's Mustafa al-Nahhas that

Arab unity could only be accomplished once Greater Syria had become a political reality.[101]

When representatives of the Arab states gathered in Alexandria in September 1944 to discuss the possibility of establishing a regional organization, Transjordan's delegation expressed a clear preference for an entity that would possess "executive authority" with regard to its members.[102] In addition, the delegation "repeatedly pressed for unification of the 'Syrian provinces.'"[103] It exhibited considerably less enthusiasm for the idea of a league of sovereign states. Prime Minister Tawfiq Abu al-Huda remarked to the Syrians during the course of the deliberations that even if such a league were to come into existence, "there was nothing to prevent Syria and Transjordan from uniting. Palestine could join them later if this proved possible."[104] Transjordanian representatives played a key role in ensuring that the protocol that emerged from the Alexandria conference contained a provision stating that further discussions concerning regional unity would be undertaken under the auspices of the provisional Political Subcommittee.[105] When it became clear that this mandate would receive little more than lip service, the leadership in 'Amman lost interest in the proceedings. Prime Minister Samir al-Rifa'i observed in the interim between the promulgation of the Alexandria Protocol and the signing of the Arab League pact "that regardless of the results of the Cairo conference, his government would continue to believe in and work for a Greater Syria."[106] 'Abdullah subsequently dismissed the Arab League as "a sack into which seven heads have been thrust . . . with remarkable haste."[107]

With the formal termination of the British mandate over Transjordan in March 1946, Amir 'Abdullah took the title of king. But, as he bluntly informed the Egyptian government at the time of his coronation, "The complete independence of Transjordan will be attained only after the realization of the Greater Syria plan."[108] Syria's de facto independence a month later prompted 'Abdullah to announce that the establishment of Greater Syria was "a basic principle of Transjordan's foreign policy."[109] The king subsequently told a group of Egyptian journalists that "my demand for Greater Syria is as natural as Egypt's desire for the unity of the Nile valley."[110] When the Lebanese government threatened to end its affiliation with the League of Arab States rather than acquiesce in Transjordan's continuing efforts to manipulate the League's institutions to promote the creation of a Greater Syria, 'Abdullah backpedaled: "Nothing will prevent my ascent to the throne of Damascus. . . . I have received formal and definite promises on that subject. [But] my Greater Syria does not include the Lebanon. I have all intentions to respect the independence and sovereignty of that country."[111] Nevertheless, the king and his foreign minister reiterated their commitment to forging a unified Arab entity throughout the last quarter of the year.[112] That December 'Abdullah asserted that "I shall never cease my efforts to achieve the unity of Syria."[113]

In fact, 1947 represented the zenith of the Transjordanian government's campaign to form a Greater Syria. At the end of March, King 'Abdullah went so far as to tell the Lebanese newspaper *Kulli Shai* that "my policy is clear: I want a state which includes Syria, Transjordan, Palestine and Lebanon. Yes, Lebanon."[114] Two months later, the leadership in 'Amman "issued a 300-page Greater Syria Plan White Paper in which it attempted to justify its policy, and on the 25th [of May], on the first anniversary of Transjordan's new independence, Abdullah pleaded again for the adoption of his Greater Syria plan."[115] A succession of large-scale military exercises along the kingdom's northern borders during the first half of the year prompted warnings from Beirut and Damascus that the Hashemite regime planned to annex Syrian territory by force of arms.[116] That summer, King 'Abdullah openly complained that the institutional structure of the Arab League stood in the way of serious attempts to achieve Arab unity, because it preserved the sovereignty of the various member-states.[117]

The drive to forge a Greater Syria climaxed in August 1947, when the Transjordanian leadership summoned the heads of the existing "regional governments of all Syria" to 'Amman to discuss ways in which immediate unification could be carried out.[118] The summit's proposed agenda entailed a series of measures designed to enable the participants "to arrive at a decision regarding Syrian unity; to determine the position of Palestine with respect to the Syrian union in order to stop Jewish immigration; and to call a federal convention to write a constitution for the union." Furthermore, the organizers pledged that "as soon as the state of Greater Syria is established, it will be followed by the formation of the Fertile Crescent in fulfilment of the ideas of the Great Arab Revolt."[119] Despite the antagonism that the invitation provoked throughout the Arab world, 'Abdullah continued throughout the autumn to declare his intention to pursue the unification of geographical Syria.[120] Moreover, at a secret meeting in Naharayyim that November, the king informed the Zionist leadership that he stood ready to grant the Yishuv a substantial degree of autonomy within the confines of a more extensive political entity encompassing Transjordan and mandatory Palestine.[121]

Paradoxically, the 1948 war buttressed the Transjordanian government's disinclination to recognize the territorial boundaries that divided the Arab world. The nationalist leadership in 'Amman did its best to strengthen the joint military committee that the Arab League set up in October 1947, and persistently resisted Syrian and Lebanese efforts to convince the League to authorize the deployment of each Arab country's regular army along its own border with mandatory Palestine. Instead, the authorities in 'Amman advocated the creation of a unified military formation under Transjordanian command, and any Arab guerrilla units that crossed into the kingdom without subordinating themselves to the local authorities were put under strict supervision.[122] Only after the Zionist forces' initial successes on the ground during March and April did King 'Abdullah order these strictures to be relaxed; even then, he only did so "provided he were commissioned to head the Arab armies' general headquarters."[123] At the same time, the king became increasingly outspoken in urging the Jewish inhabitants of Palestine to abandon their struggle to form a separate state and instead accept an arrangement based on local autonomy within the context of an overarching Greater Syria; 'Abdullah warned Golda Meyerson, when the two conferred in 'Amman on 10–12 May, that immediate unification represented the only way to avoid outright warfare.[124] By the same token, the Transjordanian leadership strenuously resisted the Gaza-based All-Palestine Government's efforts to set up an autonomous administration in the districts of Mandatory Palestine that remained in Arab hands when the fighting finally slackened that fall.[125]

Transjordan's leaders elicited little sympathy for Greater Syria among the military officers who seized power in Damascus in March 1949. The prospects for Transjordanian-Syrian unity brightened somewhat following Colonel Sami Hinnawi's countercoup that August, however, and King 'Abdullah remarked that the advent of the Hinnawi regime made the creation of Greater Syria "a natural necessity."[126] When Colonel Adib al-Shishakli, in turn, ousted Hinnawi and his allies four months later, the door to unity with Syria appeared to slam shut. It was under these circumstances that the newly redesignated Hashemite Kingdom of Jordan opted in April 1950 to take the first step toward achieving Greater Syria by annexing the districts of Palestine that remained outside Israeli control.[127] When the Political Committee of the Arab League threatened to expel Jordan in retaliation for the annexation, King 'Abdullah riposted that "if expulsion comes as a result of unifying the two parts of this besieged nation, it will be welcome. We do not wish to be of those who oppose unity in the name of the Arab League, from which we had hoped good would come." The contrast between the Jordanian leadership's notion of Arab unity and the kind of integration that was represented by the existing Arab League (i.e., integration predicated on the sovereignty of each member-state) was reiterated in the king's address to the newly elected parliament on 24 April 1950: "While we welcome the idea of collective security and of inter-Arab economic cooperation on a sound basis, we discern no security for an Arab nation without genuine unification of its component parts wherever possible through the general will of the people and without violating any pact or covenant."[128]

Despite the general opprobrium that the annexation of the West Bank engendered throughout the Arab world, leaders in 'Amman persisted in their quest for Arab unity. During the course of a visit to the Jordanian capital by the Iraqi regent in June 1950, King 'Abdullah discussed the possibility of amalgamating Jordan and Iraq after his death.[129] Jordanian officials responded favorably to the Syrian prime minister's call that November for a redoubled commitment to regional unification. More tellingly, the government categorically rejected the Iraq-sponsored Arab Collective Security Pact, whose institutional structure was designed to guarantee the sovereign prerogatives enjoyed by its individual member-states.[130]

In the spring of 1951, the Jordanian authorities made an even more serious bid to unify with Iraq.[131] The effort was undertaken in the context of growing concern on King 'Abdullah's part that his elder son Talal might prove incompetent to act as his successor: The king confided to Lebanon's Riyad al-Sulh, "I do not see in Talal or Na'if a suitable man to mount the throne and administer the country. For this reason, I have been turning this subject over in my mind for a long time. To my mind, the best way to solve this problem is an agreement with Iraq on a unification or union of the two countries under my crown, with the proviso that the whole kingdom revert after me to His Majesty Faisal the Second."[132] Unlike earlier unity proposals, however, this one envisaged "the creation of a High Federal Council, with the chairmanship alternating between the two countries' prime ministers; [the] development of 'a single foreign policy'; and [a] consolidation of diplomatic representation," rather than comprehensive amalgamation. In fact, as Robert Satloff observes, the Jordanian authorities "had been careful to add that nothing should infringe on either kingdom's 'present rights and constitution in full.'"[133] The assassination of King 'Abdullah that July piqued Baghdad's interest in a merger with Jordan; the Iraqi delegation that attended 'Abdullah's funeral even tried to pursue the matter with Prime Minister Samir al-Rifa'i during breaks in the ceremonies.[134] But by this time, powerful actors in 'Amman had begun to harbor serious misgivings about Arab unity in general and an immediate merger with Iraq in particular.

Chief among those who now backed away from the Greater Syria project were the reinstated prime minister (Tawfiq Abu al-Huda), the regent (Prince Nayif), and the newly acknowledged successor to the crown (King Talal).[135] Despite fundamental differences with one another, these three personages colluded in a campaign to reorient Jordanian foreign policy so as to affirm the kingdom's willingness to cooperate with other Arab states on the basis of mutual recognition and sovereign equality. Throughout the summer of 1951, the prime minister "publicly renounced any attempt at either a separate peace with Israel or a Hashemite-focused Greater Syria plan, and he let it be known that his was a policy of live-and-let-live with the rest of the Arab world."[136] Prince Nayif opened parliament in early September by declaring that the regime's priorities included "ensuring the safety of the Throne, [the] development of conditions of political stability in the country by safeguarding the constitutional government, [the] realization of national aspirations, [the] initiation of vital reforms [and the] maintenance of closer relations with Arab and friendly states."[137] Abu al-Huda's own policy statement to the Assembly of Representatives two weeks later "denied that the [interim] government had been approached" by the Iraqis and "emphasized the need for stability in Jordan and preservation of the Crown."[138] As the year ended, the prime minister explained his cabinet's abandonment of further unity discussions with Iraq by remarking that the two countries' leaderships possessed divergent conceptions of the form that unification should take: "If the suggested union were aimed at unification of defense or the Army, or at any other practical joint action, we would have considered it useful and promising. But the written and unequivocal plan is confined to unification of the Crown, leaving the Army to receive aid from abroad, as before, and preserving its present character and composition for another five to ten years."[139]

By mid-1952, Jordan had completed the turn to Westphalian sovereignty.

At the beginning of the year, the leadership in 'Amman finally signed the Arab Collective Security Pact. This move was followed by a series of overtures to the State of Israel, during the course of which the senior Jordanian representative on the Mixed Armistice Commission worked out with his Israeli counterparts a plan to exchange barren land around the Dead Sea for a collection of villages in the district around Qalqiliyyah. More important than the specific arrangement at hand were the prospects that the deal might set "the precedent of territorial rectifications with Arab states individually, not collectively."[140] King Talal's return to Switzerland for medical treatment that May prompted Prime Minister Abu al-Huda to proclaim that the government no longer intended to explore possibilities for amalgamation with Iraq and would instead take steps to preserve the monarchy for the young crown prince, Husain bin Talal.[141] Immediately after ascending to the throne in May 1953, King Husain directed the new prime minister, Fawzi al-Mulqi, to "aim at safeguarding the national sovereignty and Arab rights through full co-operation and understanding with all the Arab countries."[142] When Israeli commandos attacked the border village of Qibya that October, officials in 'Amman pointedly avoided issuing an invitation to the armed forces of neighboring states to take up forward positions inside the kingdom; the authorities instead solicited funds from the League of Arab States to expand and upgrade the country's own military establishment.[143] With these developments, Jordan's long-standing crusade to replace the Arab states that had been created during the mandate era with a more extensive political entity finally evaporated.

Iraq's Late Adoption

Despite Britain's decision to grant de jure independence to Iraq in 1932, the nationalist leadership in Baghdad consistently worked to replace the existing Arab states with a more comprehensive polity. King Faisal bin al-Husain had undertaken a series of such initiatives throughout the 1920s and into the early 1930s.[144] The country's influential minister of foreign affairs, Nuri al-Sa'id, furthered the campaign, beginning in 1935 with a proposal to create a union of Iraq and Transjordan.[145] A year later, the Iraqi government informed British authorities that it intended to work for the unification of the Arab world, this time in the shape of "a loose union of states, a commonwealth such as the (then) British Empire, in which each state would be as autonomous as any dominion."[146] Enthusiasm for a more extensive regional entity waned in Baghdad during the months between October 1936 and December 1938, when Nuri al-Sa'id found himself exiled first to Egypt and then to Saudi Arabia.[147] But as soon as he and his allies regained power, the drive to forge a united Arab East recommenced. In March 1939, Nuri al-Sa'id (now acting as prime minister) corresponded with a prominent Syrian politician, urging him to place the issue of immediate Iraqi-Syrian union before the parliament in Damascus.[148]

Baghdad stepped up its efforts to establish a larger Arab entity as 1939 went by. Nuri al-Sa'id devoted considerable attention to the task of convincing Amir 'Abdullah of Transjordan to join him in working out the "details of a scheme for establishing a Hashimite Kingdom in Syria and uniting Iraq, Syria, Trans-Jordan and ultimately Palestine also under the same royal house."[149] The Iraqi regent and prime minister met with the ruler and prime minister of Transjordan in March 1940, and attempted to persuade their Jordanian counterparts to amalgamate with Palestine as a first step toward a more extensive Hashemite polity.[150] Interest in regional unity peaked immediately following the fall of France that June. Officials in Baghdad proposed to undertake joint action with the National Bloc in Damascus to achieve Syria's immediate independence, either by moving units of the Iraqi army across the border into Syria or by providing arms to the Syrian people to enable them to rise up against the French.[151] Although the military officers who seized power in Baghdad in April 1941 focused their attention on abolishing Britain's remaining prerogatives inside Iraq, they retained at least a modicum of interest in regional amalgamation as well. A draft Iraqi-German military agreement drawn up that month, for example, provided for the annexation of Kuwait. It also envisaged the creation of an Arab federation consisting of Iraq, Syria, Lebanon, Palestine, and Transjordan, whose governing Federal Council would be situated in Baghdad.[152]

Plans for Iraq to merge with surrounding countries received a fillip in June 1941, when British troops ousted the regime of Rashid 'Ali al-Kailani and reinstated King Faisal. Senior Iraqi officials expected subsequent British military operations in Syria to provide them with the opportunity to unify the two countries.[153] After the British government recognized Syria as an independent state that October, Baghdad pointedly refrained from following suit, on the grounds that French officers continued to exercise an inordinate degree of control over the civil administration in Damascus.[154] Instead, the Iraqi government demanded complete independence for Syria, as the first step toward creating a larger regional entity. This posture culminated in Nuri al-Saʿid's Fertile Crescent Unity Plan of 1942–43.[155] As the plan showed signs of foundering in the spring of 1943, officials in Baghdad actively lobbied their counterparts in Damascus and ʿAmman to persuade them of "the necessity of building the foundation of Greater Syria as the preliminary to eventual Arab confederation."[156] And when the Syrian regime refused to fall in with such an arrangement, Nuri al-Saʿid offered to dispatch Iraqi troops to Damascus, "not only as a contribution to the allied war effort but also because of Arab unity and the possibility of achieving it."[157]

Baghdad continued to try to forge a unified Arab entity as 1944 began. In January, the prime minister embarked on a tour of neighboring capitals, and succeeded in badgering his hosts in Damascus into agreeing to form a federation in the near future, "whatever the other Arab states did."[158] At the October talks in Alexandria to lay the foundations for a League of Arab States, Iraqi representatives "advocated the maximum amount of cooperation possible short of a central government, to be embodied in a League Council with considerable powers, particularly in mediating and arbitrating disputes among members."[159] Throughout the first three years of the League's existence, officials in Baghdad praised the organization for being both a symbol of inter-Arab cooperation and "a national project that stands above [the] individualistic and selfish goals" of the member-states.[160] On the eve of Syria's de facto independence in the spring of 1946, Nuri al-Saʿid returned to Damascus to discuss the possibility of Iraqi-Syrian union with Syria's Prime Minister Saʿdallah al-Jabri.[161] Rebuffed once again by the Syrians, the Iraqi government drafted a unity agreement with Transjordan instead.[162]

Meanwhile, Baghdad seized the initiative in attempting to coordinate the Arab League's response to the escalating crisis in Palestine. As early as June 1946, the head of Iraq's delegation to the Bludan conference sharply criticized the evident absence of unity among the participants, charging that "the conference has been one more example of the opposing view-points and the conflicting interests of the Arab countries which are voiced at every conference and find expression in every resolution of the League."[163] Iraqi representatives argued forcefully at Aley in October 1947 that popular military formations, rather than the regular armies of the countries surrounding

Palestine, should take primary responsibility for prosecuting the conflict with Zionist forces. Nevertheless, a senior Iraqi commander, General Isma'il Safwat, was put in charge of an inter-Arab military committee assigned to explore the possibility of joint intervention by the regular armed forces.[164] After assessing the general strategic situation, Safwat recommended at the end of October that the Arab governments subordinate their respective armies to a unified command structure. They delayed taking this step until the first week of May 1948, when the Arab League finally authorized Iraqi General Nur al-Din Mahmud to take up the post of supreme commander.[165] Pervasive infighting among the disparate Arab general staffs shaped both the course and outcome of the 1948 war.

In the aftermath of the first Arab-Israeli conflict, Iraq's commitment to Arab unity wavered. Baghdad hastily disengaged itself from multilateral negotiations concerning the implementation of a formal ceasefire with the new State of Israel, perhaps in order to avoid "incurring the odium of recognizing Arab defeat."[166] More important, the government adopted an ambiguous posture toward the new Syrian regime of Husni al-Za'im, which came to power in Damascus following a coup d'etat in March 1949. Although influential members of Iraq's political elite—including the regent—advocated an immediate merger of the two countries in the aftermath of the coup, others—among them Nuri al-Sa'id—insisted that Baghdad wait to see how matters might fall out between al-Za'im and his rivals.[167] A high-ranking Syrian delegation traveled to the Iraqi capital in mid-April to propose a mutual defense treaty that would entail "immediate co-operation in the event of attack by Israel; a joint command in time of war headed by an officer from the country first attacked; [and] a joint planning staff in peacetime."[168] The Syrians also asked that two Iraqi infantry brigades be permanently deployed along the Syrian-Israeli border. Officials in Baghdad rejected the proposal, partly because it was clear that the general staff in Damascus intended to exercise control over all units stationed inside Syria and partly because the Iraqi high command hesitated to take responsibility for defending Syrian territory.[169]

In an attempt to find a more acceptable basis for collaboration, Prime Minister Nuri al-Sa'id paid a return visit to Damascus in the company of the minister of defense, minister of foreign affairs, and chief of the general staff. The prime minister did his best to convince al-Za'im that a mutual defense treaty was unnecessary, because "the world is progressing with speed and taking dangerous steps so that soon it will be possible to sign a charter which will be greater than a pact between two states."[170] The Iraqi delegation went on to alienate its hosts by meeting with prominent private citizens and promising them that Baghdad would support any unity proposal that originated from the Syrian people.[171] In the wake of the trip, relations between the two governments frosted. Not even al-Za'im's ouster in mid-August at the hands of officers led by Colonel Sami Hinnawi improved the chilly atmosphere between Damascus and Baghdad. Only when the new Syrian leadership proffered a plan to create "a federation under the crown of Iraq's young King Faysal II," which would include the establishment of "a Federal council that would draft a constitution and a Federal Parliament, composed of equal numbers of Syrian and Iraqi deputies, which would sit one-half of the year in Damascus and one-half in Baghdad" did Iraqi officials take serious notice.[172] But their response was lukewarm, and discussions soon turned to the possibility of forming a bilateral military alliance instead.[173]

By the time the Hinnawi regime was itself overthrown in December 1949, the government in Baghdad appears to have abandoned its long-standing campaign to unify Iraq and Syria.[174] Iraqi representatives initialed a draft agreement with Egyptian officials in January 1950 that pledged their respective governments to abjure "intervention, either direct or indirect, in Syrian internal affairs and from any agitation and encouragement which might be considered as intervention," explicitly including a revival of the Fertile Crescent Unity Plan.[175] Furthermore, Baghdad responded—perhaps mischievously—to Damascus's proposal to reconfigure the Arab Joint Defense Pact along the lines of the North Atlantic Treaty Organization by suggesting that the revised agreement be extended to cover attacks on the part of any aggressor, not just Israel.[176] Iraqi diplomacy toward Syria subsequently revolved around the comparatively minor matter of whether to grant formal diplomatic recognition to the regime of Colonel Adib al-Shishakli, rather than the grander issue of how to construct a political entity that would supersede the two states.[177] In fact, the government of 'Ali Jawdat al-Ayyubi that formed in December 1949 quickly cut its ties to the few politicians in Damascus who persisted in calling for a merger with Iraq.[178]

Still, the dream of Iraqi-Syrian unity died hard. Prime Minister Tawfiq al-Suwaidi publicly affirmed in February 1950 that the two countries shared an "imperative need to unite."[179] Iraqi officials responded positively to Syrian Prime Minister Nazim al-Qudsi's January 1951 proposal that the increasingly fragmented Arab League be replaced by a United Arab State, although they made no effort to salvage the scheme after al-Qudsi's cabinet collapsed that March. When a group of military officers opposed to the Syrian leadership fled to Baghdad in early 1952, the authorities permitted them to organize a "Free Syrian Government" in the city, but did not insist that the émigrés include unification as one of their objectives.[180] Merger with Syria remained a stated objective of the cabinet of Prime Minister Muhammad Fadil al-Jamali in 1953–54, but the government's underlying opposition to the reform program espoused by the al-Shishakli regime precluded any concrete steps toward unity.[181]

Meanwhile, Baghdad pursued amalgamation with Jordan.[182] When King 'Abdullah suggested in the spring of 1951 that the two countries form a loose federation, Iraqi representatives responded by proposing instead "a closer form of union," to be preceded by two years of provisional confederation.[183] The authorities in 'Amman sidestepped this proposal in the wake of 'Abdullah's assassination that July, but senior Iraqi officials continued to cultivate support for union among key Jordanian politicians during the brief reign of King Talal.[184] The regent tried once more to push for Iraqi-Jordanian unity after Talal decamped to Switzerland in June 1952. This time, however, the leadership in 'Amman blasted the initiative as an example of "direct interference in Jordan's internal affairs," and turned it down flat.[185] Iraqi officials made one last attempt to persuade the British government to support unification with Jordan in the fall of 1953.[186] When London ignored this appeal, the leadership in Baghdad finally abandoned its long-standing campaign to create a political entity that transcended the territorial boundaries that the Arab world had inherited from the mandate era. By the summer of 1954, Iraq's leaders were focusing their attention on how to forge a strategic alliance with Turkey, Iran, and Pakistan—a project clearly predicated on narrowly defined Iraqi interests rather than intimate collaboration with other Arab states.

Syria's Turn

Throughout the 1930s, the nationalist leadership in Damascus—the National Bloc (al-Kutlah al-Wataniyyah)—pursued a foreign policy that linked Syrian independence to the establishment of a more extensive Arab political entity. Prominent members of the Bloc took part in the deliberations that led to the publication in Jerusalem of a Pan-Arab National Covenant at the end of 1931. This manifesto proclaimed "that Arab countries are an indivisible unity and the Arab Nation does not recognise nor agree to any kind of division" and that "the endeavours in each Arab country should be directed towards the sole aim of total independence, safeguarding their unity and resisting any idea of being content with action for local and regional policies."[187] Similar sentiments lay behind the emergence two years later of the Homs-based League of National Action ('Usbah al-'Amal al-Qawmi), whose platform equated "total Arab sovereignty and independence" with "comprehensive Arab unity."[188] It was in this tradition that a group of influential nationalists from Aleppo petitioned the Iraqi government in March 1939 to take steps to implement "the Union of Syria and Iraq, under the shadow of the flag of the heir of Faisal for the realisation of the great Arab unity."[189] At virtually the same time, students at Damascus University took to the streets not only to protest the transfer of the district of Iskandarun to the Turkish Republic, and the French government's concurrent abrogation of the 1936 treaty, but also to call for King Ghazi of Iraq to be installed as monarch of Syria.[190]

During the first years of the Second World War, Syrian nationalists continued to lean toward amalgamation with neighboring countries. The National Bloc's perennial foreign minister, Jamil Mardam, in exile in Baghdad at the beginning of 1941, convinced his colleagues in Damascus to collaborate with the rulers of Iraq, Saudi Arabia, Egypt, and Yemen in "calling on the belligerent powers to refrain from turning Arab lands into a battlefield and to grant all Arab countries their full independence."[191] Mardam himself orchestrated the formation of a provisional higher committee charged with coordinating policy among the five leaderships, but the possibility of further cooperation was abruptly quashed when Britain intervened to overthrow the Iraqi government of Rashid 'Ali al-Kailani that spring. After British troops went on to occupy Syria in June 1941, Mardam put together a united front with Bishara al-Khuri of Lebanon and Mustafa al-Nahhas of Egypt to exert pressure on Britain and the Free French National Committee to recognize Syrian independence.[192] The National Bloc then "proposed that an all-Arab committee should be established in order to frame the demands that the Arabs would submit to the Peace Conference when the war was over. Such a step would in itself promote the desired Arab union, declared the Syrian Prime Minister, and would establish it in the real world."[193] Initiatives such as these provide firm grounds for concluding that as the 1940s opened, Syrian nationalist leaders "regarded political unity as a practical goal and as a means to ensure general Arab backing in their struggle against the French."[194]

It was not long, however, before the National Bloc abandoned a multilateralist posture and committed itself to establishing a fully autonomous, territorially limited Syria instead. As early as February 1933, the Bloc had issued a proclamation that promised "to the noble [Syrian] people, in the interior and the littoral, their attachment to the rights of the country based on its unity and sovereign nationality."[195] By the fall of 1941, this sentiment became the predominant force driving the nationalist leadership in Damascus. That October the Bloc asserted that "the Syrian nation has, in the course of its recent history, been a nation desirous of progress, a militant nation who raised the flag of independence and sovereignty and never ceased her struggle to raise high her standard and to consolidate her independence until the declaration of the World War of 1941 [sic]. The Syrians, full of faith in this independence, set out to prove it by joining the Allies and fighting in their ranks to attain the goal of sovereignty and freedom."[196] A year later, President Taj al-Din al-Hasani commemorated the anniversary of General Catroux's pronouncement of de jure Syrian independence by proclaiming that "the independence which has been granted us is complete. . . . We will not sacrifice any of our rights and will renounce none of the manifestations of our sovereignty and of our dignity."[197]

More important, Syrian officials flatly rejected the Fertile Crescent Unity Plan advanced by the Iraqi government in the winter of 1942–43, arguing that such an arrangement "was impossible since Iraq was a monarchy and Syria a republic and the former was bound by a treaty to Britain, whereas the latter was free of any contractual obligation to any foreign power."[198] When asked in the summer of 1943 what Damascus thought of the possibility that the Arab states might form a Commonwealth, Foreign Minister Na'im al-Antaki replied, "We can't federate until we have something to federate *with*—and that is why our national development comes first."[199] After the National Bloc recaptured control of the state apparatus that August, the newly installed president, Shukri al-Quwwatli, proclaimed that his government would pursue "the attainment of complete independence and sovereignty, the maintenance of close cooperation with the rest of the Arab world, and the development of

Syria's international relations in accordance with the principles of the Atlantic Charter."[200] The following month, Prime Minister Sa'dallah al-Jabri informed the nationalist leadership in Beirut "that the Syrian president and all the members of his government supported an independent Lebanese entity and accepted Lebanon's rightful regime and its present frontiers, provided that its independence was total and real in the sense that no foreign power could use Lebanon as a base to undermine the interests of Syria."[201] Syria's willingness to recognize a self-governing Lebanon defined by its existing territorial boundaries was reiterated in a memorandum submitted to the Egyptian government in October. This document went on to suggest that an Arab federation would be the appropriate institutional arrangement "to institute total political, economic, social and cultural cooperation amongst the eight states of Syria, Egypt, Iraq, Saudi Arabia, Yemen, Palestine, Transjordan and Lebanon."[202] That any such federation would be predicated on the sovereignty of the individual member-states was emphasized during the course of al-Jabri's discussions with Egyptian officials in late October 1943, as well as during Mardam's visits to the Iraqi and Saudi capitals in December 1943 and February 1944, respectively.[203]

In June 1944, the National Bloc leadership invited Soviet representatives to come to the Syrian capital to discuss the possibility of establishing formal diplomatic relations between Moscow and Damascus. Following a banquet for the Soviet mission on 24 July, the Syrians released a communiqué stating that "the recognition by the Soviet Union of the Syrian Republic as an independent and sovereign State is a full recognition, unvitiated by any reservation."[204] Similar sentiments lay behind telegrams dispatched to Britain, the United States, and the Soviet Union in mid-September, at the height of tensions with France over the disposition of the Syrian armed forces: "The British Minister and the French Representative in Syria have suggested that the Syrian government enter into negotiations with the French for a treaty under which France should obtain a privileged position in Syria. This suggestion is contrary to the high principles proclaimed in the United Nations Atlantic Charter. . . . The Syrian government considers the Mandate to have been terminated both de jure and de facto since the establishment in Syria of liberal, democratic and independent institutions and also since the recognition by Great Britain, the Soviet Union and the United States and other countries of Syria's independence."[205] Meanwhile, Prime Minister al-Jabri informed the newly appointed Transjordanian consul in Damascus that "the

Syrian government favored the formation of Greater Syria but without alteration of [Syria's] present republican regime."[206]

Damascus's interest in promoting Westphalian sovereignty was equally evident at the preliminary conference on Arab unity that convened in Cairo at the end of September 1944.[207] Prime Minister al-Jabri at the outset of the meeting declared Syria's willingness in principle "to give up its sovereignty," while expressing "the wish that the other Arab states would do the same." Nevertheless, this pronouncement was immediately tempered by his further suggestion "that in view of the apprehensions of some states, it could be affirmed that the independence of each would be respected and defended."[208] As the conference went on, the Syrian delegation steadily backed away from the prime minister's opening declaration. Ahmed Gomaa reports that by the fourth session, "all the delegates present ruled out the idea of a union with a central government." Syrian representatives continued to raise the possibility of forming "an organization with executive authority" until it became clear that the majority would oppose such an arrangement;[209] they then recommended that the new grouping be designated an "alliance," rather than a "league." This proposal was also rejected, with Egypt's al-Nahhas observing "that the word 'League' was in fact [the] stronger and more comprehensive" of the two terms.[210] Foreign Minister Mardam went on to parry the Transjordanian prime minister's call for the immediate unification of Greater Syria, recommending that explicit assurances of Lebanese sovereignty be added to the protocol that resulted from the conference.[211] Not long after the meeting adjourned, President al-Quwwatli traveled to Cairo to signal his government's solidarity with the leaders of Egypt and Saudi Arabia, who had argued most forcefully in favor of the creation of a league of sovereign Arab states. Moreover, he "made a very important speech soon after his return from Egypt, in which he reiterated his country's determination to preserve her independence."[212]

As the Second World War drew to a close, Syria's nationalist leadership reaffirmed its commitment to the consolidation of a sovereign, territorial state. In February 1946 Prime Minister al-Jabri flatly rejected the Iraqi government's demand to join it in concluding a mutual defense pact with Turkey.[213] Three months later, Damascus sealed the country's border with Transjordan in order to prevent pro-Hashemite notables from attending the coronation ceremonies for Amir 'Abdullah, "fearing that the presence either of any important Syrian dignitaries or large numbers of ordinary Syrians would be used by Transjordan to promote its Greater Syria plan."[214] When King ʿAbdullah stepped up his efforts to create a Greater Syria that autumn, Mardam informed Syrian parliamentarians that Syria "has no desire (to join) any union . . . that would encroach upon the rights and privileges which she has gained and which are (commonly) enjoyed by sovereign states."[215] At the same time, the Syrian leadership insisted that the Greater Syria scheme be placed on the agenda of the fifth Arab League Council meeting, where it was subjected to intense criticism.[216] As the *Arab News Bulletin* remarked, "during the fifth meeting held on November 26 the attention of the Council was called to the reports circulated regarding the so-called Greater Syria question and it was declared that perfect agreement had been reached among Arab states to consider the idea as definitely dropped."[217] ʿAbdullah's attempt to revive the plan once more in August 1947 prompted President al-Quwwatli to charge that "this false federation violated the sacredness of the Arab League Charter . . . by meddling in [Syria's internal] affairs."[218]

When tensions mounted along the border with Palestine in the fall of 1947, Syria joined Iraq, Lebanon, and Transjordan in forming a higher committee to coordinate Arab military operations. But Damascus dragged its feet on the crucial issue of whether to authorize Iraqi troops to take up forward positions inside Syrian territory.[219] Syrian delegates to the conference in Aley that October argued instead that each Arab country's regular armed forces should be given responsibility for engaging Zionist forces in the areas adjacent to its own border with mandatory Palestine.[220] The leadership in Damascus subsequently earmarked virtually all of its resources to support the operations of the Syrian military and the Damascus-based Popular Army led by Fawzi al-Qawuqji, virtually ignoring units loyal to the Arab Higher Committee and other guerrilla formations.[221] Syria's commitment to Westphalian sovereignty, which was evident as early as the mid-1940s, thus held firm even when it clashed with the common Arab interest in prosecuting the struggle against the State of Israel.

Conclusion

One might think that nationalist leaders would gravitate immediately toward foreign policies congruent with Westphalian sovereignty, particularly by the early twentieth century. The great powers of Europe had long since adopted patterns of interaction and terms of diplomatic discourse that established Westphalian sovereignty as a foundational international institution, however hypocritical their overall adherence to its principles might have been. The steady expansion of European influence during the eighteenth and nineteenth centuries led or forced international orders in other parts of the world to adjust along European lines.[222] Aspects of Westphalian sovereignty were codified into universally recognized principles of international law, and incorporated into the charters of key international organizations.[223] Furthermore, as Benedict Anderson argues, nationalist elites might be expected to have been socialized by the imperial experience to conceive of their communities as sovereign states. Because the educational and career paths of future nationalist leaders tended to be fixed by structures of governance that were imposed by the imperial overlords, and because opportunities outside one's native country were severely restricted (at least for anyone who was not a child of European parents), the boundaries of nationalist vision and ambition most often coincided with the territorial extent of the local administration.[224]

Yet for nationalist movements in the Arab world, the emergence of a states-system rooted in Westphalian sovereignty was neither immediate nor automatic. An alternative conception of regional order, in which the Arab countries merged to form a united political entity, dominated nationalist rhetoric and diplomatic practice during the first two decades of the twentieth century. The shift to an international arena made up of narrowly self-interested, territorially bounded states took place over a considerable period of time. Some nationalist leaderships made the transition comparatively early, while others did so much later. Explaining why this profound transformation in Middle Eastern affairs occurred involves accounting for the divergent trajectories that one finds among different Arab states.

CHAPTER TWO

Regulation, Surveillance, and State Formation

One explanation for the emergence of Westphalian sovereignty in the Arab world can be gleaned from an influential body of sociological literature that asserts that the appearance of external sovereignty is intimately related to the intensification of state control over domestic society. Agrarian empires and city-states, neither of which exercised firm or exclusive authority over the local political economy, interacted with one another in a wide variety of ways, but their foreign relations tended to remain circumscribed by the existence of "a normative community of shared norms and perceptions, some very general, others shared by specific transnational classes or religions; some peaceful, others violent."[1] The rise of well-articulated, centralized polities, by contrast, accompanied the emergence of an anarchic states-system, as rulers started to recognize one another's existence and other basic prerogatives, and interstate alliances formed on the basis of strategic interest, rather than according to ascriptive commonalities. In the terms introduced by Michael Mann, the unprecedented infrastructural power of the modern state led to "a tightening state-society relation, caging social relations over the national rather than the local-regional or transnational terrain, thus politicizing and geopoliticizing far more of social life than had earlier states."[2]

Anthony Giddens offers the most compelling account of how these complex processes fit together. He argues that Westphalian sovereignty takes shape whenever a country's central administration substantially augments its capacity to monitor and regulate the daily activities of the local population, and in particular when the extent of routine government surveillance approaches the geographical limits of state authority. Empires and city-states possess at best a tenuous grasp over internal affairs, both in terms of the extent to which state officials are able to extract resources and orchestrate collective projects and in terms of how much ideological hegemony the ruler enjoys over allies and subordinates. Furthermore, what little capacity the central administration has to monitor internal affairs is inherently "segmental," that is, split into distinct "political" and "economic" components.[3] As a result, government oversight tends to diminish sharply across space: districts situated close to the capital tend to be monitored and regulated much more closely than ones lying farther away. State surveillance is weakest at the fringes of society, where "the political authority of the centre is diffuse or thinly spread."[4] Such zones Giddens designates as "frontiers," and they represent regions where groups that have no allegiance to any particular polity can congregate unmolested by the surrounding authorities. Relations among premodern states thus prove to be inherently fluid and multifaceted: raiding, conquest, tribute, trade, and negotiation are all equally likely to be evident in the interactions of such polities.

Three dynamics enable states to augment their capacity to monitor and manage domestic affairs: "(i) the centralization and expansion of administrative power; (ii) the development of new mechanisms of law; and (iii) alterations in modes of fiscal management."[5] Such developments set the stage for the rise of the "absolutist state." This kind of polity provides the institutional framework in which capitalist relations of production can most readily coalesce. With the rise of capitalism comes a more integrated network of power relations that steadily supplants the segmental system of the precapitalist era.[6] More important, absolutist rulers generally succeed in suppressing periodic outbreaks of local violence. The process of "internal pacification" picks up momentum as state officials benefit from improvements in information storage capacity and other enhancements in what Giddens, following Michel Foucault, calls "disciplinary power" or surveillance. The upshot "is the withdrawal of the military from direct participation in the internal affairs of the state" and "a concentration of military power 'pointing outwards' toward other states in the nation-state system."[7] Under these circumstances, frontiers no longer represent "areas of territory (usually peripheral but often internal too) where the power of the state is weak."[8] On the contrary, the diffusion of more effective means of administrative supervision and control steadily pushes the least efficient form of domination — physical force and violence — to the very edges of society. At the same time, the borderlands between neighboring states take on greater salience, as they come to constitute the primary nodes through which external shocks can enter the internal arena. State officials therefore make a concerted effort to preclude the leaders of surrounding countries from engaging in any activity that might pose a threat to these exceptionally sensitive locales, while relinquishing whatever ambitions they might have to manipulate developments on the other side of the border. In this fashion, frontiers get transformed into "boundaries," and the absolutist state metamorphoses into the modern nation-state, which Giddens labels "a bordered power-container."[9]

Egypt's Surprisingly Weak State

Egypt's comparatively early adoption of Westphalian sovereignty is hard to explain in these terms. In many respects, the country's central administration became firmly entrenched in local society during the course of the nineteenth century. Officials in Cairo took charge of military conscription and the construction and maintenance of virtually all economic infrastructure as early as the 1820s. By mid-century, state agencies had captured pivotal roles in the supervision and management of agriculture, manufacturing, public health, and education.[10] More important, the operations of government agencies became increasingly depersonalized and rule-governed as the decades passed.[11] British administrators introduced further measures designed to enhance the efficiency of state control over domestic affairs after British troops occupied the country in the fall of 1882. In the words of one senior adviser, "The British Officials were the servants of [the Government of Egypt], the Consul-General was, by legal status, merely one of many accredited representatives of foreign powers. But by fortunate accident there was in Egypt an army belonging to the Power which he represented — and the happy result of this astonishing phenomenon was that what the British Consul-General said had to be listened to by the Egyptian Government."[12] Consequently, state agencies steadily tightened their grip on local society, while government expenditures more than doubled between 1881–84 and 1910–13.[13]

Still, key aspects of Egyptian society remained outside the purview of the central administration as the twentieth century opened. Government officials exercised little control over domestic capital investment. Foreign banks and expatriate financiers descended on the country en masse during the early 1860s, when the outbreak of civil war in the United States led to an unprecedented jump in demand for Egyptian cotton on world markets. The strongest of these financial institutions took advantage of the postwar collapse of cotton prices to seize a dominant position in local banking.[14] By 1900, virtually all decisions concerning the allocation of capital in Egypt were being taken by outside actors.[15] Not even the crisis of 1907 prompted state officials to take significant steps to augment their meager capacity to intervene in the country's financial affairs.[16]

External control over investment and finance complemented a general paucity of state regulation throughout the domestic economy. Not until 1911 was there a government department charged with supervising agriculture, although the ministry of public works had long administered the country's extensive irrigation system.[17] Roger Owen notes in this respect that "British policy toward other sectors of the economy [besides agriculture] was very much less interventionist, very much more in line with the conventional laissez-faire economic thinking of the day. . . . Laws affecting business activity were as unrestrictive as possible, and even then not always applied to foreign-owned enterprises covered by Capitulatory privileges."[18] Tariffs remained fixed at minimal levels, arguably as part of a comprehensive British strategy aimed at stifling local manufacturing.[19] Egypt's largest industrial enterprises, such as the Société Anonyme des Sucreries et de la Raffinerie d'Egypte and the Egyptian Salt and Soda Company, went about their day-to-day business with neither the active support of nor sustained interference from government regulatory agencies.

Meanwhile, the presence of British advisers at all levels of the central bureaucracy created a peculiar sort of dual administration that effectively undermined the state's capacity to implement policy or regulate domestic affairs. In early 1908, for instance, Consul-General Eldon Gorst proposed that the provincial councils that had been in existence but essentially dormant since 1883 take over responsibility for advising provincial governors regarding the administration of irrigation, the supervision of district police, and the organization of local markets.[20] British advisers in the provincial branches of government ministries were instructed by their superiors in Cairo to scale back their activities; this order in effect augmented the power of provincial governors, the great majority of whom owed their positions to personal connections with the minister of the interior. No longer constrained by British advisers and the informal links that the advisers enjoyed to the central administration, the governors ignored the councils. As a result, nepotism and law breaking became endemic in districts outside Cairo and Alexandria during the years just prior to the First World War. British officials tried to restore order by creating a new inspectorate of provincial police as part of the ministry of the interior, but "the new Inspectors' powers were more restricted — the continuity of their authority had been broken — and their functions were a compromise which, to be successfully carried out, required greater knowledge of the country and more experience than they actually often possessed."[21] Lines of administrative responsibility between the center and the periphery grew even more blurred following the declaration of martial law in November 1914.[22]

Dual authority was equally pronounced in Egypt's legal system. The bifurcation of the judiciary can be traced to the system of capitulations that had been established during the Ottoman era, which mandated that any legal disputes that involved Europeans be adjudicated differently from ones that involved Egyptians.[23] In 1875, state officials attempted to rationalize the judicial system by creating a network of Mixed Tribunals to handle cases involving foreign nationals; the European consular corps acquiesced in the creation of these tribunals, but insisted that their authority be restricted to civil and commercial disputes, while reserving for the existing consular courts the right to try criminal offenses. Subsequent attempts to reform the judiciary failed to produce an integrated, hierarchical court system, and as late as 1914 "the Egyptian judicial structure was composed of the following courts: 8 central tribunals, 90 summary tribunals, 28 markaz [provincial] courts, 235 cantonal [district] courts; with the central tribunals divided into first instance and appeal courts." The upshot was that "the new [British-sponsored] legal system failed to operate as effectively as anticipated."[24] Similar sorts of jurisdictional conflicts and administrative redundancies plagued the police and gendarmerie until an integrated public security agency was finally set up in February 1920.[25]

Dual authority characterized not only the central bureaucracy and legal system, it also pervaded provincial administration. Beginning in the 1890s, Mixed Commissions were established in the larger towns to assess and collect taxes on foreign nationals residing within their boundaries. Such bodies appeared initially in Alexandria and al-Mansurah, then in Tanta, Zagazig, and Damanhur, and in 1911 in al-Minya, Zifta, and Port Sa'id.[26] The commissions operated alongside a network of municipalities, which was loosely attached to the ministry of the interior. By 1915, there were in fact four distinct forms of local councils in the country: the Mixed Commissions, which relied on the voluntary compliance of foreign citizens for the revenues required to support their activities; two kinds of municipalities, one that collected taxes levied by local officials and the other that disbursed funds allocated by the ministry of the interior; and town (or village) councils, whose resources consisted exclusively of annual grants from the authorities in Cairo. As a result, programs that each municipality head approved and implemented often ran at odds with ones that interior ministry officials in Cairo authorized.

These trends were reflected in the ambiguous position that the port city of Alexandria occupied vis-à-vis the central administration in Cairo. By the end of the nineteenth century, Alexandria had become home to a sizable population of European merchants, speculators, and rascals, most of whose activities lay outside the jurisdiction of the local police and civil courts. Foreign nationals who resided in the city routinely turned to the European consular tribunals to adjudicate disputes not only among themselves but also between expatriates and Egyptians. In 1913, the British consul-general in Cairo appointed a commission to explore the possibility of abolishing the consular court system, but its findings were "irretrievably pigeon-holed until they were out of date" due to the outbreak of the First World War.[27] Along the same lines, European enterprises that operated in Alexandria regularly refused to pay the tax assessments that Egyptian-owned companies were compelled to remit to the municipal and central authorities.[28]

Officials in the capital exercised even less control over Egypt's southern provinces than they did over European neighborhoods in Alexandria. 'Ali Mubarak recounts the story of Qaw, an Upper Egyptian village whose inhabitants

> were like nobody else, and considered themselves different from the inhabitants of other villages; they spoke another dialect, pronounced the consonants differently. . . . Hence their faculty for self-preservation and fecundity; hence, too, their imperviousness. It was not by chance that the wheat of this village was said to contain precious substances, or that its tobacco, its vegetables, its poppy-seeds were valued so highly. Nor was it by chance that, from time to time, there were outbreaks of violence which the central power crushed without understanding them.[29]

In an attempt to impose a modicum of order in the south, British officials in 1904 promulgated an Arms Act that prohibited individuals from owning or carrying firearms. The ordinance had little impact on Upper Egypt, however, and in 1906 fighting erupted between Muslims and Christians throughout the region.[30] Jacques Berque reports that as late as 1920–21, "the countryside was overrun by bands of brigands who had practically become masters of every 'izba [agricultural laborers' village], particularly in Upper Egypt."[31] Central authority fared little if any better after the British Protectorate was formally abolished in February 1922: Lord Lloyd reports that "crime was very prevalent in the provinces, and Mudirs [provincial governors] were showing an inclination to slacken their supervision and take things easy."[32]

In addition, British advisers tightly restricted the Egyptian government's ability to raise and sustain regular military formations. Beginning in the 1890s, the total strength of the country's armed forces was capped at 6,000 troops, the majority of whom were deployed to scattered outposts in northern Sudan. Units stationed inside Egypt proper were usually attached either to the provincial gendarmerie or to the municipal police corps.[33] The post of operational commander of the armed forces (*sirdar*) was reserved for a British general, whose primary responsibility was to act as governor-general of the Sudan. Pivotal leadership positions throughout the military establishment were monopolized by British officers under secondment to the authorities in Cairo. Furthermore, the annual budget of the Egyptian armed forces was kept secret from civilian ministers by order of the sirdar.[34]

Egypt did enjoy comparatively well-demarcated territorial boundaries in the opening decades of the twentieth century. The country's northeastern border with the Syrian provinces of the Ottoman Empire was clarified as a direct result of the 1906 Sinai crisis. Almost all of the western border with Cyrenaica was formally defined two years earlier, during the course of a particularly intense episode of strategic jockeying between Istanbul and London.[35] Nevertheless, British commanders took advantage of the 1911–12 Libyan war to extend the boundaries of Egyptian control around the port at Sollum, and further disagreements over the disposition of enclaves west of Sollum persisted into the 1920s.[36] A more important ambiguity surrounded the southern limits of the central administration's authority. Egypt's rulers had seized control over vast areas of Dongola, Sinnar, and Kordofan in a series of military campaigns in 1810–11, and won title to strategically important coastal districts adjacent to the ports of Masawwa and Suwakin in 1865.[37] However, Egyptian command over the Red Sea littoral turned out to be both tenuous and short-lived: Ghada Talhami observes that "the British finally stripped away the last vestiges of Egyptian authority when the Mahdist Rebellion of 1882 spread to the eastern Sudan."[38] In the years following the revolt, British military officers and civilian administrative personnel steadily extended their influence westward from the Red Sea coast into the Nile basin.[39]

By 1901, policy decisions regarding the Sudan had devolved almost entirely onto a small group of senior British advisers, to the exclusion of the Egyptian government in Cairo. New regulations promulgated that year prohibited the authorities in Khartum from raising taxes and transferred responsibility for overseeing Sudanese finances from Egypt's council of ministers to the ministry of finance, a move that put effective control over the region's fiscal affairs in the hands of a British financial officer.[40] Three years later, the governor-general of the Sudan proposed to raise revenues to support the local administration by levying a tax on livestock exported to Egypt; the proposal was immediately quashed by the consul-general in Cairo, on the grounds that "the Sudan was an Egyptian province and could not impose separate export duties."[41] More crucially, military and internal security arrangements throughout the Sudanese provinces remained the exclusive prerogative of the sirdar, who tended as time went by to act without bothering to consult the war ministry in Cairo, "and in certain cases the Egyptian minister of war only learnt of a military engagement from the Egyptian press." As for more routine matters, "Sudan ordinances which, according to the first draft of the Condominium Agreement [of 1899], had to be submitted to the [Egyptian] council of ministers for its approval, were later only submitted as a matter of form and the council of ministers had no right to amend them.[42] The longtime British governor-general in Khartum, Reginald Wingate, in fact came to the opinion around 1907 "that the Sudan should become a separate political entity," and did his best to divorce the two countries from one another. This view was not shared by Eldon Gorst, the British consul-general in Cairo from October 1907 to July 1911, but it was tacitly endorsed by Gorst's successor, Lord Kitchener.[43] By the time Kitchener decamped to London in June 1914, lines of authority with regard to the Sudan had become almost hopelessly tangled.[44]

The outbreak of the First World War a month later precipitated a momentary jump in state intervention in Egypt's domestic economy. Strict limits were imposed on the exportation of cereals, in order to ensure an adequate supply of food to the cities. Local farmers immediately protested such restrictions, however, and in the spring of 1915 the prohibitions against exporting maize, beans, and wheat were quietly rescinded. That September the ceiling on the amount of land that could be devoted to cotton production was lifted as well.[45] The Supplies Control Board was set up by the council of ministers in November 1917 to supervise the allocation of staples among both civilians and the armed forces, but even though "some of its activities were beneficial, others [proved to be] irritating and ineffective, others prodigiously unbusinesslike."[46] Robert Tignor concurs: "Lacking an efficient administrative organisation, the Board was unable to enforce its rulings, and goods were sold in market places at prices well above those fixed by the state."[47] Enforcement was particularly lax in provincial towns, such as Damanhur.[48] Similarly, and after prolonged debate, the government set up a commission in June 1918 to oversee the purchase and distribution of locally grown cotton. Yet this board seldom managed to get prices right, and tended to act in ways that enriched elite cotton merchants at the expense of growers.[49] The food controller had no greater success regulating the price of foodstuffs on domestic markets.[50] Only with regard to the local labor force did government officials manage to tighten their grip as the war went along: the first paramilitary workers' battalions were organized in August 1915, and by the fall of 1917 the Labour Corps and Camel Transport Corps together boasted some 100,000 conscripts.

As the war drew to a close, state officials finalized plans to construct a new network of dams across the Blue Nile and White Nile rivers, the water from whose combined reservoirs was expected to increase the amount of arable land in southern Egypt and northern Sudan by almost 50 per cent.[51] Regulations to govern foreign trade, on the other hand, remained virtually nonexistent. Imports consequently flooded back into local markets in 1919–

20, sharply reversing the fortunes of local industry, which had prospered during the war.[52] State involvement in investment and finance remained equally minimal: the new national bank set up in March 1920, Bank Misr, had almost no connection with the central administration. Instead, as Tignor remarks, this institution "represented the most strikingly nationalist, even antiforeign, wing of the domestic bourgeoisie in Egypt. . . . Its official language was Arabic, for its founder wanted to demonstrate that Arabic could be a language of finance. No less significantly, he barred foreigners from being shareholders or directors in the bank."[53] Widespread unrest among urban workers prompted the authorities to establish the Labor Conciliation Board in August 1919. "Yet," according to Joel Beinin and Zachary Lockman, "in keeping with the principles of classical liberalism, the LCB was granted only very limited powers, for it could not impose binding arbitration, or enforce compliance with agreements reached under its auspices, but merely report its findings and make recommendations."[54]

In short, Egypt's nationalist leadership adopted a posture of Westphalian sovereignty at a time when the central bureaucracy in Cairo possessed little more than a rudimentary capacity to monitor and regulate domestic affairs. In the vivid words of Lord Lloyd, at the time the country gained de jure independence from Britain in March 1922, "the situation remained profoundly obscure in the growing maze of [political] intrigue, and the year 1922 ended without a Protectorate, without a Constitution, with an indemnity, and with martial law still in force."[55]

Tunisia's Comparatively Strong State

Giddens's argument appears to fit the Tunisian case a good deal better than it does that of Egypt. Tunisia's central administration steadily extended its purview over both far-flung agricultural villages and unruly pastoral districts as the nineteenth century passed.[56] The bey and his senior advisers imposed a unified command structure over the country's heterogeneous armed forces, and introduced systematic conscription, as early as the mid-1830s.[57] Military reforms accompanied concerted efforts to set up an integrated internal communications network, along with economic policies intended to create a complex of state-sponsored industrial enterprises. To obtain the revenues necessary to pay for these programs, innovative forms of taxation were imposed on olive and date cultivation, as well as on the sale of other major crops and livestock.[58] Political and economic centralization accelerated once again during the 1870s, under the direction of the visionary prime minister Khair al-Din.[59] After French troops overran the country in April 1881, French officials implemented a wide range of measures aimed at reinforcing and augmenting the state's capacity to supervise local affairs.[60]

Nevertheless, large areas of Tunisian society remained outside the reach of the central administration as the twentieth century got under way. Much of the high steppe that makes up the interior of the country continued to be governed not by the authorities in Tunis but rather by a collection of powerful tribal confederations, most notably the Hammamah, the Zlass, and the Majir. In districts dominated by these confederations, "a tribal council regulated tribal life, made collective decisions concerning production, irrigation, and transhumance. . . . The council orchestrated the life of the tribal group, made all important decisions about moves on tribal pasture lands, regulated internal conflicts and, in case of crime, decided on punishment and compensation."[61] Equally beyond the control of the state were the desert marches of the south, where the commanders of scattered military garrisons did their best to organize public works, education, and tax collection, while at the same time maintaining some degree of order.[62] Government authority rarely extended farther than the perimeter of these outposts, however, and large-scale revolts against French rule flared on a regular basis.[63] Beginning in 1911 and continuing through the initial years of the First World War, the incidence of raiding between tribes based in Tunisia and those of neighboring Tripolitania reached new heights. It was only when food supplies in the far south began to dry up in 1917 that French commanders found themselves at last able to gain the upper hand by manipulating the distribution of scarce staples.[64]

Even in those parts of the country where the authority of the central administration was more widely recognized, state officials exercised almost no influence over the way in which capital was invested. Exclusive long-term concessions to exploit the most profitable sectors of the domestic economy were held by French companies, which most often took steps to integrate their Tunisian and Algerian operations. The Tunisian Company for Iron and Railroads, for example, had originally been formed to exploit the rich mineral deposits around Constantine in northeastern Algeria. Other large enterprises, such as the Company for Phosphates and Railroads of Gafsa and the

Franco-African Agricultural and Property Society, were in fact little more than subsidiaries of major French banks.[65] Investment decisions were routinely taken by the directors of these companies without bothering to consult either the French authorities in Tunis or their superiors in Paris. As Noureddine Dougui remarks, "the Compagnie [des Phosphates et du Chemin de Fer de Gafsa], as a quasi-'sovereign' power, stood as an equal with the state itself at the pinnacle of the small economic realm of the Protectorate."[66]

In fact, the Tunisian state possessed only a rudimentary capacity to regulate domestic economic affairs in the years prior to the First World War. An Inspectorate for Agriculture and Viticulture was not set up until May 1913. This agency was not expanded into a comprehensive Agricultural Service until October 1924, when it was assigned responsibility for coordinating government programs to augment farm output in the regions around Bizerte, Tunis, Le Kef, Sousse, and Sfax.[67] A Public Office for Indigenous Agricultural Credit started operations a year later.[68] About the same time, the government created two organizations to oversee exploration for mineral and petroleum deposits: the Société de Recherches Minières de Tunisie and the Syndicat d'Etudes et de Recherches Pétrolières.[69] The first policies intended to regulate labor conditions can be traced to a June 1910 directive that limited the workday to ten hours; at the same time, a law was enacted that prohibited children under the age of 12 from working as wage laborers.[70] But state regulations governing other aspects of industrial labor were not promulgated until December 1919 and April 1921.[71] Similarly, although a complicated set of import duties and export taxes had been introduced in October 1884, the administration of foreign trade remained essentially haphazard until July 1904, when a more streamlined body of ordinances was put in place.[72] Tariffs were further rationalized in the spring of 1914, and amended yet again in 1926 and 1928.[73]

As in British-dominated Egypt, Tunisia's state apparatus exhibited a fundamental bifurcation — what Daniel Goldstein calls "la confusion des pouvoirs"[74] — throughout the Protectorate era. Mounira Charrad notes that during the years of French control, "as the de jure ruler, the bey issued decrees in his own name, but a decree took effect only if the resident general, the de facto power holder, gave his approval."[75] At lower levels of the government bureaucracy, French civil controllers were attached to key administrative offices and agencies.[76] Each civil controller was explicitly instructed not to engage in day-to-day administration, "but, within the extent of his circumscription, he alone is qualified, outside the Tunisian government, to oversee the administration of the native chiefs, to summon them and to correspond with them, to give them orders." As Lisa Anderson points out, "the distinction between administering and giving orders was a fine one — so fine, in fact, that it eventually escaped most of the controllers and most Tunisians."[77] Moreover, a melange of so-called technical agencies started to take shape in the decades following the French occupation to deal with such matters as public services, communications, and agriculture. Anderson observes that these agencies "were formally under the control of the Tunisian prime minister. In fact, [though,] they were independent ministries, controlled and staffed exclusively by French nationals."[78]

One area over which the civil controllers made a concerted effort to assert their authority involved Tunisia's extensive network of pious endowments (awqaf or habus). Such endowments reserved the proceeds generated by specific urban and rural properties in perpetuity to support a wide range of charitable institutions and activities. Both the management of the habus themselves and the charities that they funded remained outside the grasp of state agencies long after the French occupation. Instead, each endowment was administered by an agent (*muqaddam*), who was appointed to the post by the bey. The muqaddams were in turn loosely organized into a countrywide habus administration (*jama'iyyah al-ahbas*), which was one of the institutional legacies of the reform program orchestrated by Khair al-Din in the 1870s.[79] By one estimate, just under half of the local economy consisted of habus during the first decade of the twentieth century. French officials tried to force habus lands onto the open market as early as 1898.[80] But it was not until the mid-1920s that the central administration was able to exert a significant degree of control over the disposition and management of these properties.[81]

On the other hand, Tunisia's armed forces during the Protectorate boasted a highly centralized command structure, headed by a French general bearing the title Commandant Supérieur des Troupes des Tunisie.[82] Recruits from Senegal and Morocco made up the large majority of the 18,000 troops under this officer's direct command. Tunisian soldiers generally found themselves relegated to mixed companies of scouts and sappers. They were, however, expected to flesh out the reserve units that would be mobilized in time of war, and all 19-year-old males were required by law to register for potential military service. Registration and enlistment in each locality were supervised by the district headman (*qaid*), who was authorized to grant individual exemptions from active duty in exchange for cash payments.[83] Equally important, a French gendarmerie was set up in the coastal areas of the north and east in September 1888, and was extended to most other parts of the country during 1897–98. A separate corps of indigenous gendarmes, under the joint supervision of the qaids and the civil controllers, assisted in enforcing order and collecting taxes, "but only for the natives" ("mais pour les indigènes seulement").[84]

The coming of the First World War witnessed a substantial increase in the degree of state intervention in domestic affairs. During the months after August 1914, the French gendarmerie undertook to "assure the surveillance of the country; look for deserters, malefactors, and the unruly; strengthen the recruiting system; oversee prisoners of war; and supply the armed forces with valuable goods as ordered."[85] State agents seized control of the distribution of wheat and sugar at the outset of the war, and imposed price controls on other key staples as the fighting dragged on.[86] Unprecedented restrictions on imports and exports were also put in place.[87] Between 60,000 and 80,000 Tunisians were conscripted into the French armed forces, and more than 10,000 of these troops died fighting on European battlefields.[88] In addition, shortages of agricultural and industrial laborers inside France prompted Protectorate officials to enact a law in April 1918 that accorded them "wide latitude in requisitioning workers" in an effort to keep French farms and factories operating at full capacity.[89] Inspired by the wartime initiatives undertaken by the French authorities, the bey took steps in the fall of 1917 to impose extraordinary taxes on the profits generated as a result of the wartime boom in trade and manufacturing.[90]

Thanks to such measures, the central administration exercised an unprecedented degree of influence over local society when the war came to an end. In 1919, the newly appointed resident general set up five Grand Commissions to coordinate postwar policy regarding colonization, finance, administration, social issues, and public works.[91] Conscription of agricultural workers for work on French-owned farms and in the French mining companies continued during the two years following the armistice.[92] The Resident General in May 1920 ordered that all "unproductive" land in the country be sequestered by the government and sold to new owners who would bring it into immediate production. Determining the extent of such land, as well as its precise legal status, necessitated a comprehensive survey of all real estate, whether privately held or designated as habus.[93] Redoubled efforts by state officials to modify the restrictions on habus properties sparked widespread discontent among mainstream Islamic scholars and the heads of religious brotherhoods alike.[94] In response, the French authorities created a ministry of justice in 1922 to take over many of the duties of the local Islamic courts.[95] Small-scale manufacturers and shopkeepers found their activities exposed to heightened scrutiny on the part of government-appointed market inspectors, while the number of Tunisians imprisoned for infractions of currency regulations reached unprecedented levels.[96] Furthermore, general rates of taxation jumped immediately after the war ended.[97] Even more galling, Tunisians employed in French institutions and enterprises were subjected beginning in 1919 to strict ceilings not only on the positions they might hold but also on the amount of monetary remuneration to which they were entitled.[98]

Moreover, Tunisia's eastern and southern boundaries came to be clearly delimited during the course of the First World War. Skirmishes between rival tribal groups broke out along the border with Tripolitania with increasing frequency and intensity beginning in early 1915.[99] In response, French commanders stepped up their efforts to regulate all movement into and out of southern Tunisia. Military operations against restive tribes in the south proved more successful than ever before due to the expansion of a telegraph network to link isolated garrisons throughout this vast region. In September 1919, the authorities in Tunis signed a treaty with officials in Tripoli that formally demarcated the boundary between their respective domains.[100] Consequently, by the time the war ended, the French armed forces had managed not only to establish a distinct line between the territory under its own control and the Italian-held lands next door, but also to establish a firm hold over far-flung districts that had previously been subject to no more than nominal French authority.

Tunisia therefore looks like a case in which the turn to Westphalian sovereignty did in fact accompany a steady increase in state surveillance and supervision over domestic affairs. The U.S. consul in Tunis even opened a report to Washington in October 1925 with the pithy observation that "There is too much Government in Tunisia."[101] Yet the regime's very success in consolidating central administrative control in the years leading up to the First World War makes it hard for historical sociologists to explain why

Westphalian sovereignty took hold as late as it did. Whereas the nationalist leadership in Cairo adopted a posture toward the outside world predicated on the notion of a self-interested, territorially bounded Egypt a good deal sooner than Giddens might predict, nationalist leaders in Tunis held off a bit too long before making the shift.

Jordan's Surprisingly Strong State

Given this line of argument, one might have expected Westphalian sovereignty to appear in Jordan at a comparatively late date. It is a truism among Middle East specialists that of all the Arab states that were set up in the aftermath of the First World War, Transjordan was by far the most fragile. As late as 1957, one well-informed observer remarked that "the ultimate fate of Jordan hangs in the balance. Whether the state can long exist independently remains to be seen."[102] In a similar vein, Mustafa Hamarneh's overview of the political economy of the amirate period concludes that "by 1946, Jordan was one of the most backward and underdeveloped countries" in the world, "unable to generate enough surplus from within to maintain itself as a separate state."[103] More recently, Nazih Ayubi asserts that at its birth, Transjordan constituted no more than "a 'corridor' country without a distinct history, or focal point, or even a native royal family"; British officials dominated the rudimentary administrative apparatus and military establishment, while "Syrian merchants continued to be prominent in Amman's marketplace for several decades."[104]

Yet the central administration gained virtually unchallenged control over the country's internal affairs comparatively early on. Amir ʿAbdullah bin al-Husain and his retainers experienced little difficulty subordinating the disparate collection of district governments that sprouted in al-Salt, Irbid, ʿAjlun, Jarash, and Karak in the months immediately after the First World War.[105] Armed uprisings against the new regime erupted in al-Kurah in June 1921, around Karak the following winter, and in the Balqa district a year later, but these revolts were suppressed quite handily by the regime's embryonic armed forces with the assistance of Britain's Royal Air Force.[106] Moreover, the outspoken Syrian and Palestinian expatriates who comprised the membership of the handful of political parties that played an active part in the country's internal affairs during the 1920s soon found themselves ousted from positions in the central bureaucracy; they were then denied Transjordanian citizenship according to the terms of the restrictive 1928 nationality law.[107]

Meanwhile, the Hashemite leadership's chosen capital, the sleepy town of ʿAmman, quickly captured a predominant position in the local political economy. Other urban centers that had been the primary loci of earlier trade and manufacturing, most notably al-Salt and Karak, lost not only population but also prestige compared to ʿAmman in the early 1920s.[108] Prominent commercial houses relocated their main offices to the new capital almost as soon as ʿAbdullah and his entourage arrived.[109] ʿAmman-based merchants set up the country's first chamber of commerce in 1923, thereby reinforcing the growing economic and political importance of the city.[110] Physical proximity to the amiri court ensured that powerful commercial interests located in the capital enjoyed regular access to the central administration, while enhancing the role of elite merchants in shaping economic policy.[111] By the mid-1930s, ʿAmman stood as the country's unchallenged political and economic center.[112]

Furthermore, the central administration exercised control over a comparatively well-demarcated territory. British and French officials mapped out the border separating Transjordan from Syria in the fall of 1920, and ratified the arrangement through a series of bilateral negotiations that took place during October 1931.[113] Disputed districts around ʿAqaba and Maʿan were incorporated into the amirate in 1925, during the course of severe fighting between supporters of the Hashemite ruler of al-Hijaz and forces allied to the Al Saʿud of Najd.[114] Meanwhile, a succession of skirmishes in August 1922 involving the powerful Bani Sakhr confederation and formations of Muwahhidi Ikhwan ranging north out of central Arabia not only cemented a crucial strategic alliance between the Bani Sakhr and Amir ʿAbdullah but also extended ʿAmman's purview all the way to the desert frontier with Saudi Arabia.[115] The actual contours of the Transjordanian–Saudi Arabian border were drawn up under British auspices that October.[116] On the other hand, Britain's mandate over Palestine complicated the question of Transjordan's western boundary. But the uncertainty that was engendered by this particular territorial ambiguity inspired neither secessionist nor irredentist sentiments inside the amirate.

In fact, state surveillance steadily permeated Transjordanian society in the first two decades of amirate's existence. District gendarmes and urban police were integrated into a centralized command structure during the spring of 1923.[117] A central prison was constructed in ʿAmman two years later to replace the patchwork collection of district jails that had previously dotted the countryside.[118] In April 1926, the Transjordanian Frontier Force was set up to patrol the amirate's eastern marches.[119] This military formation, renamed the Desert Patrol, was attached to the 'Amman-based Arab Legion in 1930 and was equipped with armored cars, two-way radios, and modern small arms provided by the British garrison in Iraq.[120] Meanwhile, "a tribal control board was formed so the British authorities could have more control in bedouin matters, and small salaries were paid to 'leading' sheikhs on the condition that they assumed responsibility for public order among their tribesmen."[121] This network of institutions, in conjunction with astute diplomacy on the part of the commander of the Desert Patrol, effectively consolidated the central administration's control over the eastern desert, perhaps as early as 1932 and certainly by 1934.[122]

In the economic arena, the authorities in 'Amman promulgated an initial Customs and Excise Law at the end of 1926, whose terms spelled out the routes whereby imported goods might legally enter the country.[123] A year later, the government instituted the Palestine pound as the amirate's sole legal currency; it concurrently "unified all measures and measurements (which formerly had given rise to constant complaints by the merchants)."[124] December 1927 saw the beginnings of a comprehensive survey of Transjordan's agricultural land, which eventuated in the adoption of a revised land tax code in the spring of 1933. Full implementation of the code required an additional two years, but by the end of 1935 "all villages in Transjordan were operating under the new law."[125] Plans to construct and maintain a network of paved roads throughout the country were adopted that same year.[126] In 1936, the postal service was reorganized in such a way as to make motor vehicles the primary means of collecting and distributing local mail, thereby significantly improving the efficiency and reliability of communication inside the amirate.[127]

State officials introduced more stringent controls over foreign trade as the decade drew to a close. At the end of 1936, the Directorate of Customs and Trade started issuing government licenses regulating the importation of grain into the country.[128] In July 1938, the authorities announced their intention to abrogate a 1923 agreement with Syria that had exempted all goods produced in one country (with the exception of tobacco products and alcoholic beverages) from customs duties levied by the government of the other.[129] Additional restrictions on external commerce were put into effect in September 1939.[130]

The outbreak of the Second World War precipitated a wide range of policies that substantially augmented what Mann would call the infrastructural power of the Transjordanian state.[131] Extraordinary duties were imposed during the early 1940s on imported tobacco products, electronic equipment, and other goods.[132] Thousands of underemployed tribespeople were recruited in 1941–42 to construct roads and railway lines in the area between Ma'an and 'Aqaba.[133] Michael Fischbach reports that in 1944 the Department of Lands and Survey introduced a cluster of emergency measures designed to provide government assistance for heavily indebted small farmers.[134] The following spring the finance ministry levied an unprecedented income tax on local merchants. Although the head of the 'Amman Chamber of Commerce convinced the prime minister to put off collecting the first year's assessments, the Legislative Council ratified the scheme in the fall of 1945.[135] Most important of all, the Department of Customs, Trade, and Industry actively cooperated with the Cairo-based Middle East Supply Center (MESC) in supervising the distribution of lucrative import and export quotas among prominent members of Transjordan's rich merchant community. The activities of the MESC not only boosted indigenous capital accumulation but also accelerated the diversification of the local economy.[136]

So by the time the British mandate ended in March 1946, Transjordan's state apparatus possessed most if not all of the attributes that Giddens associates with the appearance of Westphalian sovereignty. Nevertheless, the leadership in 'Amman persisted in claiming authority over extensive territories outside the recognized borders of the kingdom for more than half a decade after Jordan won de jure independence. This position poses a significant puzzle for sociological accounts of the emergence of self-interested, territorially bounded states: Why did Jordanian leaders continue to predicate their foreign policy on an exceptionally broad notion of political community for so long after the central bureaucracy had established effective control over domestic society?

Iraq's Comparatively Strong State

According to the argument advanced by historical sociologists, Westphalian sovereignty should also have appeared in Iraq much earlier than it did. The central administration in Baghdad exercised a considerable degree of control over domestic affairs even before the country was granted de jure independence from Britain in 1932. As Roger Owen remarks, "already by the early 1920s the most politically active groups within both the Shiʿi and Kurdish populations had accepted the realities of the new order and focused their attention on trying to exert pressure on the power centre in Baghdad."[137] This state of affairs arose largely out of the experience of the armed uprising of 1920, which melded the country's diverse populace together in active resistance to British rule. In Hanna Batatu's words, during the course of the revolt "for the first time in many centuries, Shiʿis joined politically with Sunnis, and townsmen from Baghdad and tribesmen from the Euphrates made common cause. Unprecedented joint Shiʿi-Sunni celebrations, ostensibly religious but in reality political, were held in all the Shiʿi and Sunni mosques in turn: special *mawlids*, Sunni ceremonial observances in honor of the Prophet's birthday, were on occasions followed by *taʿziyahs*, Shiʿi lamentations for the martyred Husain, the proceedings culminating in patriotic oratory and poetic thundering against the English."[138] British-sponsored institutions — such as the Divisional Councils, which were set up at the end of the First World War "to secure the full benefit of co-operation by tribal leaders and large landowners,"[139] and the Tribal Disputes Regulation of 1924 — provided concrete mechanisms whereby authorities in the capital could contain popular discontent and, on occasion, channel it in directions favorable to the regime.

State control over domestic affairs heightened during the 1930s as a result of several overlapping dynamics. First, the centrality of Baghdad as the national capital was deliberately fostered by government officials, and was bolstered by the implementation of a number of economic and infrastructural projects.[140] The growth of manufacturing and construction enterprises in and around the city encouraged a steady stream of immigrants from the provinces, as well as a proliferation of new residential neighborhoods.[141] As a result of these developments, Batatu observes that by the early 1940s "to speak of the towns is to all effective purposes to speak of Baghdad, to which, with the decline of the tribal world, the political center of gravity had definitively and decisively shifted, and which in the space of a few decades absorbed unto itself much of the vitality of the entire country."[142] Neither Mosul in the north nor Basrah in the south posed the kind of challenge to Baghdad's primacy in the Iraqi political economy that Aleppo did to Damascus during this period.

In addition, the size and scope of the central administration increased steadily in the decade after independence. The total number of persons employed in government agencies rose from 8,247 in 1935 to 10,754 in 1940, then jumped to 15,259 in 1945.[143] Although a state-sponsored Date Association set up in 1933 failed to ameliorate conflicts between growers and packers of this important crop, the Supervisory Commission for the Date Trade that was formed two years later enjoyed the capacity to "fix the price of dates, make loans to producers in financial straits . . . , and enforce previous provisions relating to hygienic conditions."[144] The commission's powers expanded dramatically when prices on regional markets collapsed after 1938.[145] An even more important indicator of the expanding scope of central authority can be discerned in what Phebe Marr calls "the increased effectiveness of tax collecting, which now reached groups and individuals who previously were only marginally involved. By the end of the mandate [in 1932]," she continues, "virtually all citizens of every class were liable for taxes, which included an income tax, land revenue taxes, rent on miri (state land), an animal tax, a property tax, and finally, a municipal tax on artisans and workmen."[146] Revenues derived from such assessments rose steadily from the time of independence to the end of the Second World War.[147]

Sporadic outbursts of popular disorder persuaded the country's rich merchants and larger landholders to cast their lot with the central government. Increased activism on the part of artisans and laborers at the beginning of the 1930s heightened what Charles Tripp calls "the prospect of a Shiʿi-Sunni alliance dominated by the former, or the sight of urban and rural elites collaborating with workers' organizations in the towns."[148] The persistence of unrest led the commercial aristocracy of Baghdad to look to state officials to keep order in the cities, while large estate-holders acquiesced in the repeated bombardment of rural areas by units of the Royal Air Force. In this way, powerful forces whose interests might otherwise have clashed with those of the central bureaucracy ended up supporting the consolidation of state authority and surveillance over local society.

Government officials benefited from the professionalism and ésprit de corps of the Iraqi armed forces, particularly after the suppression of the Assyrian rebellion of 1933.[149] Immediately following the revolt, the authorities in Baghdad introduced a law that mandated universal male conscription for military service. The law took effect in June 1935, and "active measures were soon taken to register eligible males between the ages of eighteen and twenty-one."[150] Iraq's armed forces gained strength and prestige as a result of their success in suppressing a further series of uprisings in the provinces during the mid-1930s, and emerged as a major actor in domestic politics when troops loyal to generals Bakr Sidqi, 'Abd al-Latif Nuri, and Muhammad 'Ali Jawad seized control of the state apparatus in October 1936.[151] This coup d'état undermined the authority of the cabinet that it ousted from power, but the policies that the military leadership pursued in the wake of the coup substantially enhanced the strength of the central administration vis-à-vis opposition parties and provincial notables alike. Consequently, "state consolidation through conscription and other methods continued and the extension and entrenchment of a landowning interest proceeded undisturbed."[152] During the course of 1944–45, the armed forces were reorganized so as to enable them to respond more efficiently to internal and external threats to the regime.[153] Between 1932 and 1947 the size of the military establishment increased by more than 400 per cent.[154]

Central authority in Iraq received a further boost in 1934, when petroleum began to be exported in commercial quantities. As oil revenues flowed into state coffers, the government set up the Economic Council, whose assigned task was "thoroughly to study important development schemes."[155] Two years later, steadily rising income from oil production made it possible for state officials to launch the Agricultural and Industrial Bank, whose primary purpose was to encourage innovative food processing and manufacturing ventures.[156] Oil monies made it possible for successive governments to allocate one-third of total state expenditures to capital development projects between 1935 and 1940.[157]

Finally, the territorial boundaries of Iraq stood relatively well-defined at the moment that Iraq became independent. Nationalist leaders in Baghdad made little secret of their desire eventually to regain control of the strategically situated desert marches south of Basrah, out of which Britain had created the autonomous amirate of Kuwait at the beginning of the twentieth century.[158] And they periodically expressed concern that the Turkish Republic might revive its long-standing claim to the profitable oil-producing region around the northern cities of Mosul and Kirkuk. Nevertheless, the boundary between Iraq and Transjordan was clearly demarcated in an exchange of notes in September 1932, while outstanding disagreements with Syria concerning the precise location and administration of their common border were resolved a month later by a special commission acting under the auspices of the League of Nations.[159] Iraq thus ended the 1930s largely free from the pervasive uncertainties regarding territorial demarcation that complicated the diplomacy of other Arab countries.

In short, the years preceding the Second World War evidenced a continuous rise in the infrastructural power of the Iraqi state. Wartime exigencies accelerated the expansion of central administrative control even further. September 1939 saw the promulgation of a pair of administrative orders that greatly augmented the scope of state surveillance over internal affairs. The first declared a nationwide state of emergency and authorized the ministry of the interior "to order general or partial black out in any area of the country" and "impose a curfew in any place or district of Iraq." The second, designated the Decree for Organizing the Country's Economic Life during the Present International Crisis, empowered the government "to take steps for the storage, supply, and sale of 'essential commodities'; to monopolize their sale to the public; and to fix prices and take steps to ensure the effective execution of measures decided upon."[160] At the same time, the government created a state-affiliated Central Supply Board, and charged it with supervising the equitable distribution of foodstuffs and other staples. When this agency proved unable to suppress widespread profiteering in the wake of the June 1941 British occupation, it was replaced with the Supreme Supply Committee, which tried to regulate the supply of essential commodities by issuing licenses to authorized distributors.[161] Persistent inflation prompted the government to introduce a system of price controls in 1942.[162] A year later, the cabinet adopted a wide-ranging package of labor reforms, which gave state officials considerable latitude in monitoring working conditions in private sector companies and arbitrating disputes between owners and workers.[163] In 1944, rationing of coffee, tea, and textiles was introduced.[164] By that time, ministries in the capital were reported to exercise command "in almost every detail [over] the provincial administration."[165]

When the Second World War ended, Iraq's central administration possessed most if not all of the attributes that historical sociologists connect to the emergence of Westphalian sovereignty. Yet the leadership in Baghdad continued to pursue a foreign policy that was explicitly oriented toward the creation of some form of amalgamated Arab political entity. This line of argument offers little insight into the puzzle of why Iraq, with its comparatively well-established state apparatus, adopted the fundamental characteristics of Westphalian sovereignty so tardily.

Syria's Comparatively Weak State

In marked contrast to Iraq, Giddens would expect Westphalian sovereignty to have appeared in Syria a good deal later than it actually did. Throughout the Second World War, the country's state bureaucracy remained circumscribed by the French imperial administration that had been set up during the 1920s and 1930s. The leadership of the National Bloc confronted two fundamental difficulties in its efforts to win Syrian independence in the years between the two world wars. First, it had to persuade influential provincial elites to recognize Damascus as the country's permanent capital. Most strongly opposed to subordinating themselves in perpetuity to rule from Damascus were the elite merchants of Aleppo. Such sentiments were shared by the inhabitants of the rural districts outside the coastal city of Latakia and the southern highlands around al-Suwaida (Jabal Druze). Notables from Aleppo constituted a separate branch of the Bloc, whose members actively challenged the predominance of the Damascene wing during the 1930s and early 1940s.[166] More important, jockeying between the Bloc's northern and southern factions provided openings for a variety of popular associations whose programs envisaged a radical reconfiguration of Syria's political institutions.[167]

Agitation against the central administration on the part of 'Alawis in the coastal districts south of Latakia and Druze from the countryside around al-Suwaida escalated sharply after 1937, when the hero of the 1925 rebellion against the French, Sultan Pasha al-Atrash, returned to southern Syria from exile in Transjordan.[168] Government officials exercised little control over day-to-day affairs in either 'Alawi or Druze territory until the late 1940s.[169] Meanwhile, the Kurds, Armenians, and Assyrians who populated the towns of the Euphrates basin (al-Jazirah) in the northeast "launched their own autonomous movement . . . demanding administrative and financial autonomy, the continuation of the French Mandate, and the appointment of local functionaries under a French governor."[170] Under these circumstances, the leadership in Damascus found it virtually impossible to construct what Philip Khoury calls "a new national identity for Syria."[171]

Second, the nationalist leadership remained sharply divided over the question of whether to accept the territorial boundaries that had been imposed on geographical Syria by the French. The Aleppo branch of the National Bloc consistently championed the creation of a more extensive political entity. As early as February 1934, a congress of northern Bloc activists adopted a platform that called for the reintegration into independent Syria of four Ottoman administrative districts that the French had transferred to Lebanon in 1920.[172] By contrast, the Damascus wing of the National Bloc tended — largely out of tactical necessity — to acquiesce in the demands of successive French governments that Syria's existing borders remain intact, as well as in their insistence that the 'Alawi and Druze homelands retain a substantial degree of autonomy after independence.[173] The Damascus leadership's proclivity to compromise during the course of its protracted negotiations with France culminated in its acquiescence in the transfer of the former Ottoman sanjak of Iskandarun to Turkey in 1938–39.[174]

State surveillance over the territory inside Syria's nominal borders remained tenuous as the Second World War got under way. The central administration's lack of effective control was particularly evident in military and security affairs. Instead of a regular armed forces, the French-led Troupes Speciales du Levant garrisoned border posts and maintained a modicum of order in the provinces. This military formation suffered from a persistent shortage of funds during the late 1930s, which greatly reduced its operational capabilities.[175] Furthermore, the creation of a new irregular Circassian cavalry formation (the Groupement Partisan Tcherkess) in November 1940 engendered serious friction between Druze veterans in the Troupes Speciales and the newly recruited Circassians.[176] As the war moved east in early 1941, it became clear that the Troupes Speciales stood "woefully underarmed, with practically no heavy offensive or defensive weapons." Discipline was in equally short supply: one French commander complained that his Syrian companies had turned out to be "little more than [armed] bands with a superficial layer of military discipline."[177]

In addition, the Troupes Speciales du Levant enjoyed almost no legitimacy among the general population. Nacklie Bou-Nacklie reports that on the eve of the war the Syrian minister of the interior begged the Vichy high commissioner, Gabriel Puaux, to prevent Circassian units from entering the cities and towns "for fear of riots by the Arabs, who detested the Tcherkess."[178] Tensions mounted in the spring of 1941, after Vichy officials ordered Druze and Circassian troops to be segregated from the local population in an effort to stop the flow of desertions to Palestine and Transjordan.[179] When Syria gained de jure independence from France in August 1943, influential members of parliament argued forcefully against the state's taking charge of the Troupes Speciales, partly on fiscal grounds but also "because of its close association with the French." Faris al-Barzawi's impassioned assertion "that the 'people' were prepared to pay higher taxes to defray the money needed to support the army" elicited shouts of derision in the assembly.[180]

Even after units of the Troupes Speciales reverted to Syrian control in June 1944, they proved largely incapable of carrying out their assigned duties. Bou-Nacklie observes that "in the spring of 1944 under British pressure, the French decided to hand over the mehariste companies to the Syrian [authorities]. Unfortunately for both the meharistes and the Syrian government, famine struck Iraq in that year and thousands of bedouins streamed into northeastern Syrian looking for food. The 1ere and 2eme companies meharistes, which were stationed in that region, found themselves unable to keep law and order."[181] To make matters worse, "the French waited for the Syrians to fail and did not propose to help the efforts of Syrian government officials by offering any of their units stationed in that region. It was when the Syrian government publicly stated that it was unable to control the situation that the French sent the Tcherkess in."[182] French officials pointed to this episode as a reason to delay relinquishing the remainder of the Troupes Speciales du Levant to Syrian command. Orders to complete the transfer were not issued until July 1945, and the Troupes Speciales were at long last divided between the Syrian and Lebanese governments that August.[183]

As the Second World War drew to a close, state officials took steps to strengthen the embryonic military establishment. The Syrian government asked the United States in August 1945 for drill instructors, technical advisers, and modern equipment as part of a comprehensive program to improve the army's operational effectiveness.[184] When the U.S. Department of State at last decided to turn down the request, Damascus turned to Switzerland and Sweden for assistance, albeit without success.[185] Finally, in August 1946 a former British field commander, Lieutenant-Colonel Gordon Fox, was appointed to take charge of training the Syrian armed forces. Fox's efforts quickly collapsed, partly because "the British government opposed his attempt to hire retired British officers to help him" and partly because "he was suspected by the Syrians to be a British intelligence officer and was therefore never truly trusted in his mission."[186]

Furthermore, Syria's foreign trade continued throughout the war to be regulated not by the central administration in Damascus, but rather by the

French-run Conseil Supérieur des Intérêts Communs. This organization governed not only the joint Syrian-Lebanese customs administration but also a wide range of public sector enterprises, including the two countries' combined railroad system, the post and telegraph office, and the public utilities.[187] Negotiations concerning the disposition of these joint agencies took place between French representatives and the National Bloc leadership during the course of 1944, and "by the end of the year," Albert Hourani reports, "almost all the services in question had been formally handed over, including the Customs Administration, the Financial and Economic Services, the control of the tobacco monopoly and concessionary companies, the Press Censorship, the Beduin control and the 'Sûreté Générale.'" As a result of these talks, Hourani remarks, the Syrian state obtained "almost all the attributes of independent governments."[188] Nevertheless, local control remained more apparent than actual: despite the formal agreements, "the transfer was more in name than in reality, since for reasons of efficiency the French personnel of the services was retained temporarily."[189] Not until February 1948 was the Conseil Supérieur finally abolished.[190]

Syria's central administration exercised little more control over the domestic economy than it did over foreign trade. Wartime measures that were intended to supervise local industry, manage prices, and regulate the supply of staples proved generally unsuccessful.[191] Spiraling prices and persistent shortages of bread, sugar, and heating oil sparked popular demonstrations in Damascus and Aleppo in January and February 1941, which in turn prompted the authorities to order French troops into the major cities in an attempt to restore calm.[192] When protests broke out once again in March, the new high commissioner, General Henri Dentz, announced that the government would allocate more resources and devote greater attention to creating jobs and providing affordable food.[193] Nevertheless, these programs turned out to be "generally ineffective. . . . An Economic Congress summoned at Damascus could debate and form its busy sub-committees, but could neither increase supplies nor facilitate distribution; an ambitious programme of public health measures made hopeful reading, but a new interstatal Rationing Committee, to meet alternately at Beirut and Damascus, made but a slow start."[194] Efforts to stabilize wholesale and retail prices fared no better.[195]

In short, the Second World War did little to enhance the infrastructural power of the Syrian state. On the contrary, "the years 1946 and 1947 were characterized by a rapid disorganization and deterioration of the governmental processes, parliamentary and administrative."[196] Measures designed to replace French and British wartime subsidies with domestic revenues precipitated widespread popular protest, to which the leadership in Damascus responded by launching "a campaign to destroy its critics by a policy of arrests and suppression of political opposition."[197] In October 1946, President Shukri al-Quwwatli took the extraordinary step of releasing all government agencies from the supervision of the Accounts Office (Bureau des Comptes), thereby acknowledging the state's incapacity to regulate even the routine operations of its own departments.[198]

So by the time that Syria gained de facto independence in August 1946, the state apparatus possessed few if any of the attributes that historical sociologists link to the emergence of Westphalian sovereignty. Nevertheless, the nationalist leadership in Damascus had long since adopted a foreign policy posture that was predicated on a conception of Syria as a narrowly self-interested, territorially bounded political entity. This fact poses the opposite puzzle to the one raised by the cases of Jordan and Iraq: Why did the relatively feeble Syrian state take on the defining features of Westphalian sovereignty with such alacrity?

CHAPTER THREE

Commercial Interests and Elite Bargains

A promising way to address the conceptual and empirical puzzles associated with the emergence of Westphalian sovereignty in these five Arab countries can be extrapolated from Hendrik Spruyt's analysis of the origins of external sovereignty in early modern Europe. In *The Sovereign State and Its Competitors*, Spruyt argues that those European polities that exercised control over fragmented urban commercial centers took on important attributes of Westphalian sovereignty under two broad circumstances: (1) when the economies in which they were situated experienced a steady expansion of foreign trade and (2) when that trade consisted primarily of low-profit, high-volume goods. Given these conditions, it proved virtually impossible for any single merchant house to capture a monopoly position in external markets, and all commercial enterprises were highly sensitive to both increases in transaction costs and the adverse effects of foreign competition.[1] Powerful trading interests therefore formed a political alliance with their respective rulers, which entailed the establishment of fully autonomous, territorial states as a way to regularize and limit transaction costs. In other words, rich merchants had a clear incentive to tolerate the new constraints and burdens that accompanied the coming of external (as well as internal) sovereignty, because subservience to a single, recognized monarch was preferable to continued domination and predation by unruly local nobles.

On the other hand, rich merchants located in countries whose foreign trade consisted mostly of high-profit, low-volume goods had very little incentive to acquiesce in the formation of autonomous, territorially bounded states. Such merchants' profits were much less severely affected by fluctuations in transaction costs, and many of these traders might reasonably have expected to capture a monopoly position in regional or global markets. Under these circumstances, members of the commercial elite made little attempt to work with one another to advance their collective interests, and tended instead to take steps that effectively undercut each other.[2] More important, merchants engaged in high-profit, low-volume trade did their best to resist falling subordinate to a sovereign overlord, and preferred instead to take their chances as independent actors in the unregulated external market. Consequently, Westphalian sovereignty appeared at a relatively early date in low-profit, high-volume France and took shape a good deal later among the high-profit, low-volume city-states of the Italian peninsula.

Egypt's Low-profit, High-volume Trade

Spruyt's argument goes a long way toward explaining why Westphalian sovereignty emerged at a comparatively early date in Egypt. Low-profit, high-volume agricultural goods dominated Egypt's foreign trade at the beginning of the twentieth century. The most important of these goods—long-staple cotton and its various derivatives—accounted for more than 90 per cent of total export earnings as of 1910–13.[3] Three other staple crops—rice, beans, and sugar—made up almost all of the remainder. Major industrial exports consisted of similarly low-profit items, most notably the coarse cotton, wool, and silk cloth produced by provincial artisans for sale on markets in the Sudan and eastern Mediterranean.[4] None of these goods was one in which Egyptian merchants might reasonably have expected to capture a monopoly position in either regional or international markets. Producers of cotton, rice, beans, sugar, and coarse cloth therefore shared a fundamental interest in keeping transaction costs to a minimum.

Egypt's foreign trade registered a steady rise at the turn of the twentieth century. The value of cotton and cottonseed exports almost doubled between 1885–89 and 1900–04, and rose by another two-thirds between 1900–04 and 1910–13.[5] More generally, Bent Hansen and Edward Lucas calculate that Egypt's terms of trade exhibited "a strong upward trend [from the mid-nineteenth century] until about 1910, followed by a prolonged downward trend until World War II."[6] This finding turns out to be remarkably robust, whether it is measured by means of net barter terms of trade, income terms of trade, or income terms of trade per capita.[7] Export volume per capita shows a similar pattern, with a marked increase at the end of the nineteenth century leading to "a fairly constant high plateau from 1902 to 1913."[8]

From its introduction in the 1820s until the arrival of the British in 1882, cotton tended to be cultivated for export by a small collection of wealthy landholders, who could afford the comparatively steep startup costs that were associated with this crop. Aggregate capital formation in agriculture accelerated during the first quarter century of the British occupation, but slowed markedly after 1906. The sudden deceleration in agricultural capital formation can be attributed on one hand to the cuts in state investment in infrastructure that followed the completion of the Aswan Dam and its associated network of barrages and canals. On the other, the slowdown reflected the unanticipated evaporation of credit that accompanied the U.S. stock market slump of 1907. The ensuing financial crisis made it almost impossible for Egypt's larger landholders to raise sufficient amounts of operating capital, and precipitated a sharp drop in purchases of new and replacement agricultural machinery.[9] At the same time, persistent overcropping and burgeoning drainage problems combined to generate a significant fall in agricultural productivity. Capital formation in agriculture consequently stagnated between 1909 and 1913, then plunged with the outbreak of the First World War.[10]

Egyptian manufacturing was even less capital intensive than was cotton farming at the turn of the twentieth century. A survey of local industry compiled by the Alexandria branch of the British Chamber of Commerce of Egypt in 1899 lists only twenty-three joint-stock companies, the largest of which were two sugar processing firms, a salt company, and two cotton cloth factories.[11] Over the next eight years, another 160 large-scale industrial enterprises formed, including a cement factory, a second salt company, a pair of cold storage companies, and an ice supply company. Still, such firms accounted for only a small fraction of the country's overall manufacturing capacity. They employed an equally minute proportion of the total labor force: John Chalcraft estimates that large-scale, highly mechanized enterprises employed around 3 per cent of industrial workers during the 1910s.[12] The picture had changed little as late as 1927, when the first comprehensive industrial census was undertaken.[13]

Small-scale enterprises tightened their hold over Egyptian manufacturing in the wake of the 1907 crisis. Twenty-six large industrial and mining companies, including the Egyptian Cotton Mills Ltd. and Société Anonyme Egyptienne des Presses Allemandes, ended up going bankrupt during the course of the crisis. Artisanal factories, by contrast, flourished in the period leading up to the First World War. This trend can be inferred from the steadily rising share of total imports that was made up of the various inputs such enterprises used.[14] Even more compelling is the final report of the wartime Committee on Trade and Industry, which concluded that as of 1917 small-scale industry constituted the "most important" component of local manufacturing "because it occupies the greatest number of workers and extends its network in all towns and farmsteads of Egypt."[15] Disruptions in the flow of imported manufactures occasioned by the war set the stage for a substantial rise in the number of small workshops operated by tailors, dressmakers, shoemakers, haberdashers, and cane and umbrella makers.[16] There is some evidence that the war resuscitated artisanal production of different sorts of cotton cloth as well, particularly in the major cities.[17]

As Spruyt might expect, producers of low-profit, high-volume agricultural goods were among the strongest proponents of policies associated with the emergence of an autonomous, territorially bounded Egyptian state. Cotton growers began to call for greater government intervention in the domestic economy in the immediate aftermath of the 1907 crisis.[18] State officials eventually responded to these demands, promulgating in 1912 a Five Feddans Law that prohibited foreign financial institutions from carrying out foreclosures on loans secured by properties that were smaller than five feddans, or approximately five acres, in area.[19] More important, provincial cotton merchants played a pivotal role in raising the initial capital for the country's first indigenous financial institution (Bank Misr) during the spring of 1920. They further demanded "that the Bank Misr replace the British controlled National Bank of Egypt as the state bank."[20] It is therefore not surprising that such traders, along with medium-scale cotton farmers, represented a core constituency of the avowedly pro-independence Wafd Party led by Sa'd Zaghlul.[21]

Producers of low-profit, high-volume manufactured goods also advocated more extensive state intervention in the local economy. The country's largest sugar company, the Société Anonyme des Sucreries et de la Raffinerie d'Egypte, turned to the central administration for assistance when it suffered severe financial difficulties in 1905–06.[22] Five years later, government officials authorized a group of wealthy landholders and merchants led by 'Umar Lutfi, Prince Husain Kamil, Alfred Eid, and Tal'at Harb to set up the Co-operative Finance and Trading Company of Cairo. The company is reported to have "extended many loans to small businesses in Cairo during its first few years of operation."[23] More to the point, the leadership of al-Hizb al-Watani made a concerted effort to win sympathy for the party's program among small-scale manufacturers. Urban artisans provided the primary basis of support for the Manual Trades Workers' Union (Niqabah 'Ummal al-Sanai' al-Yadawiyyah), set up by the party in 1909.[24] Members of this organization championed the adoption of a wide range of government policies to protect local manufacturers from foreign competition.[25] In a similar vein, the Egyptian Federation of Industries encouraged small-scale manufacturers to throw their weight behind the fledgling Bank Misr, on the grounds that "the growth of the Bank Misr was crucial if Egypt was to establish and expand native industries."[26] Most owners of smaller factories subsequently rallied to the banner of the Wafd as well.

By contrast, those engaged in the production and trade of high-profit, low-volume goods tended to resist programs that heightened the degree of state involvement in the domestic economy. Eric Davis observes, for example, that "large merchants involved in the [luxury] import-export trade and who had extensive ties with foreigners, such as Amin Yahya Pasha, were not forthcoming with support [for Bank Misr] as they had little to gain from it."[27] As a general rule, Egypt's commercial elite and wealthiest landholders gravitated away from the Wafd and toward the Liberal Constitutionalist Party, whose platform advocated incremental steps to develop profitable, market-oriented domestic industry as a necessary precondition to national independence.[28]

Spruyt's explanation thus illuminates several key aspects of the turn toward Westphalian sovereignty in early twentieth-century Egypt. However, this line of argument runs afoul of two significant empirical problems. In the first place, it is not at all clear that long-staple cotton should be considered a low-profit, high-volume crop, rather than a high-profit, low-volume one. There are three plausible reasons to place it in the former category: (1) local growers took considerable pains to expand the total acreage devoted to cotton cultivation during the early 1900s; (2) they exerted almost continuous pressure on state agencies to improve the country's irrigation and transportation systems in order to reduce unit production costs; and (3) even the richest of Egypt's cotton producers and export merchants had little prospect of carving out a monopoly position in either regional or European markets. These points persuade me that Egyptian cotton deserves to be categorized as a low-profit, high-volume good. Nevertheless, it is worth noting that as well-informed and insightful an observer of the country's economic history as Roger Owen considers locally grown, long-staple cotton to represent a "high value product."[29]

Second, the turn toward Westphalian sovereignty occurred not when Egypt's foreign trade was expanding but rather as it was experiencing significant difficulties. According to Hansen and Lucas, "export volume per capita had already reached its peak by the end of the nineteenth century. During the twentieth century the trend is persistently downwards. There is a tendency toward a fairly constant high plateau from 1902 to 1913. . . . But even during the period 1902–13 . . . the trend is unmistakably downward."[30] In fact the sharp drop in cotton exports that took place following the outbreak of the First World War prompted local growers to set up the Egyptian General Agricultural Syndicate, whose stated objective was "to pressure the Egyptian government to purchase and store cotton until the harvest could be sold under more favorable conditions."[31] Exports continued to be depressed throughout the 1920s, particularly in comparison with the generally high levels that had characterized the last decades of the nineteenth century.[32] More recent calculations confirm Hansen and Lucas's findings: A new series of estimates of Egypt's gross domestic product indicates that even though the first decade of the twentieth century may have been less dismal than earlier studies claim, the decline in local economic activity that occurred from 1912 to 1920 was a good deal worse.[33] Whatever collaboration occurred between powerful commercial interests and state officials therefore took shape under circumstances that were almost precisely the opposite of those one would expect on the basis of Spruyt's analysis.

Tunisia's Low-profit, High-volume Trade

This line of argument offers an equally promising explanation for the comparatively early appearance of Westphalian sovereignty in Tunisia. During the initial decades of the twentieth century, low-profit, high-volume agricultural goods — most notably wheat, barley, and olive oil — accounted for some 70 per cent of the country's total output and around two-thirds of the total value of exports.[34] Locally harvested sponges were shipped from the eastern port of Sfax to markets throughout the Mediterranean basin as well.[35] Phosphates and other low-profit minerals were also sent to Europe in substantial quantities, particularly in the years just before and immediately after the First World War. Mahfoud Bennoune reports that in the extractive sector of the local economy, "the volume of production increased threefold between 1908 and 1919 alone. Mining enterprises increased from 38 [companies] in 1914 to 57 in 1924."[36] These companies continued to gravitate toward the extraction and exportation of bulkier, less valuable ores as Tunisia's railway network expanded. Overseas shipments of iron ore, for instance, exhibited a steady rise during the 1920s, while exports of phosphates, lead, and lead ore, which reached their zenith in 1910, remained generally stable. Shipments of more valuable minerals such as zinc, on the other hand, also peaked in 1910 but then declined steeply throughout the 1920s. At the same time, exports of even rarer and more expensive metals, most notably manganese and copper, shrank into insignificance.[37]

Low-profit, high-volume agriculture received a boost shortly after the First World War ended, as large estate-holders sold off a considerable proportion of their lands to small-scale cultivators. British intelligence agents estimated that some 14 per cent of the total acreage that French grandées had previously held was transferred to Italian and Tunisian farmers during the months immediately following the armistice.[38] These lands were for the most part planted in olive trees, which quickly emerged as the predominant cash crop in the arid districts to the west and south of Sfax. Olive oil extraction plants and soap factories, which had been centered in the established olive-producing region south of Sousse, quickly spread into the area around Sfax as well, creating dynamic, export-oriented agricultural and industrial sectors of the local economy. For the most part, the olive oil and soap factories of Sousse and Sfax consisted of small-scale, family operated enterprises, although two larger companies, the Société Générale des Huileries du Sahel

Tunisien and the Société de l'Huilerie Franco-Tunisienne, were to be found in Sfax as well.[39]

Not only was the Tunisian economy oriented toward the production of low-profit, high-volume goods, but the late 1910s and early 1920s also witnessed a general expansion of the country's foreign trade. The total value of grain exports averaged just over 47 million francs during the war (1914–18), but jumped to 122.5 million francs in 1919, thanks to a massive increase in the amount of wheat shipped overseas during that year. Mineral exports took somewhat longer to catch up, reaching a total value of 175 million francs in 1920 after averaging less than 46 million francs from 1914 to 1918.[40] Wartime disruptions in regional and international commerce also created new opportunities for local manufacturers, who stepped up their output of silk fabric, clothing, hats, and household goods after 1914 for sale on southern European, North African, and eastern Mediterranean markets. A new lead foundry and chemicals plant started operations at this time as well.[41] In addition, exports of cotton cloth rose sharply during the war years, and continued to increase in the immediate postwar period.[42]

As Spruyt's argument would predict, proponents of an autonomous, self-interested Tunisia clustered in those parts of the country where low-profit, high-volume goods predominated. Residents of the towns located in the rich coastal plains surrounding Sousse and Sfax, which had by the late 1910s become not only the country's major olive- and olive oil–producing zone but also a center of artisanal cotton cloth making, constituted a major constituency for the nationalist cause in the early 1920s.[43] Among the early activists who hailed from this region was Shaikh Muhammad Karkar, who played a leading role in cultivating support for Tunisian independence among local students during the years following the First World War.[44] These same districts later became the primary locus of support for the more militantly independence-oriented Neo-Destour Party led by Habib Bourgiba.[45]

Sympathy for the establishment of a fully autonomous Tunisia was equally strong among small-scale manufacturers in the cities. The artisans and craftspeople of Tunis, Kairawan, Sousse, and Sfax suffered severely as French goods inundated local markets at the end of the nineteenth century.[46] They found themselves further marginalized and impoverished when French-owned factories began to appear in the larger towns after 1900.[47] With the coming of the First World War, the fortunes of small manufacturers started to improve, as the items that they produced not only captured local markets but also began to be shipped overseas in sizable quantities. Wartime prosperity turned out to be short-lived, however, and European manufactures once again flooded into the country beginning in 1919. By 1921, manufactured goods made up 53 per cent of total imports, while industrial raw materials and machinery constituted another 25 per cent. Small-scale tradespeople suffered further as a result of sharp increases in export fees and other forms of taxation that were imposed in the months following the war.[48] Consequently, in the words of Ali Mahjoubi, "the suqs where artisans and traders were generally clustered constituted fertile ground for the activities of the Tunisian nationalists" ("les souks ou les métiers d'artisans et de commerçants sont généralement imbriques, constituent un terrain d'éléction pour l'activité des nationalistes tunisiens").[49]

Sentiment in favor of a more extensive form of political entity, by contrast, lingered among rich merchants and senior Islamic scholars. It was among the commercial elite of Tunis that the idea of restoring a worldwide Islamic order led by the khalifah in Istanbul had taken root during the first decade of the twentieth century.[50] And it was scions of the wealthiest urban families, with the best connections overseas, that emigrated to the Ottoman capital and Europe after 1911, and acted as the champions of "the Algerian-Tunisian people" during early years of the First World War. But not all advocates of restoring the caliphate fled the country. As late as 1915, local notables with ties to Tunisia's premier olive oil companies exhibited pronounced Turcophile attitudes.[51]

At odds with Spruyt's explanation is the fact that high-profit crops made significant inroads into Tunisian agriculture during the years surrounding the First World War. In particular, a growing proportion of the country's most productive farmland started to be planted in grapevines, whose output was earmarked for the manufacture of first-quality wine for export to Europe. Just prior to the war, French landholders cultivated grapes on a little more than 9,000 hectares; by 1920, over 9,400 hectares were devoted exclusively to vineyards. Even more startling was the turn to viticulture on the part of members of the local Italian community: in 1912 Italian farmers worked just over 5,600 hectares of land planted in grapevines; by 1918, the total had jumped to more than 10,000 hectares.[52] The spread of vineyards accompanied a marked increase in wine exports, the value of which soared from a little more than 4 million francs in 1913 to almost 21 million francs in 1921. Only phosphates, olive oil, and iron ore brought in greater revenues by 1921.[53]

More important, the period of relative prosperity that followed the First World War tended to undermine, rather than promote, efforts by Tunisian nationalists to mobilize popular support for a fully autonomous, territorially bounded polity. The early 1920s were years in which the authorities carried out policies of sustained repression against the Destour Party and its affiliated journals and newspapers, accompanied by widespread public indifference to the nationalist cause.[54] When wheat and barley harvests suddenly plummeted in 1924, though, at the same time that major export markets for Tunisia's artisanal manufactures unexpectedly disappeared, popular enthusiasm for the Destour and its program quickly revived. Meanwhile, the party's publications grew more strident in demanding complete independence from France.[55] By the same token, improved economic conditions in the years after 1926 contributed to an evident return to "lethargy" in nationalist circles, which persisted through the second half of the decade.[56]

There is thus much to recommend Spruyt's theory as a way to understand the early emergence of Westphalian sovereignty in Tunisia. The predominance of low-value, high-volume goods in the country's foreign trade provided export-oriented farmers and manufacturers with strong incentives to support the creation of an autonomous, territorially bounded polity. And the shift away from more extensive notions of Arab or North African independence accompanied a secular rise in trade with the outside world. Nevertheless, this line of argument has a hard time accounting for the fact that arguably the most dynamic sector of the local economy at the time that the nationalist leadership began to articulate the demand for a fully independent Tunisia consisted of a comparatively high-value, low-volume product. Moreover, popular backing for the nationalist project appears to have waxed whenever the country experienced a pronounced economic downturn and waned with the return to prosperity. It is therefore plausible but in the end unpersuasive to trace the emergence of Westphalian sovereignty in Tunisia to a political compact between powerful commercial interests and state officials.

Jordan's High-profit, Low-volume Trade

Spruyt's argument goes an equally long way toward explaining the relatively late emergence of Westphalian sovereignty in Jordan. The economic system that took shape in the country during the early 1940s under the auspices of the MESC was characterized by a peculiar kind of high-profit, low-volume trade. The MESC allocated exclusive import licenses to a limited number of well-connected local merchant houses. Those merchants who gained possession of such licenses imported set quantities of cloth, sugar, grain, and other staples into Transjordan, then re-exported these goods to neighboring countries where they were in much shorter supply.[57] A handful of local traders profited handsomely as a result of this arrangement, then used the proceeds they derived from their advantageous position to corner the market in a wide variety of scarce products. Abla Amawi goes so far as to observe that "MESC policies were geared specifically to the creation of monopolies" in the Transjordanian economy.[58]

This small group of privileged import-export merchants, which Amawi calls the "quota coterie," had little incentive to support the establishment of a self-interested, territorially bounded state. When government revenues fell short during the last months of the Second World War, for instance, and state officials proposed to impose an income tax on the commercial elite to raise funds, influential members of the quota coterie quickly mobilized to resist. Amawi reports that the well-connected "Chairman of the ʿAmman chamber of commerce, Sabri al-Tabbaʿ went to Prime Minister Tawfiq Abu al-Huda and asked about the amount the government hoped to collect from the new income tax. Tabbaʿ was told approximately £100,000. He, in turn, informed the prime minister that he would collect this figure from the merchants directly and that there was no need for the new tax. Through this maneuver, the merchants were able to escape paying income taxation for a year."[59] When the measure was finally implemented in October 1945, rich merchants organized a general strike in the larger cities and appealed directly to Amir ʿAbdullah for relief. Nevertheless, the tax was upheld by the Legislative Council, largely due to the fact that large landholders represented a majority in the council and were "only too anxious to see the merchants pay a greater share of the national income."[60]

As the Second World War drew to a close, the quota coterie extended its activities farther afield. Several of its members "formed connections directly with sources of supplies, such as India, Argentina, and the United States."[61] In addition, local trading companies started to concentrate on the distribution and sale of specific goods: "Prior to the war and especially during the war years," Amawi observes, Transjordanian "merchants engaged in all kinds of trade. Their stores were general stores selling items such as shoes, food stuffs, wheat, wool, perfume, sweets, and textiles. After the war, [however,] specialization of trade occurred. Companies opened up dealing specifically with manufactured merchandise, construction materials, and textiles."[62] This process buttressed the position of the commercial elite in both local and regional markets. As late as 1951, "imports could be made only by registered importers, who received foreign exchange allocations in hard or soft currencies on the basis of the government's import program for each commodity group."[63] Influential import-export merchants even organized a political party to further their collective interests. As Spruyt would expect, this party, called Hizb al-Nahdah al-'Arabi, actively supported government policies aimed at establishing a Greater Syria.[64]

Groups associated with low-profit, high-volume goods, by contrast, tended to favor greater state intervention in a less expansive domain. Jordan's small-scale food-processing, cloth-dyeing, and pottery-making plants sold their products exclusively on the domestic market.[65] The owners and workers attached to these factories made up the bulk of the membership of the Muslim Brotherhood (Ikhwan al-Muslimin), which took root in 'Amman, al-Salt, Karak, and Irbid in the late 1940s.[66] Although the principles and rhetoric of this movement advocated the unity of believers and, at least implicitly, criticized existing political structures throughout the Muslim world, the Jordanian Ikhwan in practice tended to look out for the interests of its local members and sympathizers.[67] The heightened level of political organization among disgruntled tradespeople convinced the government in October 1949 to rescind import licenses for goods that could be produced in local factories and workshops. This move was immediately followed by the formation of the Development Board to coordinate agricultural and industrial projects in the kingdom.[68]

With the annexation of the area between the Jordan River and the borders of the State of Israel (viz., the West Bank) in April 1950, small manufacturers and merchants based in Nablus and al-Khalil (Hebron) contributed more forcefully to this political current.[69] Three weeks before the annexation, West Bank retailers formed a delegation to complain to the authorities in 'Amman that the existing distribution of import licenses worked to their direct disadvantage.[70] This complaint was repeated on the very eve of the annexation.[71] After the West Bank was formally incorporated into Jordan, owners of industrial plants in and around Nablus demanded that state officials either raise tariff duties to protect their operations or put pressure on surrounding countries to accept greater quantities of locally produced exports.[72]

Other disaffected tradespeople filled the ranks of Jordan's early communist parties. The first such organization, the Union of Jordanian Workers (al-Ittihad al-'Ummal al-Urduniyyin) appeared in 1932; it was followed four years later by a successor association, whose objectives included "overthrow[ing] 'Abdullah's regime, driv[ing] the British out and set[ting] up a republican Arab Union which would include Syria." By the time the communists reorganized a second time in 1946, the goals of the organization had changed to reflect more closely the economic interests of its primary backers. Aqil Abidi reports that the newly reconstituted League of National Liberation ('Usbah al-Taharrur al-Watani) demanded "the revision of the powers of the Amir and his relations with the British government, termination of the Anglo-Jordanian Treaty and free elections for the parliament."[73] British officials were a bit more cavalier in describing the party's program: in the weeks leading up to the August 1951 parliamentary elections, "some fifty manifestos in the form of hand bills and announcements in the press have appeared, of which the most extreme example has come from the quasi-communist elements of the so-called Jordan Popular Bloc. This asks for cancellation of the Anglo-Jordan treaty and settlement of the Palestine problem on the basis of the partition scheme of 1947. Two other manifestos ask for revision of the Jordan constitution. The rest follow the usual slogans promising relief from economic conditions, improvements for the refugees, etc."[74]

Although this way of explaining Jordan's prolonged delay in shifting to a foreign policy posture predicated on Westphalian sovereignty displays considerable merit, it nevertheless has trouble dealing with the broader context in which sovereignty took shape in this case. Spruyt argues that the emergence of sovereign states in early modern Europe was stimulated by a marked increase in foreign trade. Yet the boom years of the Second World War coincided with the nationalist leadership's unequivocal repudiation of the notion of a self-interested, territorially bounded Transjordan.[75] The positive correlation between expanding external commerce and the Jordanian government's efforts to promote Greater Syria persisted into the immediate postwar period: large quantities of Transjordanian fruits, vegetables, olive oil, and wool continued to be shipped to Syria and Lebanon in exchange for manufactured goods and cereals throughout the late 1940s.[76]

It was only when foreign trade started to contract that the authorities in

'Amman backed away from their long-standing advocacy of an amalgamated Arab entity. Soon after the dissolution of the Syrian-Lebanese customs union in March 1950, the government in Damascus unexpectedly imposed strict controls on a wide range of imports.[77] Jordanian officials quickly followed suit, raising tariffs on almost all goods coming into the kingdom. As a result, commerce among the three countries plummeted.[78] The leaderships in Damascus, Beirut, and 'Amman attempted to "salvage" the situation by negotiating a collection of bilateral trade and payments agreements during the course of 1952–53.[79] But except for a set of protocols governing the exchange of a limited number of agricultural items, such arrangements failed to resuscitate regional commerce. By 1953, the collapse of Jordan's foreign trade left the country dependent on regular infusions of foreign aid to ameliorate recurrent balance of payments difficulties.[80]

Stagnant trade sparked widespread demands for more extensive state intervention in the local economy. Abidi reports that

> a number of merchants, importers, tribal leaders, [parliamentary] Deputies and representatives of various organizations met in a conference at Ramallah on 13 November [1951] and resolved to petition the government to frame a comprehensive development plan for Jordan "so that the whole country, and not only Jordan (Transjordan) will benefit." The suggestions made were that the local industries be protected and encouraged, prices of essential goods be reduced and controlled, aid and relief be given to farmers and agricultural laborers, and the import of luxury goods be cut down.[81]

Moreover, the commercial downturn of 1951–52 accompanied the rise of the ministry of the economy under the direction of the outspoken nationalist Hamad al-Farhan. From its inception in 1951, this agency pursued an "agenda [that] included state-led industrialization and the adoption of a more flexible monetary system through the creation of an independent central bank and the reduction of the 100 per cent currency cover, both of which would release frozen domestic funds for development."[82] British officials attempted to undermine the new ministry by channeling economic assistance funds through the Development Board, which remained firmly under British control.[83] Such tactics prompted Prime Minister al-Mulqi to take the Village Loans Scheme out of the board's hands in May 1953 and turn the program over to the state-run Agricultural Bank. A month later the cabinet proposed the formation of a Higher Economic Council that would assume the duties of the Development Board. At the same time, the ministry of the economy set up a planning department of its own.[84] These agencies posed a direct challenge to Britain's position as the éminence grise behind economic policy making in Jordan, and provided the institutional underpinnings for the state's campaign to "break the patterns of the Mandate period."[85]

It thus seems clear that Jordan adopted a posture of Westphalian sovereignty in the context of slumping, rather than expanding, foreign trade. It may even be the case that powerful 'Amman-based merchants actively resisted the trend toward greater state intervention in the local economy, although the quota coterie did tend to support the government's efforts to improve transportation and other kinds of infrastructure during the early 1950s.[86] In any event, positing a congruence of interest between elite commercial interests and state agencies offers a less than compelling explanation for the comparatively late emergence of Westphalian sovereignty in Jordan.

Iraq's High-profit, Low-volume Trade

Spruyt's argument offers an explanation for the relatively late emergence of Westphalian sovereignty in Iraq that looks promising on its face. Two components of the country's foreign trade in the years before the Second World War might well be considered high-profit, low-volume activities. One component was the exportation of dates, in both raw and processed form. Geographical factors severely limited the range of lands that could be devoted to date cultivation, which greatly augmented the profitability of the crop. By the same token, any effort to increase the output of locally produced dates tended to reduce the overall quality of the harvest, which in turn dampened prices on overseas markets. Estate-holders consequently took considerable pains to restrict the planting of new date palms, while at the same time monopolizing the ownership and operation of local pitting and pressing operations.[87] The result was a highly concentrated industry that employed a relatively small number of skilled and unskilled laborers.[88]

Dates accounted for more than 37 per cent of Iraq's total exports at the time of the country's de jure independence. After a marked drop from 1929 to 1930, the value of date exports rose steadily throughout the remainder of the decade, despite a decline in the aggregate tonnage of dates shipped overseas.[89] Even when prices for agricultural goods fell on regional markets in 1938, dates made up one-fourth of Iraq's nonoil export earnings. Overseas shipments plunged sharply during 1942–43 due to poor harvests and increased domestic demand, but exports recovered in 1944 and continued to rise until 1948. Such trends confirmed Iraq's longstanding position as the largest exporter of dates in the world, and by far the most important supplier to the major markets of the Middle East and South Asia.

Second, a high proportion of Iraq's foreign commerce consisted of transit trade, particularly such luxury items as carpets from Iran and specialty tobaccos from Turkey.[90] This trade accounted for around 20 per cent of the country's total foreign commerce in the early 1930s. After the Iranian government began restricting the flow of imports entering the country from Iraq at mid-decade, the proportion fell to around 12 per cent. But transit shipments recovered quickly following the outbreak of the Second World War, and made up almost 38 per cent of Iraq's total trade in 1941. High-profit, low-volume goods therefore played a key role in the Iraqi economy throughout the 1930s and on into the war years. As a result, the small group of elite merchants who controlled the lucrative trade in dates, carpets, and specialty tobacco had little incentive to collaborate with state officials to regularize and limit transaction costs.

Political organizations tied to the commercial elite played an important part in pushing for Iraq's unification with surrounding countries. Of the parties that actively contested elections during the late 1940s and early 1950s, the Independence Party (Hizb al-Istiqlal) most closely reflected the interests of the rich merchant community both in internal affairs, with its studied silence with regard to economic issues, and in foreign policy, with its outspoken advocacy of Arab unity.[91] It was occasionally overshadowed by such competing organizations as the Socialist People's Party (Hizb al-Ummah al-Ishtiraki) and the Constitutional Union Party (Hizb al-Ittihad al-Dusturi), which drew their primary support from educated professionals and landholding tribal shaikhs, respectively. But Hizb al-Istiqlal nevertheless remained a pivotal player in parliamentary politics until formal parties were finally banned in the summer of 1954.

Arguably the most serious electoral challenges to the Independence Party came from political organizations that appealed directly to the interests of low-profit, high-volume producers. Such organizations included the National Democratic Party, or NDP (al-Hizb al-Watani al-Dimuqrati), whose membership was drawn largely "from the middle walks of life, and comprised merchants, shopkeepers, small property owners, craftsmen, students, teachers, lawyers, and other professionals."[92] The NDP's program "stood for political freedoms, land reform, the abolition of monopolies, and a more equitable distribution of wealth to be achieved mainly through tax measures." Furthermore, the party exhibited a pronounced "lack of interest in pan-Arab schemes."[93] Smaller, more ephemeral parties like the Liberal Party (Hizb al-Ahrar) and the National Union Party (Hizb al-Ittihad al-Watani) also advanced platforms emphasizing the importance of promoting a "national bourgeoisie" in order to achieve "complete independence" for the country.[94] These groupings suffered continual harassment from the police, and were forced to deal with electoral procedures that were systematically biased in favor of pro-regime parties. In addition, they found themselves struggling against an almost hegemonic bloc of forces committed to preserving the high-profit, low-volume oriented political-economic order.

Nevertheless, low-profit, high-volume goods made substantial inroads into the local economy during the course of the Second World War. Grain exports represented no more than 14 per cent of the total value of Iraq's foreign trade in 1937, the high point for the decade. But the outbreak of the war sparked a sharp rise in cereals production, which went largely for export. The country's output of barley, for instance, jumped in the 1942 crop year, as British officials purchased this particular grain in large quantities to feed troops and civilian populations all over the Middle East. Under pressure from London, the Iraqi government in February 1943 fixed the selling price of barley, but did so at an unusually high level, thereby encouraging farmers to expand cultivation of that particular crop the next growing season.[95] British purchases stopped abruptly in 1944, but resumed a year later due to largely strategic rather than economic considerations. Beginning in 1945, British officials shifted from government-to-government barter arrangements to buying barley on the open market. This change led to a significant increase in both the area devoted to barley production and the total amount produced, because the reopening of trade with Europe made it possible for consumers there to purchase cereals imported from the Middle East at prevailing world prices.[96]

A similar trend was evident in the industrial sector of the Iraqi economy. Capital investment in manufacturing remained minimal throughout the 1930s and 1940s.[97] As late as 1950, the International Bank for Reconstruction and Development reported that "industry is little developed. Although perhaps as many as 60,000 people are engaged in industrial production (other than oil), virtually all of these are employed in small undertakings where the work is done largely by hand and productivity is accordingly quite low."[98] Nevertheless, the disruptions in foreign trade that accompanied the Second World War enabled many local manufacturers to flourish: cloth and cigarette factories operated at a substantial profit, despite the lack of sophisticated machinery.[99] Metalworking picked up as well, as local foundries were actively encouraged to transform scrap metal into hand tools and household items.[100] Soap making, on the other hand, suffered from a lack of raw materials, as increased quantities of vegetable oil were consumed as food.

When the war ended, the state-owned Agricultural and Industrial Bank, which had been set up in 1936, was split in two. The new Industrial Bank almost immediately set out to promote large-scale, mechanized manufacturing by providing investment capital for several large-scale projects, including a cotton spinning and weaving complex, a concrete factory, a handful of food-processing plants, and several cereal mills.[101] Local industry received a further boost in 1950 when the government promulgated a revised version of the 1929 Law for the Encouragement of Industry, and then set up a Development Board to evaluate proposals and allocate the funds necessary to carry them to fruition. The conclusion in December 1951 and January 1952 of a pair of new agreements concerning the distribution of oil revenues between the Iraqi state and the oil companies effectively tripled the amount of capital reserved for the Industrial Bank, from 1 million to 3 million Iraqi dinars.[102] Still, the industrial census drawn up in 1954 shows that no more than 7 per cent of all manufacturing establishments employed more than five people, and only 1 per cent of all enterprises had more than twenty employees.[103]

Finally, it is not at all clear that Iraq's foreign trade exhibited steady growth during the 1940s and early 1950s. The total value of imports and exports dipped from 1937 to 1939, then fluctuated widely in the years between 1940 and 1946. Oil exports and the transit trade displayed an even greater degree of instability up to and during the Second World War. There was a generally positive trend in the overall value of the country's foreign trade between 1932 and 1946, but this pattern most likely reflects successive bouts of severe inflation rather than real commercial gains. In the two years after the war, total exports increased, and overseas shipments of dates, barley, and rice spiked in 1951.[104] But nonoil export income remained generally stagnant throughout this period, and the country's balance of payments tended to run a substantial deficit.[105]

Spruyt's argument thus sheds light on important aspects of the appearance of Westphalian sovereignty in Iraq. Yet it is ultimately unpersuasive. Nationalist leaders in Baghdad continued to pursue a foreign policy that rejected the notion of a narrowly self-interested, territorially bounded Iraq at a time when low-profit, high-volume goods were steadily displacing the high-profit, low-volume goods that had dominated the local economy during the period up to the Second World War. Moreover, the leadership's commitment to a unified Arab polity persisted despite the general stagnation of Iraq's external trade, which might have been expected to convince powerful commercial interests to tolerate, if not actively demand, greater government intervention in economic affairs. It is thus hard to explain the emergence of Westphalian sovereignty in Iraq in terms of a mutually beneficial compact between elite commercial interests and state officials.

Syria's Low-profit, High-volume Trade

This line of argument offers a more problematic account of the emergence of Westphalian sovereignty in Syria. It is true that low-cost, high-volume goods — most notably cereals, wool, milk products, fruits and vegetables, and other agricultural items — accounted for more than three-fourths of local exports in 1931.[106] Producers tended to target these products toward markets in surrounding countries as a way to minimize transportation and other transaction costs. The few locally produced high-profit items, most notably silk cloth manufactured in Aleppo and Damascus, experienced a sharp decline during the early 1920s, partly owing to the disruption of trade with Anatolia that resulted from the establishment of the Turkish Republic and partly due to heightened competition from less expensive Japanese imports.[107] The generally small profit margins that characterized Syria's foreign trade is indicated by the government's decision to rescind the 1 per cent duty on exports when regional markets began to feel the effects of the Great Depression in Europe.[108]

Throughout the Second World War, the MESC encouraged Syrian farmers to specialize in cereals and other low-profit, high-volume staples. Grain production in the arid plains northeast of Aleppo expanded dramatically as a result of the MESC's policies: "In the years 1943–53 grain production doubled, while population increased by about 33 per cent, from 2.9 million to 3.9 million."[109] By 1944, Syria's trade with Egypt consisted primarily of potatoes, dried apricots, licorice, walnuts, and olive oil.[110] A rapid expansion of agricultural production took place in precisely those parts of the country where surpluses tended to be most evanescent. Doreen Warriner points out that the districts watered by the Euphrates and Khabur rivers were ones in which "transport is expensive, roads are bad, labour is scarce, credit dear, and land tenure confused and insecure.'"[111] Under these circumstances, merchants based in Aleppo made use of farm machinery provided by the MESC at subsidized rates to bring unused land into cultivation, but their operations hovered on the brink of insolvency: Warriner reports that the wartime activities of the new class of "merchant-tractorists" led to "no improvement in soil fertility or in grain yields, a risk of soil erosion, and no stability."[112] Consequently, "the dry-farming expansion [that occurred in the mid-1940s turned out to be] inevitably precarious and speculative."[113]

Meanwhile, small-scale manufacturing experienced a pronounced revival. The output of cotton yarn from workshops located in and around Aleppo increased by more than 500 per cent between 1939 and 1946.[114] The Damascus newspaper *al-Nidal* reported on 1 May 1943 that cloth and glass factories throughout the country "have received an exceptional impetus" as a result of the "shortage of overseas products" in the local marketplace.[115] Cotton cloth became a major item of Syria's foreign trade as the war went on. Alfred Musrey observes that exports of cotton fabric to Iraq "increased from 100,754 square meters valued at I.D. [Iraqi dinars] 1,540 in 1939 to 2,191,961 square meters valued at I.D. 1,263,776 in 1944." Cotton and woolen textiles made up a significant proportion of Syrian trade with Palestine during the mid-1940s as well.[116] Virtually all of these goods were manufactured in small-scale workshops, which "rose once again like a Phoenix from the ashes" during the course of the war.[117]

In this fashion, the war stimulated the proliferation of low-profit, high-volume manufacturing throughout the local economy. Mechanized textile factories had appeared in the suburbs of Aleppo as early as 1922, and the large-scale Syrian Spinning and Weaving Company started operations in 1936.[118] Nevertheless, not until the war years did mass production become firmly entrenched. The interruption of imports of cotton yarn in the summer of 1940 led to a marked increase in the number of spinning mills in and around Aleppo.[119] A survey undertaken in 1944 on behalf of the American chemical supplier DuPont lists fourteen large cloth factories in Aleppo and Damascus, most of which initiated production at the end of the 1930s and all of which were scrambling for access to imported dyes in order to satisfy the growing demand for locally manufactured cotton and silk fabric.[120]

These factories provided the foundation on which Syria's capital-intensive industrial sector was constructed in the years immediately after the war. Edmund Asfour remarks that "both the war[time] shortage of imported goods and the demand created by the needs of foreign troops had given a strong impetus to industrial expansion during the war but the required capital goods could not then be obtained." It was not until the Second World War came to an end that "accumulated profits and foreign exchange balances made it easy for entrepreneurs to expand their old firms and to establish new industries."[121] Whereas only seven joint-stock manufacturing companies with a total capital of just over 19 million Syrian pounds formed during the period from 1928 to 1944, six such corporations possessing a combined capital of over 40 million were established in 1946 alone. By 1949 there were twenty-one large-scale, capital-intensive industrial enterprises operating in the country.[122]

As Spruyt would expect, Syria's smaller-scale producers tended to collaborate with state officials in an effort to regularize and limit the costs associated with low-profit, high-volume commercial transactions. As early as July 1941, the government announced plans to issue import and export licenses to assist traders who were having trouble laying their hands on the hard currency they needed.[123] Two years later, state officials found themselves castigated in the local press for administering price controls in an irregular and "confusing" fashion.[124] Similar complaints arose over the way in which the authorities implemented the new income tax statute.[125] Persistent popular demands that the government adopt measures to stabilize wild fluctuations in the value of the paper currency circulating in the country led by July 1943 to a press campaign in favor of the establishment of a national bank.[126]

Political organizations that drew their primary support from the producers of low-profit, high-volume goods tended to be proponents of local sovereignty, no matter what their ostensible political ideologies. The leadership of Syria's Muslim Brotherhood (Ikhwan al-Muslimin), for example, championed the independence of a territorially bounded Syrian polity throughout the 1940s. Umar Abd-Allah notes that at this time "the struggle for independence was certainly primary" for the Ikhwan; among the movement's key principles during these years was the notion that "a strong, independent national economy must be created and protected from the inroads of major world powers like the United States, the Soviet Union, France, and Great Britain."[127] As soon as Syria gained nominal independence from France in the spring of 1943, the Ikhwani leadership moved the organization's headquarters from Aleppo to the new national capital of Damascus.[128] When popular enthusiasm for federation with Iraq peaked once again in October 1949, the general supervisor of the Syrian Brothers proclaimed that "we welcome unity of the Arab countries on a wide scale, by which all artificial frontiers and restrictions would be abolished. It is only natural that we welcome union with Iraq as a first step toward the longed for Arab unity. However," he continued, "we do not want this union to be a means for binding free and independent Syria with new bonds. We want a union with free and independent Iraq which is the master of itself. As to the form of rule, we insist on the maintenance of the republican regime which has been accepted by all parties and blocs."[129]

Equally firmly committed to the consolidation of Westphalian sovereignty was the powerful agricultural laborers' movement led by Akram al-Hawrani. From its beginnings in the late 1930s, this movement pursued the twin objectives of "independence from the French and a just redistribution of the national wealth."[130] In December 1949, al-Hawrani played a key role in organizing those members of the newly elected Constituent Assembly who stood opposed to the idea of Syrian-Iraqi federation into an informal grouping called the Republican Bloc.[131] Majid Khadduri observes that the parliamentary Republicans cooperated with Ba'th Party activists in stirring up "agitation outside the Assembly against unity with Iraq."[132] Prominent landholders joined the Republican Bloc and the Ba'th in spearheading resistance to any diminution of Syrian sovereignty.[133]

Syria's Communist Party also advocated the creation of an autonomous, territorially bounded state. Beginning in the mid-1930s, Gordon Torrey observes, "Communist Party policy was to collaborate with the Arab nationalists and to promote Syrian unity. In accordance with this tactic, it strongly supported the abortive 1936 Syrian treaty and railed against the cession of Alexandretta to Turkey."[134] Philip Khoury concurs: "The Communist Party enjoyed a new lease on life during World War II largely because the increasingly astute [party leader Khalid] Bakdash kept it on an almost purely nationalist footing. . . . The Party strengthened its pragmatic orientation during the war, becoming pronouncedly Arab nationalist in character rather than socialist."[135] Bakhdash campaigned for a seat in the Constituent Assembly during the summer of 1943 on a platform that called for the "independence and liberty of Syria," as well as the "encouragement of national industries and protection of national capital."[136] Khoury reports that "the Party's new National charter of January 1944 spoke of the importance of complete national liberation, of close relations between the Arab peoples, and of national education."[137] A joint meeting of the Central Committees of the Syrian and Lebanese parties issued a sharp denunciation of the Greater Syria scheme in early March 1945.[138] Not until much later did the communist leadership adopt the kind of "anti-nationalist" program that is generally associated with Marxist-Leninist organizations.

Merchants who specialized in high-profit, low-volume trade, by contrast, consistently opposed the emergence of Westphalian sovereignty and advocated the creation of a more extensive political entity instead. Noureddine Bouchair reports that a group of rich import-export merchants petitioned the British consul in Damascus in February 1939, demanding the immediate unification of Syria, Transjordan, and Palestine; the leader of the delegation took pains to reassure the consul "that he and the people he represented were not involved in any politics and that they wanted the union for economic reasons only."[139] Similarly, influential members of Aleppo's commercial elite agitated during the winter of 1942–43 in favor of cultivating a special relationship with Turkey.[140] The following summer, the prominent Halabi politician Rushdi al-Kikhya was widely suspected of preferring federation with the Turkish Republic to independence under the rule of the Damascus-centered National Bloc.[141]

This political current persisted throughout the decade. A delegation of northern notables met with King ʿAbdullah in February 1947 and "apparently presented letters of allegiance to the King from Aleppo and is reported to have said that 75 per cent. of the population of Syria were Royalist sympathizers."[142] The British consul in Aleppo relayed to the Foreign Office in early 1948 "the alacrity with which pro-monarchist and anti-republican sentiment has taken root in Aleppo, Homs and Hama."[143] That August, some sixty representatives from north-central Syria gathered in the Lebanese town of Falugha to set up a political organization to challenge the Bloc's successor, the National Party. Delegates to this founding congress of the People's Party (Hizb al-Sha'b) agreed that state-to-state alliances perpetuated fundamental splits in the Arab world, and must be superseded by active steps toward regional unity. The newly installed leadership of Hizb al-Sha'b sent a letter to President Shukri al-Quwwatli in December 1948 demanding immediate unification with other (unspecified) Arab countries as the most efficacious way to strengthen Syria's strategic position vis-à-vis the State of Israel. The president responded by attempting to turn popular sentiment against the People's Party, and publicly charged that the letter advocated immediate amalgamation with monarchical Iraq at the expense of Syria's established republican institutions.

Spruyt's analysis of early modern Europe thus illuminates several key aspects of the appearance of Westphalian sovereignty in Syria. Nevertheless, it suffers from a fundamental empirical difficulty: Sovereignty emerged not in the context of expanding foreign trade, but rather at a time when trade was at best stagnant. Commercial activity in the northern provinces had been severely disrupted by the cessation to Turkey of the region around Iskandarun in 1939; difficulties escalated and spread throughout the country after Great Britain imposed an economic blockade on Syria in the summer of 1940. Meanwhile, "a relatively poor crop, combined with an unknown but considerable amount of hoarding and profiteering, as well as contraband export to neighboring countries where prices were much higher, . . . created a near-crisis" in the local economy a year later.[144] Agricultural exports remained depressed throughout 1942, "a year of disastrous harvests."[145] At the same time, the newly established MESC imposed strict limits on the importation of a wide range of consumer goods.[146]

Syria's foreign commerce showed some signs of recovery during the course of 1943, when the aggregate value of exported vegetable products, shoes, minerals, and lumber and other construction materials registered a marked increase.[147] Still, the elite merchants who handled the country's trade in such items found themselves too weak to exert much influence over economic policy making until after the Second World War.[148] It is therefore hard to account for the emergence of Westphalian sovereignty in Syria in terms of a political bargain between the haute bourgeoisie and the central administration.

Conclusion

Hendrik Spruyt's theory that countries whose foreign trade consists primarily of low-profit, high-volume goods provide fertile ground for the growth of autonomous, territorial states goes a long way toward resolving the puzzles that result from trying to explain the emergence of Westphalian sovereignty in the Arab world in terms of concepts advanced by historical sociologists. The states that made the turn to a self-interested, territorially bounded foreign policy relatively early turn out to be the same ones whose trade involved low-profit, high-volume exports, while the leaders of high-profit, low-volume Jordan exhibited a pronounced reluctance to abandon the quest for a more comprehensive form of Arab polity. In Iraq, where the local economy was shifting toward the production of low-profit, high-volume goods, two well-entrenched high-profit, low-volume sectors nevertheless buttressed the leadership's long-standing drive for regional unity. And in Syria, the external preferences of influential political actors corresponded remarkably closely to the kind of goods they handled.

Nevertheless, the emergence of narrowly self-interested, territorially bounded Arab states took place not in the context of expanding trade but rather at moments when foreign commerce was either stagnant or in decline. This finding undermines Spruyt's theory in two ways. First, and most obviously, it contradicts the underlying logic of the proposed argument. A drop in foreign trade might be expected to put merchants who deal in low-profit, high-volume goods in a substantially weaker position vis-à-vis the state, and lead them to fear predation by government officials almost as much as by local nobles. Under these circumstances, their willingness to acquiesce in the consolidation of a more activist state is hard to understand. Second, the ability of forces to exercise political power successfully while experiencing a deterioration in their economic circumstances runs counter to the basic assumptions of neoclassical economics on which Spruyt's analysis rests. For neoclassical economists, actors are assumed to enjoy or gain power when they are prospering or are in a position to prosper, and lose influence as their fortunes decline. Thus Ronald Rogowski argues that landholders exercise a great deal of influence in expanding land-rich economies, whereas capitalists prevail in expanding capital-rich economies.[149] But if political outcomes end up reflecting the interests of actors that are losing rather than gaining ground, some other kind of argument is required.

CHAPTER FOUR

Domestic Conflict and Regime Maintenance

Existing theories offer important insights into the complex process whereby anarchic states-systems take shape and flourish. There is clearly some kind of link between internal state formation and external sovereignty, and the dynamics associated with domestic political coalitions have been shown to be useful in explaining a wide range of foreign policy outcomes.[1] But the specific arguments that Giddens and Spruyt propose fail to provide a persuasive explanation for the divergent trajectories whereby nationalist leaderships across the Arab world turned away from the quest to create a unified regional polity and began instead to promote the narrow self-interest of their respective territorially bounded states.

A more compelling way to explain the shift to Westphalian sovereignty in this part of the world can be formulated in terms of fundamental conflicts of interest that pitted each country's commercial and industrial elite against the small-scale manufacturers and shopkeepers who supplied goods to the domestic market. Changes in foreign trade had a direct impact on the distribution of power between these two broad coalitions of social forces. In particular, marked contractions in trade with the outside world tended to weaken rich import-export merchants and large-scale export-oriented manufacturers vis-à-vis artisans and traders. The threat to the commercial and industrial elite was compounded whenever low-profit, high-volume goods dominated a country's foreign trade, making elite merchants and industrialists more vulnerable to marginal increases in transaction costs. If, on the other hand, trade consisted primarily of high-profit, low-volume goods, then commercial and industrial elites found themselves in a better position to ride out challenges from the petite bourgeoisie, because small manufacturers and tradespeople stood a good chance of suffering ruin as a result of even a brief period of economic difficulty.

What mattered even more than aggregate changes in the level or value of trade was the extent to which commercial fluctuations provided an opportunity for small-scale manufacturers and shopkeepers to form an alliance with other social forces actively opposed to the regime. More precisely, whenever a downturn in external trade took place in the context of escalating political activism on the part of urban workers or rural laborers, it became possible for small-scale manufacturers and tradespeople to threaten to ally with more radical challengers, greatly increasing their leverage vis-à-vis the authorities. Under these circumstances, the already-weakened commercial and industrial elite could offer little support to state officials, who had a strong incentive to explore innovative, even risky, ways to prop up the deteriorating domestic order. New government agencies designed to regulate trade, banking, and labor were among the institutions that most often appeared as a direct response to heightened internal threats to the regime.

Such institutional innovations contributed substantially to the emergence of self-interested, territorially bounded polities, in which the central administrative apparatus exercised an unprecedented degree of supervision over domestic economic and social affairs. At the same time, nationalist leaderships took steps to limit or undercut the appeal of radical dissidents by mobilizing popular sentiment in support of platforms, slogans, and symbols that highlighted the country's coherence and distinctiveness as an autonomous political entity. This effort proved most effective whenever the internal political arena was dominated by organized parties, which competed against one another for electoral support. Consequently, the existence of liberal democratic institutions throughout the Arab world in the three decades following the First World War greatly facilitated the emergence of an anarchic Middle Eastern states-system.

Stagnant Trade and Popular Unrest in Egypt

As Egypt's foreign trade contracted in the years after 1910, elite commercial establishments and the large-scale industrial enterprises with which they were associated steadily lost ground relative to smaller-scale manufacturing and trading concerns. This trend was most evident in food processing and staple consumer goods. In 1911, the country's five highest-capitalized companies included the Société Anonyme des Sucreries et de la Raffinerie d'Egypte, the Egyptian Salt and Soda Company, and United Egyptian Salt. Almost as large were the Port Sa'id Salt Association and the Rosetta and Alexandria Rice Mills.[2] Such enterprises not only exported a substantial proportion of their total output, but also relied heavily on overseas suppliers for vital raw materials and equipment. The steady deterioration of foreign trade led capital formation in these companies to stagnate from 1911 to 1914, then drop sharply at the start of the First World War.[3] By contrast, artisanal workshops expanded and proliferated, not only in the major cities but also throughout the provinces. No fewer than 568 "plus ou moins primitifs" sugarcane-crushing plants are reported to have been operating as of 1911.[4] According to the official censuses taken in 1907 and 1917, the total number of domestic manufacturers jumped from some 380,000 before the war to more than 491,000 at its height.[5]

Large-scale, staples-producing firms responded to the deterioration of their position in the local economy by taking steps to seize control of the supply of locally grown inputs, not only to reduce production costs but more importantly to cripple smaller competitors.[6] This strategy enabled the major sugar and salt companies to profit handsomely from wartime scarcities by boosting production for the internal market, which had burgeoned with the arrival of thousands of British troops. The Société Anonyme des Sucreries generated profits of more than 469,000 Egyptian pounds in 1916–17, compared to less than 79,000 three years earlier.[7] Efforts to monopolize the flow of raw materials generated severe conflicts of interest between the larger companies and artisanal manufacturers, but so long as wartime conditions heightened profits for producers across the board, these tensions remained latent.

By early 1918, the shrinking availability of petroleum products began to raise the cost of this vital input for a wide range of industrial operations. Among those hurt most were the artisanal sugar and molasses makers of

Upper Egypt, who faced sharp increases in the price of fuel oil during the winter of 1917–18.[8] With smaller producers in trouble, the Société Anonyme des Sucreries quickly cut its output, driving prices up steeply on local markets.[9] Rich sugar merchants added to the growing panic among consumers by spreading rumors that the next year's crop was about to fail.[10] The resulting crisis prompted state officials to consider rationing sugar to consumers. But before plans to do so could be carried out, prices dropped to more manageable levels. Meanwhile, efforts on the part of large-scale cereals merchants to manipulate the supply of the staple grain durrah during the winter of 1917–18 prompted bakers to urge the government to extend price controls to all varieties of wheat.[11]

Shortages of imported yarn and fabrics in the years after 1914 revived Egypt's major cotton manufacturers, such as the Associated Cotton Ginners, the Société Anonyme Générale de Pressage et de Dépôt, Anglo-Egyptian Spinning and Weaving, and Kafr al-Zayyat Cotton Ginning. Robert Tignor goes so far as to claim that "Egypt's only large-scale textile firm, the Filature Nationale d'Egypte, was saved from bankruptcy by the war."[12] On the whole, the disappearance of European-made textiles from domestic and regional markets after 1914 offered greater profit-making opportunities for large and small enterprises alike. But unlike those in the food processing sector, workshops devoted to cloth production suffered disproportionately from wartime shortages of foreign inputs, particularly high-quality yarns and dyes.[13] In the important provincial textile center of al-Mansurah, artisanal spinning and weaving of silk all but disappeared during the course of the war.[14] Small-scale linen workshops in the nearby cities of Tanta and Zifta suffered a similar fate.[15] Some craftspeople attempted to salvage their fortunes by setting up collective enterprises, in which a number of independent producers worked side by side and shared overhead expenses.[16] Other, more fortunate artisans took steps to mechanize their operations in an attempt to offset the spiraling cost of inputs.[17]

Persistent coordination problems between large and small textile enterprises prompted state officials to set up the Commission on Commerce and Industry in 1916. Chief among the problems the commission investigated was the potential for heightened unemployment in the cloth sector, particularly in the major cities. To prevent displaced tradespeople and workers from endangering public order, the commission recommended that the government take immediate steps to encourage the diversification of the local economy through the expansion of import-substituting industry in other sectors, preferably by establishing a state-affiliated industrial investment bank.[18] In addition, it urged the authorities to erect tariff barriers strong enough to protect existing manufacturers. A year later, the ministry of the interior set up a special commission to monitor the distribution of petroleum products throughout the country.

Meanwhile, elite merchants found their activities increasingly jeopardized by government initiatives aimed at regulating the wartime economy. The Cotton Commission that was formed in June 1918 initially left the most important aspects of purchasing and distributing this crop to designated local commercial firms. As time went by, however, control over these activities passed into the hands of London-based trading companies, effectively bypassing the merchant houses of Alexandria and Cairo.[19] More active collaboration between the Supplies Control Board and the Cairo Military Tribunal led to stricter enforcement of the regulations that governed the distribution and sale of grain and other staples, at least in the capital.[20] In addition, state officials took steps during the war to curb the long-standing prerogatives of the consular tribunals and Mixed Courts, while redoubling their efforts to implement a comprehensive reform of the legal system.[21]

As soon as the war ended, imported goods of all kinds inundated the local market. Tignor estimates that the real value of manufactured imports almost doubled from 1919 to 1920. The flood of foreign-made products quickly overwhelmed such large-scale industrial companies as the Filature Nationale d'Egypte, the Société Anonyme des Sucreries, and the Egyptian Salt and Soda Company.[22] Small enterprises, by contrast, adapted to the situation somewhat more successfully. Raw materials and spare parts that had been largely unobtainable during the war could once again be procured, albeit at inflated prices. Labor costs remained significantly lower in small-scale concerns than in the larger factories.[23] Moreover, the fact that most local workshops (*al-ma'amil al-mahalliyah al-saghirah*) were specifically exempt from paying the government-imposed excise tax enabled these concerns to bear the rising costs of manufacturing more easily than large-scale enterprises could.[24]

Increasing trade did little to improve the position of Egypt's commercial elite in the months following the First World War. The ban on domestic sugar exports remained in force into the early 1920s.[25] Marked fluctuations in the supply of locally produced cotton loosened the grip of the Alexandria General Produce Association on the marketing of that crop, and opened the door for a rival organization—the Syndicate for the Protection of the Interests of Cultivators, later called the Egyptian General Agricultural Syndicate—to champion the interests of growers over those of brokers.[26] Rich merchants suffered additional setbacks as a result of the popular uprising that swept the country in the spring of 1919. Not only did sustained attacks on the railway network in March and April disrupt routine shipments of goods for export, but provincial offices of many major import-export firms were looted and vandalized during the course of the revolt.[27] The difficulties confronting the country's merchants during these months sparked the formation of chambers of commerce at al-Mansurah and Tanta, followed by similar organizations in Zifta, Mit Ghamr, and Alexandria three years later.[28] Nevertheless, the chambers remained fundamentally weak, primarily due to the fact that no more than a handful of local traders could afford to join. More precisely, the chambers of commerce tended to represent almost exclusively the interests of the country's heterogeneous expatriate merchant community, leaving Egyptians at the mercy of rapacious middlemen and the vagaries of the market.[29]

It was in this vulnerable condition that Egypt's elite merchants and large-scale manufacturers found themselves faced with unprecedented levels of labor unrest. Organized protests by dockworkers at Port Sa'id erupted as early as 1894. By the turn of the century, strikes by skilled laborers and craftspeople had become a recurrent feature of social life in Cairo and Alexandria as well.[30] Labor activism peaked during the fall of 1910 and summer of 1911, when workers stormed into the streets to demand higher wages and an end to discriminatory dismissal and promotion policies, first at the massive Egyptian State Railways repair yard at 'Anabir and then in the Société des Tramways du Caire.[31] The repressive measures that were undertaken by the Department of Public Security and the local police in the aftermath of these strikes brought organized labor protest to an abrupt halt in the fall of 1911. Benevolent associations and newspapers that covered workers' problems in a sympathetic manner were targeted by the authorities as well, tightly limiting the potential for further collective action. In the words of Joel Beinin and Zachary Lockman, "Unable to recruit aggressively or take the offensive against employers, even the strongest unions were forced to turn inward and try to preserve themselves by focusing on their mutual aid functions. Other unions went out of existence, or barely held on with only a small core of loyal members."[32]

Strikes and other forms of collective protest remained in abeyance until August 1917, when cigarette factory workers in Alexandria and Cairo abruptly walked out to demand wage levels commensurate with rising prices.[33] These laborers struck once again the following February.[34] At the end of 1918, tramway workers in the capital mobilized to demand shorter hours, higher wages, and "a more rational and equitable system of disciplinary penalties."[35] But it was in the context of the popular uprising of March–April 1919 that labor unrest blossomed into a nationwide movement. According to Lockman, "within a few days [of the arrest of Sa'd Zaghlul and his colleagues on 8 March] workers at the Cairo, Heliopolis and Alexandria tramways, the 'Anabir, the [Egyptian State Railways] printing press, the Government Press, the Arsenal and government workshops, the Helwan electric railway, the Cairo electric company and other enterprises, along with postal, port, lighthouse and customs employees, taxi and carriage drivers and others had all gone on strike."[36] The U.S. consul in Alexandria reported that at the beginning of April, "arrests were made among the native labour unions for attempts to manufacture suspicious iron instruments for use against the British soldiery."[37]

Organized labor posed a continuing challenge to the stability of the political order in the months following the 1919 revolt. Besides tram, railway, and cigarette workers, a wide range of other employees and laborers, mechanics, and independent craftspeople set up trade unions in the wake of the revolt.[38] Strikes broke out in May at the alcohol factory at Tura and the Salt and Soda Company complex at Kafr al-Zayyat.[39] Growing discontent among workers and tradespeople culminated in a cluster of industrial actions three months later:

> The great strike wave of August 1919 included the tramways of Cairo, Helipolis [sic], and Alexandria, omnibus drivers, the 'Anabir and Jabal al-Zaytun railway workers, numerous cigarette factories, the Abu Qirqas sugar mill, the Hawamdiyya [sugar] refinery, waiters and kitchen workers in the major cafes, restaurants, and patisseries of Cairo and Alexandria, shop and bank employees, bakery workers, the Ma'asara quarrymen, the Candida engineering works in Alexandria, Bonded Stores warehouses and the Spathis soda factory. There were also strikes in Suez, Tanta, and Mansura.[40]

Shortly thereafter, workers at cotton ginning factories in al-Fayyum and al-Buhairah walked off the job, followed by laborers in the sugar mills at

Komombo and Hawamdiyyah.[41] The U.S. consul in Cairo reported at the beginning of September that

> the strikes that have obtained for the past three weeks in Cairo and Alexandria and other towns in Egypt appear to grow worse rather than better. . . . The strikes of the various labor unions seem to be political as well as economic, and this gives rise to more fear of future evil. . . . From time to time one hears of resolutions adopted by the Central Committees of carpenters, printers, tailors, electricians, hair dressers, bakers, painters, bank clerks, waiters, and Zionist socialists, and other organizations, and rumors fill the air that more serious strikes are coming, that all government employees will soon quit en masse, etc., etc.[42]

Popular disorders continued into the fall and winter of 1919–20. Two days of rioting in a poor district of Alexandria in mid-October led to armed intervention by British troops, which in turn sparked strikes throughout the city by shopkeepers, students, and state employees. The protests prompted similar actions on the part of artisans and tradespeople in al-Mansurah, Dissuq, and Shibin al-Qum.[43] Students and agricultural laborers in the countryside engaged in a further outburst of mass demonstrations and sporadic attacks on government offices in February.[44]

It was in direct response to this broad wave of labor militancy that the authorities in August 1919 set up the Labor Conciliation Board, "to investigate disputes between workers and employers, appoint mediators to convene negotiations, propose measures to resolve disputes, and participate in the development of representation for workers and employers."[45] Two months earlier, a ministry of communications was formed to coordinate the operations that had previously been supervised by the separate departments of railways, river navigation, and roads and bridges.[46] Simmering popular unrest persuaded state officials to acquiesce in the creation of Bank Misr the following spring. The appearance of this pivotal indigenous institution set the stage for the formation of a state-sponsored Association of Egyptian Industries, which in 1922 became the Egyptian Federation of Industries. Both the bank and the industrialists' federation actively lobbied government agencies to implement tariff reform and adopt other forms of state protection and support for local manufacturing.[47] Meanwhile, the ministry of public works in early 1920 announced an ambitious program designed to increase the total area of farmland by one-third and convert almost one-fourth of the country's existing agricultural land from basin to perennial irrigation.[48]

Nationalist leaders responded to the heightened labor activism of 1918–19 in divergent ways. The leadership of al-Hizb al-Watani had established intimate ties to craftspeople's and workers' organizations during the first decade of the twentieth century.[49] The party played a key role in orchestrating the succession of strikes that shook the cities during the years immediately preceding the war. It also took steps to set up district syndicates of farm laborers to push for increases in agricultural wages and improvements in living conditions in the countryside. State officials cracked down on Nationalist Party activists during the war, charging that they were working in league with Ottoman and German agents.[50] As a result, party militants set up a network of underground associations, whose members initiated a campaign of intimidation and violence against the government.[51] These covert operations steadily alienated the country's growing class of well-educated, well-to-do professionals, known collectively as the *effendiyyah*, as well as more moderate political associations such as Hizb al-Ummah and the Constitutional Reform Party (Hizb al-Islah ʿAla Mabadi al-Dustur). Misgivings on the part of the effendiyyah escalated in the wake of the Bolshevik revolution in Russia, which accompanied the appearance of scattered cells of avowedly leftist revolutionaries in poor neighborhoods of Alexandria, Cairo, and Port Saʿid.[52]

Growing threats of popular violence convinced prominent members of the effendiyyah to press for greater political autonomy by peaceful means. Energized by the publication of U.S. President Woodrow Wilson's Fourteen Points in January 1918, and encouraged by Sultan Fuad, Prince ʿUmar Tusun, and other senior figures in the palace, these notables formed a delegation (*wafd*) to submit Egypt's demands to the international peace conference in Paris.[53] Nationalist historiography has clouded the crucial issues of precisely what the wafd's initial demands might have been, and how its platform evolved over time. The usual picture of the leading figure of the movement and the later Wafd Party that it engendered, Saʿd Zaghlul, portrays him as a consistently outspoken champion of Egyptian independence. But as Mahmud Zayid observes, "The post-war Zaghlul, however, began with a program which was less ambitious than is usually recognized."[54] Nationalist leaders collaborated with the palace to hammer out an elaborate scheme whereby a delegation of respected notables would first present the demand for full Egyptian autonomy to the Paris peace conference; then, if it were rejected, the delegation would immediately undertake intensive negotiations with Britain to set new terms for continuing the Protectorate.[55] It was only in the wake of the frustrating and humiliating 13 November 1918 audience with the British high commissioner in Cairo that Zaghlul and his colleagues started to issue public calls for independence. More tellingly, the Wafd's commitment to "complete independence" appears to have solidified only in reaction to pressure from militants associated with al-Hizb al-Watani.[56]

Egyptian nationalists therefore adopted a foreign policy platform whose primary components entailed the principles of Westphalian sovereignty as part of an intense struggle to win the support of the country's small-scale manufacturers and shopkeepers, who might otherwise have joined mobilized workers and farm laborers to pursue a more radical set of objectives. The turn toward advocating complete independence for a narrowly defined, territorially bounded Egypt accompanied a more-or-less conscious effort on the part of prominent members of the effendiyyah to rally popular sympathy behind the leadership of the Wafd, a strategy that blossomed in the wake of the deportation of Sa'd Zaghlul and his comrades in early March 1919. From that time on, the nationalists' shared conception of Egypt excluded any notion that the country might form part of a reconstituted Ottoman realm, just as it adamantly rejected the continuation of the British Protectorate.

Egypt's long-standing connection to the Sudan nevertheless remained problematic. At the height of the 1918–19 crisis, the Wafd's leadership expressed little if any interest in maintaining Cairo's control over the vast territories that lay south of Wadi Halfa. On the contrary, Zayid reports that Sa'd Zaghlul himself "was ready then to forget the Sudan—the rock on which many later Anglo-Egyptian negotiations were destroyed."[57] Furthermore, the government's plan to expand irrigated agriculture on reclaimed lands throughout the entire Nile valley at the beginning of 1920 sparked heated opposition from nationalist leaders, who charged "that Egyptian interests were being sacrificed to Sudanese irrigation needs."[58] Zaghlul publicly complained that the extensive network of dams and canals envisaged in the scheme would leave Egypt more vulnerable than ever to external pressure, because British military forces based in the Sudan would now be able to manipulate the flow of vital Nile River water coming into the country from the south.[59] Such sentiments reflected the Wafd's campaign to promote a comparatively narrow definition of Egypt's strategic interests in the months immediately after the First World War, but they also contained elements of a somewhat broader notion that continued to envisage the formation of some kind of integrated Egyptian-Sudanese polity.

Declining Trade and Labor Activism in Tunisia

Commercial difficulties during the early 1920s severely weakened the rich merchants and large landholders on whom the French authorities relied to prop up Tunisia's imperial order. Mineral exports faced unprecedented competition from such new suppliers as the United States and Morocco. The global glut in phosphates proved particularly detrimental to local producers, whose share of the crucial European market plunged sharply after the First World War.[60] More important, agricultural exports plummeted in 1922–23, due to an unexpectedly poor crop year for the country's major staples. The collapse of domestic grain production prompted the government to start importing large quantities of wheat, which were then sold to domestic consumers at exorbitant prices. "As a result," report Eqbal Ahmad and Stuart Schaar, "the cost of living rose by 29 per cent between 1923 and 1924, and workers began to clamor for higher wages. The postwar economic crisis thus wiped out whatever profits [well-to-do] Tunisians had gained during the war."[61]

Flagging external trade set the stage for a transformation of the social relations that had structured Tunisia's economy under the Protectorate. Urban workshops that relied on elite merchant houses for credit and operating capital now found themselves unable to raise the funds they needed to continue functioning. As a result, the years immediately after the war witnessed the ruin of the predominantly artisanal system of domestic manufacturing and its replacement by a collection of larger, more capital-intensive enterprises.[62]

At the same time, Muslim members of the commercial and agrarian elite found themselves increasingly displaced by European expatriates. The number of French and Italian owners of commercial establishments rose from 3,718 in 1911 to 4,366 in 1921, while the number of European agricultural landowners jumped from 2,919 to 3,709 during the same ten years.[63] The new expatriate bourgeoisie recruited skilled workers from Italy, Spain, Malta, and Greece, thereby supplanting large numbers of Tunisians. In addition, a wave of Sudanese, Algerian, Moroccan, and Tripolitanian laborers flooded into the country in the months after the war, taking over unskilled and itinerant jobs throughout the local economy.[64] Indigenous workers repeatedly petitioned the authorities to reinstate them in their previous positions, particularly in such comparatively high-paying industries as phosphate and zinc mining. But such petitions were routinely rejected on the grounds that they infringed on the basic rights of employers.

Besides suffering from the drop in foreign trade, Tunisia's commercial elite endured the brunt of increased government exactions in the years after the First World War. Falling revenues and heightened expenditures led state officials to impose a series of new taxes on domestic economic activities beginning in 1920. Particularly onerous were the supplemental taxes on olive trees, wheat fields, and vineyards, which cut deeply into growers' already-meager profits.[65] Manufacturers of olive oil found themselves doubly burdened due to a simultaneous increase in the export duty levied on this important product.[66]

Small-scale manufacturers, on the other hand, forged close ties to the central administration during the course of the war. Of special importance in consolidating this connection was the Services Economiques Indigènes (SEI), which was set up in 1913 to facilitate the diffusion of modern industrial equipment and techniques among local tradespeople.[67] When the war ended, the SEI took charge of a variety of artisanal activities in rural districts, and sponsored the formation of agricultural and artisanal cooperatives throughout the countryside.[68] These moves sparked sharp criticism from the French colon elite, whose members forced the Resident General to transfer the head of the SEI to Syria at the end of 1921.

Persistent difficulties in coordinating the production and distribution of manufactured goods across North Africa left smaller manufacturers increasingly disenchanted with the notion of building a unified regional market. Beginning in 1915, French military authorities ran a central office to oversee the supply of military clothing and equipment in Algiers. The overall inefficiency with which this agency carried out its operations generated considerable discontent among the artisans of Tunis, and threatened to revive the sort of anti-French activism that had erupted in 1911.[69] Even after the war came to an end, local manufacturers firmly resisted the Resident General's plans to establish a customs union with France and Algeria.[70]

Wartime shortages and price hikes sparked sporadic protests by industrial workers and government employees. But it was not until the fighting in Europe came to an end that worker activism blossomed: in the words of Daniel Goldstein, "1919 fût la grande année des luttes ouvrières."[71] That year saw the outbreak of more than a dozen major industrial strikes, including ones involving tramway and flour mill workers in Tunis, dockworkers in Sfax, and munitions workers in Bizerte. When consumer prices continued to skyrocket over the course of 1920, the residents of poor neighborhoods in the larger cities turned to plundering shops and warehouses. At the same time, striking workers in different parts of the country took steps to coordinate their activities, thereby laying the foundation for a nationwide labor organization.[72] This trend received a boost when the powerful and well-connected phosphate miners of Metlaoui and Redeyef walked out at the beginning of March.

As the frequency and severity of industrial actions grew, French labor leaders set up a Tunisian branch of the Confédération Générale du Travail (CGT). This organization quickly gained adherents among the country's skilled workers and professionals, most notably state employees, teachers, and railway and tramway personnel, along with heavy equipment operators at the mines and docks.[73] The great majority of the CGT membership during 1919–20 consisted of Italian, Maltese, French, and other European expatriates. As a result, the early leadership tended to turn a blind eye to labor practices that discriminated against indigenous Muslims, and generally adopted a patronizing attitude with regard to non-Europeans among the organization's rank and file. The CGT's obvious unwillingness to address problems associated with inequitable pay scales and working conditions pushed many Muslim workers toward the local communist movement. This movement took a variety of institutional forms in the years immediately following the First World War, but Muslim laborers and students consistently composed the core constituency of its more radical wing.[74]

Escalating tensions between the moderate and radical wings of the labor movement led the radicals in the summer of 1921 to collaborate with the communists to form a rival trade union organization to the CGT, which affiliated itself with the Moscow-oriented Confédération Générale de Travail Unifiée (CGTU). Simmering discontent inside the CGT boiled over in August 1924, when dockworkers at the port of Tunis — against the advice of the federation's leadership — walked out to demand the same wages as their counterparts at Marseilles. The strike quickly spread to the docks at Bizerte, as well as to several other larger enterprises throughout the north of the country.[75] Eqbal Ahmad remarks that this wave of industrial unrest "demonstrated, for the first time in Tunisia, the efficacy of organized mass political action."[76] More important, it encouraged radical textile, tram, and cement workers to set up trade unions of their own that remained outside the CGT. This trend prompted the U.S. diplomatic representative in Tunis to report that "the political situation during 1924 was less favorable than in 1923. An intensive communistic propaganda [campaign] was carried on among the natives."[77]

Growing activism among skilled and unskilled workers sparked similar moves on the part of small-scale manufacturers, particularly in the larger cities. Makers of the distinctive conical felt hat known as the *chechia* (or, more loosely, fez) set up a producers' association at the time of the dockworkers' strikes in Tunis and Bizerte; craftspeople specializing in the manufacture of leather apparel and household goods soon followed suit.[78] The collapse of negotiations between the striking dockworkers and the authorities sparked a wave of closures and walkouts in the shops and warehouses of the capital.[79] The possibility that influential members of the country's petite bourgeoisie might join the workers in challenging the status quo posed a significant threat to the colonial regime and the Destour leadership alike.

Meanwhile, radicals inside the Destour Party engaged in setting up a network of consumers' cooperatives to promote self-reliance in poorer districts. These activists joined striking dockworkers, led by the charismatic labor activist Muhammad Ben 'Ali Ben Mokhtar al-Ghaffani (more commonly known as Muhammad 'Ali al-Hammi) in November 1924 to form the Confédération Générale des Travailleurs Tunisiens (CGTT). Enthusiasm for the new organization spread rapidly not only in and around the capital but also across industrial areas throughout the north. In early December, Muhammad 'Ali and other members of the CGTT executive committee traveled to Sfax, where they appealed to workers in the larger olive oil and mining companies of the south to join the movement.[80] Support for the new organization proved particularly strong among miners, prompting company managers to petition the government for assistance in restricting Muhammad 'Ali's activities.[81] The CGTT's growing success inspired cement and limestone workers outside Tunis to carry out a wildcat strike in January 1925. When the leaders of the CGTT publicly expressed support for the strikers, they were immediately arrested on charges of conspiring to undermine the security of the state.[82] This episode only heightened the prestige and credibility of the union among disaffected laborers in both urban and rural areas.

State officials scrambled to deal with the growing militancy of Tunisia's workers during the early 1920s. Minor revisions of the 1884 French labor code proved to be an ineffective means by which to address the workers' demands.[83] An alternative institutional mechanism envisaged the revival of customary tribunals in each locality, made up of the heads of the artisan guilds, one or two influential patrons, and representatives of workers; these bodies were to be charged with the dual tasks of enforcing labor regulations and adjudicating disputes.[84] In October 1924 the Resident General wrote to his superiors urging them to find an innovative solution to the longstanding problems arising from the fact that French laborers were accorded very different legal rights and privileges from those granted to their Italian and Muslim coworkers.[85] These distinctions precluded any general strategy to cope with the problems posed by labor activists, and led the government to continue to discriminate among different nationalities within the proletariat. As a result, resentment against Europeans heightened among Muslim workers.

Faced with an increasingly insurrectionary situation, the French authorities set up the extraordinary Commission Consultative d'Etudes Tunisiennes to explore new ways to defuse tensions.[86] This high-level advisory committee solicited investigative reports from a variety of government agencies, both in Tunisia and in metropolitan France. The findings were passed along to the Resident General in Tunis to serve as the basis for innovative approaches to public policy.

Leaders of the Destour responded to the rise of the CGTT by focusing their activities on concrete measures that might improve living conditions for Tunisia's indigenous, Muslim population. The leadership also reorganized the structure of the party by expanding the number of local branches and increasing the frequency of open meetings and public rallies.[87] Party activists increasingly praised the actions of the CGTT leadership and encouraged workers to join the organization. Government agents reported on 4 December 1924 that party gatherings had begun to resemble union rallies, and that prominent Destourians were urging their supporters to turn their attention toward promoting labor syndicates composed exclusively of "Tunisian" members.[88] Such pronouncements undercut the major socialist unions, the CGT and CGTU, whose members prided themselves on their antinationalist ethos, while at the same time augmenting solidarity among the country's Muslim workers. The main socialist newspaper countered by calling the Destour-CGTT campaign to create Tunisians-only labor organizations "an instrument of nativist and xenophobic nationalism" ("un organe de nationalisme intégral et xénophobe").[89]

Nationalist leaders nevertheless recognized the explosive potential of the CGTT and the wildcat labor activism that its initiatives inspired. At the end of 1924, the Destour made a series of overtures to Muhammad 'Ali and his colleagues in an attempt to moderate the demands that radicals were advancing. Party and union published a joint broadsheet in Arabic and French that decried the government's attempts to break up the CGTT through the use of illegal tactics.[90] By appealing for a return to the rule of law, the leadership of the Destour hoped to restore the party's standing among small manufacturers and tradespeople, while at the same time driving a wedge between the associations that had been formed by petit bourgeois forces and more militant labor syndicates.

Furthermore, collaborating openly with the CGTT enabled the nationalist leadership to effect a crucial redirection in the groundswell of popular discontent, away from class-based grievances and toward the drive for political autonomy from France. This strategy was evident in public meetings sponsored by the party, in which prominent speakers regularly equated the rights of Muslim workers with the rights of the Tunisian nation as a whole.[91] These appeals proved increasingly effective in drawing militant workers into the nationalist fold. By the end of 1924, demands for Tunisian independence had begun to eclipse those championed by militant labor leaders. When radicals inside the CGTT tried to regain control over the labor movement that winter, they were castigated as traitors to the nationalist cause. Moreover, the campaign for independence succeeded in preventing the petite bourgeoisie from defecting to the radicals' side. Jacques Berque offers an illustrative vignette: "On 29 September 1925 a procession of protest gathered on the Place Halfawin. It caused some disturbance among those who sat smoking hashish there, or listening to the song of goldfinches. It moved along the outer street, through Bab Carthagena, crossed the Petite Malte into the Place de France, and proceeded through the suqs. It was now in the heart of the old madina, the city; and at last, by way of the rue de la Qasba, reached the seat of government. Who was leading it? An obscure bookseller, who had to some extent forced the Destour's hand."[92] As tradespeople and shopkeepers became more committed proponents of independence, the stage was set for the displacement of the Destour by the Neo-Destour — an often-told tale.

Stagnant Trade and Popular Mobilization in Jordan

Persistent commercial stagnation at the end of the 1940s and beginning of the 1950s significantly undermined the dominant position of Jordan's rich merchant community. The deteriorating political influence of the quota coterie was apparent as early as the spring of 1949, when the disruption in trade that followed the 1948 war in Palestine led the government to appoint a controller of the currency, whose office was charged with sorting out and reorganizing the existing patchwork of exclusive import licenses and foreign exchange permits.[93] By 1951, state officials had begun routinely to postpone and manipulate the issuing of import licenses in ways that enhanced government revenues at the expense of the commercial elite. According to the semiannual economic report issued at the end of the year, "the allocation of import licences for the 2nd import licencing period which was due to commence on 1st July 1951 was delayed until the beginning of September, when allocations were cut to a bare minimum and the import of some non-essential commodities was banned altogether. Whilst the news was greeted with the traditional outcry of protest from the merchants the allocations did in fact represent roughly the real needs of the country and the saving in currency enabled the Government to import further substantial quantities of cereals without drawing on their sterling reserves, a far better performance than had been anticipated."[94]

Petit bourgeois manufacturers and traders took advantage of the situation to demand greater levels of state intervention in the domestic economy. In January 1950, for instance, shopkeepers in the larger towns of the West Bank pressed the government to introduce protective tariffs that would enable them to compete successfully with the rich merchants who imported cheap consumer goods into the country. Three months later, small shopkeepers petitioned the central administration to extend the same degree of support to their businesses that it exerted on behalf of elite commercial interests.[95] Such demands became increasingly worrisome to the authorities in 1951–52, as discontent sparked by the deteriorating domestic economy flared among the urban poor and rural laborers.[96]

More important, organizations representing these groups started to play a more active role in political affairs. Members of the Muslim Brotherhood stood as independent candidates in the parliamentary elections of August 1951. Although they campaigned primarily on the basis of moral issues, at least a few of the individuals who ran for office that summer raised the question of what the government intended to do to improve the economic situation of the country's poorer citizens.[97] Six months later, an assembly of prominent Muslim Brothers gathered in ʿAmman to hammer out an economic program that would appeal not only to their supporters but also to prospective new members. Those in attendance "called for the abolition of monopoly and the introduction of price control. The appeal to [the] government [also] urged the starting of Jordan's projected development projects, thus reducing unemployment and providing [for a] better life."[98]

Growing popular disaffection generated a parallel surge in activism on the part of more radical actors. A group of militant members of the Ikhwan broke away from the main organization and set up the Liberation Party (Hizb al-Tahrir), which advocated replacing the existing state with a more just "Islamic" order.[99] Other radicals gravitated toward the communist movement, which had attempted to mobilize popular opposition to the Hashemite regime in the late 1940s.[100] The movement's potential to galvanize disaffected workers and students led the government to issue a decree in May 1948 that made it a criminal offense to engage in any action that promoted communism.[101] But the country's main communist organization, the League of National Liberation (Usbah al-Taharrur al-Watani) continued to operate underground and became increasingly active in the weeks leading up to the April 1950 annexation of the West Bank.[102] Communist agitation culminated in a public rally in Nablus at the end of March, which Amnon Cohen calls "a significant landmark: it was the first time that Communists in the West Bank had openly challenged the authorities; their overt activities up to this time had been restricted primarily to the distribution of leaflets."[103] An even larger demonstration in Ramallah followed.

Police responded to the emergence of such public manifestations of support for the communists by cracking down on the movement's leadership. A conjunction of heightened repression and increased competition from the equally radical Baʿth Party prompted a major reorganization of the League in the spring of 1951. The new leaders of the rechristened Jordanian Communist Party (JCP) opted to shift the organization's attention toward attracting greater support from well-to-do professionals and intellectuals.[104] This strategy resulted in a drop in visibility that continued for the next year. But in August 1952, JCP militants orchestrated a mass demonstration in ʿAmman, which was succeeded by a pair of similar demonstrations in Nablus that fall.[105] Encouraged by these signs of widespread support among the general public, the party leadership once again changed its priorities and took steps to win adherents among the populace at large. The distribution of JCP leaflets became increasingly common in Jordan's cities and towns; new cells proliferated in both urban and rural areas; and prominent sympathizers grew more outspoken in articulating party principles.[106] Perhaps the most striking aspect of the party's campaign to broaden its base was the conscious effort to build bridges to small-scale manufacturers and shopkeepers.[107]

State officials attempted to parry the upsurge in organized dissent by implementing a series of measures designed to prevent the formation of an alliance between the petite bourgeoisie and more radical social forces. January 1952 saw the adoption of a comprehensive workers' rights law that assigned state agencies a major role in the enforcement of regulations governing the workplace; two months later, the Assembly of Representatives reinvigorated the dormant state-affiliated Development Board and gave it primary responsibility for coordinating and supervising economic development projects throughout the kingdom.[108] More important, the assassination of King ʿAbdullah in July 1951 opened the door to a fundamental reconfiguration of the legal relationship between citizens and the crown. The outlines of the new political order were presented to the Assembly of Representatives in mid-September as a series of revisions to the 1947 constitution. The most significant of these revisions made the council of ministers responsible to the assembly rather than to the monarch, granted the assembly the right to enact laws over a royal veto with a two-thirds majority, and entrusted the assembly with the duty to ratify international treaties.[109]

This initiative was undertaken in the name of cementing the unity and independence of the Jordanian nation. Prime Minister Tawfiq Abu al-Huda explicitly linked the new constitution to the principles of Westphalian sovereignty that were enshrined in the Covenant of the League of Arab States, while affirming that the purpose of the amendments was to buttress "the stability of Jordan and maintenance of the throne." He went on to remark that "union with anyone of the Arab States would be welcomed when general Arab agreement on it was reached and provided it included a guarantee against dangers from all directions and gave adequate confidence in overcoming them."[110] But until those conditions appeared, the overriding responsibility of the state was to preserve orderly governance at home. And this entailed discrediting the radicals. In a conversation with the chief British diplomat in 'Amman in early October 1952, the prime minister smugly observed that "he had no objection to the formation of political parties, providing that their aims were in accordance with the Constitution. The Ba'ath Party, for example, wanted a republic, and could therefore not be allowed."[111]

Equally effective in forestalling an alliance of forces opposed to the regime was the Arab Legion's decision to set up a network of village militias to patrol Jordan's porous border with the State of Israel. This force, designated the National Guard, was formed in November 1949 and charged with carrying out two complementary tasks: protecting border districts from Israeli attack and inculcating a sense of Jordanian patriotism among the population of former Arab Palestine.[112] Its personnel were issued small arms and given rudimentary military training, but received no monetary remuneration for their services. As Israeli incursions into Jordanian territory escalated during 1951–52, the government introduced "a Bill making National Guard training compulsory for every male Jordanian of military age."[113] Throughout the spring of 1953, the government stepped up both the funding and training of National Guard units, sparking repeated complaints in parliament that scarce resources that might better have been used to strengthen the kingdom's regular armed forces were being diverted to the militias.[114]

What went largely unrecognized in the overly cost-conscious Assembly of Representatives was the National Guard's proven capacity to divide disaffected small-scale manufacturers and shopkeepers from the rural poor. The National Guard proved particularly successful in recruiting into its ranks members and sympathizers of the Muslim Brotherhood in rural districts: Cohen notes that "almost every branch [of the Brotherhood in the West Bank] had a few Guardsmen as members, and it was reported that most of the Civil Guardsmen in the village of Sur Bahir (near Jerusalem) were in fact members of the movement."[115] The dramatic expansion of this militia network generated intense opposition on the part of urban notables and large landholders, who feared that giving arms and military training to agricultural laborers would severely reduce their own ability to dominate the countryside.[116] The program was greeted almost as unfavorably by British officials, who recognized its potential to solidify the institutional autonomy of the

Jordanian state.[117] But as the National Guard proved to be effective in stopping Israeli raids across the border into Jordanian territory, British officials began to take a more favorable view of the experiment.[118]

In adopting the revised constitution and establishing the National Guard, the Jordanian leadership acted to preclude the formation of a tactical alliance between discontented members of the petite bourgeoisie and radical organizations actively engaged in trying to overturn the Hashemite regime. The institutional innovations that were undertaken as part of this domestic political strategy provided a firm foundation for the shift to a foreign policy posture predicated on the notion of a narrowly self-interested, territorially bounded Jordanian state. This transformation may well have been pushed along by an ambitious prime minister, who was committed to changing the course of ʿAmman's existing relations with surrounding governments. But it occurred only after the powerful commercial elite found its position undermined by a prolonged period of stagnant trade, in the context of a growing threat to the established domestic order.

Fluctuating Trade and Popular Disorder in Iraq

Immediately after the Second World War, Iraq's commerce with the outside world revived.[119] Despite a drop in the value of the transit trade passing through the country, exports of locally produced agricultural products found ready markets in both South Asia and Europe. The postwar boom tended to enrich the country's elite import-export merchants, while undercutting the position of small-scale manufacturers and shopkeepers. Hanna Batatu reports that the number of first class members of the Baghdad Chamber of Commerce jumped from 59 in 1943–44 to 156 in 1948–49.[120] Richer merchants in the larger cities diversified their business activities by investing heavily in agriculture, thereby contributing to a higher level of mechanization in the countryside.[121] They also forged close ties to the central administration, gaining control of key ministerial positions in successive postwar cabinets while at the same time voicing reservations about greater government intervention in domestic economic affairs.[122]

Small manufacturers and tradespeople, by contrast, swelled the ranks of political organizations that actively opposed the regime. In the spring of 1946, for instance, the National Democratic Party (al-Hizb al-Watani al-

Dimuqrati) appeared in Baghdad. Its initial program called for "the 'encouragement, guidance, and overseeing' by the state of 'national capital' and 'individual enterprise' in the field of industry; the setting up of special semiofficial boards for every principal branch of commerce to improve the quality and facilitate the transport and marketing of Iraq's products; . . . the 'guaranteeing of the workers' rights'; . . . and the 'completion' of Iraq's independence."[123] The party's original membership consisted of disgruntled "merchants, shopkeepers, small property owners, craftsmen, students, teachers, lawyers, peasants [and] urban workmen,"[124] whose livelihoods were jeopardized by the flood of foreign manufactured goods that inundated the country after the war. Craftspeople and shopkeepers also provided support for three smaller parties, the National Union Party (Hizb al-Ittihad al-Watani), the United People's Front Party, and the Liberal Party (Hizb al-Ahrar), whose platforms advocated complete independence from Britain and the advancement of nonexploitative "national capital."[125]

These three parties, along with the more radical Iraqi Communist Party and People's Party (Hizb al-Sha'b), played a key role in orchestrating the outbreak of popular unrest that erupted in Baghdad in January 1948. For almost three weeks, students, women, industrial workers, and the unemployed marched and rioted in the heart of the capital. In Batatu's words, "tempestuous protests pervaded the streets. Crowds, thick with Communists, and armed with huge canes, clashed with the police, who became much like aidless flotsam in a wrathful sea."[126] Demonstrators not only chanted the anti-British slogans that party leaders had approved in advance, but also raised cries against the institution of the monarchy, despite warnings from the organizers that such outbursts would work to the detriment of the movement. State officials responded to the protests by deploying heavily armed police around key bridges and intersections. The police broke up successive marches with withering gunfire, until finally abandoning their positions on 27 January. The regent then asked a prominent Shi'i religious leader, Sayyid Muhammad al-Sadr, to put together a new government, which immediately pledged to take steps to remedy the country's pervasive economic difficulties.[127]

Three things are remarkable about this episode. First, the escalating demands for radical change expressed by the demonstrators undermined the movement's appeal among small-scale manufacturers and tradespeople. Workers and students continued to engage in strikes and protests throughout the spring of 1948, but these actions failed to generate the breadth of popular support that had been so conspicuous in January. Relations between the communists and the National Democrats quickly collapsed, as the latter "set themselves unambiguously against any breach of 'tranquility.'"[128] More important, the threat of popular revolution convinced a group of reform-minded army officers to begin plotting clandestinely to overturn the monarchy.[129]

Second, the commercial elite occupied a strong enough position in local society, thanks to the upturn in trade of the late 1940s, that it was able to provide the financial and material resources necessary for the regime to prevail over its adversaries. Government officials were therefore spared from having to deploy the regular armed forces to suppress the demonstrators.[130] Sporadic strikes in the spring of 1948, particularly in the oil fields of the south, provoked only halfhearted responses from the government, despite the periodic interruptions they caused in the flow of oil exports.[131] When fighting erupted in Palestine that May, the authorities seized the opportunity to impose martial law and crack down on opposition parties. In January 1949, Nuri al-Sa'id reclaimed the prime ministership and the restoration of the old regime was complete.

Third, and consequently, state officials took no steps to expand the size or scope of the central administration in order to deal with the 1948 crisis. British entreaties to set up a development board to facilitate the coordination of economic projects were consistently ignored.[132] The al-Sadr cabinet refused even to approve new measures to offset the disruption in tax collecting that accompanied the uprising.[133] Not until September 1948 did a successor government impose greater restrictions on imports in an attempt to salvage local manufacturing. Persistent shortages of food, rising costs for housing, and growing unemployment prompted repeated requests for additional loans from Britain, instead of a sustained effort to extend state power.[134] The cabinet led by Nuri al-Sa'id in fact "reduced the amount of money allocated to all government departments by an average of 15 per cent, reduced the number of civil servants by not filling vacancies as they occurred, and reduced the cost of living allowances for civil servants."[135] Iraq's administrative apparatus therefore emerged from the 1948 uprising with a diminished, rather than an augmented, capacity to manage and monitor domestic affairs.

Widespread popular discontent flared again in 1951. Oil production and transportation workers employed by the Basrah Petroleum Company struck for two weeks in February and again in early September, demanding pay raises, free transportation to and from the job site, and reduced rents for company housing.[136] Later that fall, textile, cigarette, and mechanical and printing press workers associated with an unlicensed Permanent Bureau of Workers' Unions organized a series of demonstrations and marches in the capital. The next summer contract laborers rioted at the port of Basrah and the British airbase at Habbaniyyah.[137] Steadily escalating labor unrest persuaded the government to authorize the formation of a limited number of licensed trade unions. But when disorder continued to spread in the autumn of 1952, the official unions were summarily disbanded.[138] Workers and tradespeople in the capital joined students in a massive demonstration on 22 November, which quickly erupted into violence. When protests resumed the following day, they took on "a more distinct plebeian aspect," with laborers, craftspeople, and the unemployed playing a leading role.[139]

This time around, rich merchants found themselves less able to prop up the regime than they had been four years earlier. With the exception of oil, the value of Iraq's most important exports dipped in 1952 and continued to slide thereafter.[140] Furthermore, the demonstrators who carried out the November uprising proved more successful in winning sympathy from broad sectors of the Iraqi public than their predecessors had been. The leadership of the generally liberal Independence Party (Hizb al-Istiqlal), for instance, gravitated toward the demonstrators as the unrest took shape, and agreed to take part in an umbrella Contact Committee that was set up to supervise and coordinate the actions of the crowd.[141] By the time the disorders were suppressed, Phebe Marr observes, "the widespread alienation of critical sectors of the population was clear."[142] Consequently, the authorities resorted to the extreme step of ordering the armed forces into the streets of the capital to suppress the rioting, and General Nur al-Din Mahmud was subsequently installed as head of a new cabinet, which immediately declared martial law and outlawed the opposition parties.

More important, state officials reacted to the 1952 uprising by extending the size and scope of the central bureaucracy in order to enhance the degree of surveillance and regulation over the country's internal affairs. Two days after the rioting broke out, the cabinet issued a communiqué that promised, among other things, to "conduct an economic policy calculated to protect the national wealth," "cleanse the State of corrupt elements and to replace them by competent elements," and "expedite the enactment of the legislation necessary for social security."[143] Price controls were introduced on fresh fruits and vegetables in local markets, and a subsidy was put on common bread. Government inspectors were appointed to enforce the new regulations.[144] In addition, a state-affiliated Date Trading Company was established to coordinate the distribution and sale of this important export crop. State officials then attempted to seize control of the privately owned Baghdad Light and Power Company. At the same time, the Industrial Bank dramatically increased the number of short-term loans it disbursed, which were used primarily "to finance imports of machinery, spare parts, as well as raw materials" for light industry.[145] To buttress these initiatives, the authorities proposed to withdraw from the British-dominated Sterling currency zone and stake out an independent course in monetary affairs.[146]

Nevertheless, as popular discontent continued to simmer just below the surface through the spring and summer of 1953, the government led by Jamil al-Midfa'i crumbled.[147] The newly enthroned monarch, King Faisal II, invited Muhammad Fadil al-Jamali to head a successor cabinet that September. Prime Minister al-Jamali persuaded a group of young technocrats to accept key ministerial appointments. After terminating martial law and commuting the sentences of many of those who had been arrested during the 1952 uprising, the new government took steps to devise "a social security scheme for industrial workers, widows and orphans," to distribute state lands to small farmers, to expand the network of state-sponsored schools and hospitals, and to reform the country's tax collection system.[148] More important, state officials created a ministry of development to supplement the operations of the largely ineffectual Development Board. With the inauguration of this ministry, "the authority of the Government was strengthened and for all practical purposes the Board lost its independence because its action became dependent upon agreement with the Minister of Development."[149] As a general rule, the Development Board retained general responsibility for supervising a handful of "major development projects," while the development ministry took charge of implementing a wide range of less extensive capital works programs.[150] Spurred on by the new agency, actual investment in state-sponsored development projects jumped from one-third of planned investment in 1951 to two-thirds of planned investment in 1954.[151] State officials went on to set up a ministry of guidance, charged with formulating and propagating a national discourse centered around the monarchy.[152] Taken together, Charles Tripp points out, these policy initiatives "were intended to create a more efficient state, but also one which would be more responsive to the communities which that state claimed to represent."[153]

Opponents of more comprehensive state control over local society resisted such moves as best they could. The proposed reforms sparked vehement resistance, for instance, from the country's large landholders, who continued to occupy a powerful position in the national assembly. Agricultural grandées joined representatives of the Independence Party to demand that a number of innovative measures, including land reform and a progressive system of taxation, be shelved indefinitely.[154] The rich landholders tended to be portrayed in the popular literature of the time as working hand in hand with the commercial elite, the *tujjar al-siyassah* (political merchants), to undermine Iraqi independence.[155] Even working together, however, these forces found themselves increasingly unable to block the expansion of the oil-funded state apparatus.

Struggles over the creation and consolidation of innovative state agencies accompanied intensified contention among nationalist parties regarding the nature of the political community that the leadership in Baghdad claimed the right to govern. Influential liberal parties such as the Independence Party stood beside the palace and the al-Jamali government in championing the cause of Arab unity, whereas workers' organizations tended instead to emphasize the demand for full Iraqi independence.[156] The Iraqi Communist Party emerged in 1951–52 as the most vocal proponent of severing all ties to Britain and winning complete autonomy in both domestic and foreign affairs.[157] At the same time, the Kurdistan Democratic Party had started to advocate both the nationalization of the local oil industry and increased government support for economic projects in the poorer northern provinces. On the eve of the 1952 uprising, such demands began to infiltrate the programs of the left-leaning liberal parties — including the National Democratic Party and the Socialist People's Party — whose leaderships called on the government to adopt a foreign policy posture of nonalignment, "which," as Phebe Marr remarks, "could only have meant abrogation of the [1930] Anglo-Iraq treaty."[158]

By highlighting the demand for full independence, these parties not only gained support among craftspeople and traders, drawing them away from the more radical workers' organizations, but also attracted the votes necessary to mount a serious challenge to the palace in the hotly contested parliamentary elections of June 1954. Seeing which way domestic opinion was blowing, Nuri al-Sa'id took steps that spring to cut government backing for diplomatic machinations toward Syria. By limiting the flow of funds and propaganda across Iraq's western borders and concentrating on purely domestic matters, Nuri and his allies in the Constitutional Union Party (Hizb al-Ittihad al-Dusturi) hoped to prevent "the infiltration of dangerous influences from Syria into Iraq" that might further strengthen the opposition.[159] A potent combination of repressing radical challengers and pursuing complete Iraqi autonomy lay at the heart of the program that was implemented after Nuri al-Sa'id at last accepted the post of prime minister that August. By merging its internal initiatives with a resumption of negotiations to end the restrictive 1930 treaty with Britain, the new government not only succeeded in isolating the communists but also rallied nationalists of all stripes to stand behind the regime.

Deteriorating Trade and Popular Disorder in Syria

There can be little doubt that the slump in foreign trade that occurred in the late 1930s weakened Syria's commercial and industrial elite relative to small-scale manufacturers and traders. Heightened economic difficulties associated with the depression in Europe sparked bouts of infighting among the most powerful merchants of Damascus, further undermining their already-deteriorating influence over local politics.[160] February 1939 saw the emergence in Hamah of a new political movement whose main supporters consisted of artisans and shopkeepers; this movement openly called for the replacement of the provincial leadership of the National Bloc.[161] A month later, simmering tensions between rich merchants and small-scale tradespeople in Aleppo caused a general strike orchestrated by the Bloc to degenerate into an outburst of overtly sectarian violence.[162] By the autumn of 1940, the Bloc's leaders began actively to cultivate support among the residents of Damascus's poorer neighborhoods in an effort to offset the rich merchants' loss of control over local politics.[163]

Syria's petite bourgeoisie demanded a greater degree of state intervention in the local economy as the Second World War got under way. Growing popular resentment over the hoarding of scarce staples by elite merchants prompted the authorities to set up the Supplies Administration of the States of the Levant in the fall of 1940. At the beginning of February 1941, this agency was "divided into two services: The first will deal with all questions relative to supplies and to their distributions [sic], the organization of consumption, estimates of the specific needs of the Army and of the civilian population, the calculation and conservation of stocks on hand, the study of new costs, rationing and requisitioning, [and] control of distribution. . . . The second division will be responsible for the investigation of markets, agreements with neighboring countries, the determination and the evaluation of means of exchange, the control of foreign and domestic commerce, relations with the customs and the exchange office, tariffs, legislation and regulation, the suppression of fraud and the supervision of prices, and relations with the courts."[164] These changes elicited formal protests from the country's commercial elite, but earned state officials grudging support among struggling urban tradespeople.

Meanwhile, Syria's small but energetic proletariat grew increasingly restive. Industrial and transportation workers had engaged in collective action on a number of occasions during the 1920s and 1930s, culminating in the formation of a nationwide trade union organization, the General Federation of Workers' Unions, during the winter of 1938–39.[165] Unanticipated shortages of bread on local markets in the first quarter of 1941 sparked a resurgence of popular activism. Large-scale rioting erupted in Damascus when bread prices spiked at the end of February, and the disorder quickly spread to Aleppo, Homs, Hamah, and Dair al-Zur.[166] Radicals inside the National Bloc, who favored severing the country's ties to France as rapidly as possible, mobilized shopkeepers and tradespeople in the capital to strike in sympathy with the protesters. Those who refused to close their businesses found themselves the target of threatening handbills and other "familiar methods of intimidation."[167]

Widespread rioting broke out once again in late March, following an unsuccessful attempt by the French authorities to break up peaceful demonstrations by force.[168] The scale and severity of the new disorders led state officials to declare martial law in the larger cities.[169] An even more violent disturbance nevertheless erupted in Aleppo during the third week of April.[170] Shortly thereafter, the *New York Times* reported that "demonstrators in Hama, where a strike has been proclaimed, broke into flour mills and ransacked them after having destroyed machinery and other equipment. They then attacked a police station in an effort to release persons under arrest." This incident reignited popular unrest in Aleppo, where "French armored cars were called out to patrol the streets, while troops picketed public buildings."[171] The U.S. consul in the city observed that the "damage to property was much heavier than during [the] disturbances" that had occurred in March, with "many shops being destroyed or looted." He went on to note that "the French did little or nothing to stop the disorders and when the municipal authorities asked for help they were referred to the 'new Syrian Government.' "[172]

Confronted with the prospect of a tactical alliance between organized workers and the petite bourgeoisie in Syria's cities, state officials persuaded High Commissioner Dentz in April 1941 to authorize the creation of a constituent assembly to supersede the unelected, rubber-stamp Council of Directors.[173] At the same time, the government issued a decree ordering that all privately held stockpiles of wheat must be registered.[174] The authorities in Damascus then signed a commercial agreement with British representatives in Cairo that allowed licensed Syrian merchants to import additional supplies of grain into the country.[175] State agencies distributed these cereals at heavily subsidized prices throughout the spring.[176] At the same time, Dentz appointed a new cabinet under the prime ministership of Khalid al-ʿAzm, whose program "promised to reform the administration, to develop external trade, to pay special attention to the problems of education and youth, to ameliorate the lot of the workers and officials [viz., government employees], and to preserve strict non-partisanship in all political matters."[177]

State officials tightened their grip over the Syrian economy in the wake of the combined British–Free French occupation of the country in the summer of 1941. Licenses were mandated for all companies engaging in foreign trade; anyone who applied for a license was required to "indicate the origin and description of the products to be exported as well as the destination of the exportation and the amount and kind of foreign exchange which, as a result of the exportation, will be placed at the disposition of the Exchange Office." Somewhat more obliquely, the Supplies Administration published a "request" for "local industrialists to inform it before August 10 [1941]: [regarding] (a) the production capacity of their factories; (b) the kind and quantities of foreign raw materials which they will need during the coming year."[178] In August the Supplies Administration stiffened the regulations governing imports and exports by setting strict limits on the duration of licenses, declaring "the non-importation of products and merchandise destined for the general supply, after the delivery of the license, [to be] an attempt at disorganization of the supply" and authorizing "the special brigade controlling prices" to enforce price ceilings on all imported goods.[179] Heightened state intervention resulted in a sharp increase in the price of imports that fall.[180] In the words of *al-Hawadith*, "The cause of this is quite simple: the Allies arrived with promises of independence but not with severe laws against speculation."[181]

Strikes by workers and students broke out once again at the beginning of 1942.[182] Mid-February saw the eruption of widespread "shops' and students' strikes in Damascus, trouble in Homs and Hama and threats of strikes and minor demonstrations in Aleppo, Latakia and Tripoli."[183] At the end of March, shopkeepers in Hamah closed their doors once again, while protesters attempted to break into storehouses owned by the city's leading merchants.[184] Railway workers at Homs walked out on 23 April to protest the hiring of unskilled laborers from rural districts to repair the tracks around the city.[185] In the wake of these outbreaks of popular disorder, state officials set up the Commission for Wheat and Cereals and charged it with "assur[ing] adequate wheat supplies" to local markets in Syria and Lebanon. The new commission was granted "the monopoly of purchase and transportation of 1942 wheat crops in Syria and Lebanon as well as of flour and other derivatives."[186] Five months later, the government levied an income tax "on profits deriving from [the] industrial, commercial and non-commercial activities" of Syria's urban businesspeople.[187] In addition, state officials promulgated a decree that awarded dismissed workers severance compensation from their former employers.[188] That November, the Constituent Assembly created a pair of state agencies to regulate wage levels, one for the southern provinces and one for the north.[189]

Rather than quieting the situation in the larger cities and towns, the establishment of the Commission for Wheat and Cereals precipitated further popular disorder. Many of the strikes and demonstrations, like the ones that broke out in Aleppo in early June 1942 and in Dair al-Zur a month later, were no doubt "fomented by the middlemen, merchants, landowners, millers and others who [stood] to lose by the [Wheat] Plan."[190] Shopkeepers in Damascus closed their doors on 12 July in response to "(a) Rumours that wheat is being sent to the Lebanon and to the British army. (b) Resentment at the new income and agricultural tax, and at the refusal of permits to export vegetables to Palestine. [And as part of] (c) An indirect attack on the Government."[191] The strike appears to have been linked to the reluctance of wheat growers around the capital to turn their crops over to the commission.[192] In early September, Aleppo's shopkeepers struck for four days, and only resumed business when the governor promised to increase the availability of grain to small-scale retailers.[193] As richer farmers refused to take part in the scheme, the burden of supplying cereals to the authorities fell disproportionately on small-scale cultivators, further increasing popular disaffection.[194] Disturbances occurred sporadically in Aleppo, Homs, and Hamah throughout the fall.[195] In early November rioting erupted in Hamah over the municipality's decision to cut wheat rations from twelve to ten kilograms per person.[196]

Students in Damascus took to the streets during the last week of 1942 to protest a resolution by the U.S. Congress that supported the establishment of a Jewish national homeland in Palestine. In response to the students' actions, "shops began to close. Large crowds attended Monday prayer in the great mosque where political speeches against Zionism and voicing other grievances were made."[197] The U.S. political agent in Beirut cabled that "after the first day [the demonstrations] ceased to have any anti-American or anti-British animus. Even their anti-Zionist origin was largely lost sight of in a general airing of their grievances (notably as to flour distribution and agricultural taxes)."[198] Such grievances generated a renewed wave of rioting that swept Homs, Hamah, and Latakia in January 1943. British officials reported that these events reflected the growing influence of "communist" activists in the agricultural districts between Homs and Hamah.[199] Weavers in Homs joined the demonstrations on 20 January, after the Syrian government agreed to reduce exports of silk and cotton cloth to Palestine.[200]

Bread prices jumped once again the first week of February, generating a further round of strikes in the capital.[201] The disturbances spread to Aleppo, Homs, and Hamah over the next few days.[202] Yet another major strike took place in mid-March.[203] By mid-May, the Damascus newspaper *al-Istiqlal* reported that "the workers' movement in Syria has developed so well that the various syndicates are now in a position to express their opinions freely. The Aleppo Federation of Workers' Syndicates," the report continued, "has addressed a petition to the Chief of State asking that uniform rights be granted to workers' organization in all Syrian Muhafazas [governorates]."[204]

These incidents pushed state officials to implement measures to enhance the central administration's control over the local economy. The Supplies Administration published a unified list of fixed prices for staples in February 1943.[205] Concerted enforcement of ceilings on the prices of sugar, cotton cloth, and gold finally succeeded in reducing the cost of these three commodities as the spring went by.[206] Meanwhile, the authorities promulgated a number of laws intended to regularize the collection of the income tax; a decree issued in early May 1943, for instance, empowered the finance office to inspect the ledgers of all companies operating in the country.[207] That June, the Commission on Wheat and Cereals issued a directive prohibiting the use of stockpiled foodstuffs and cloth as security for business or personal loans.[208] Increased activism on the part of state officials to regulate the distribution of cereals led to a dramatic drop in the incidence of rioting in the larger cities as the summer began, although the arrest of a notorious opium smuggler sparked a violent protest in Tripoli that August.[209]

It was under these circumstances that campaigning got under way for elections to the revivified Constituent Assembly, which had been authorized in January by the Free French Delegate General, General Georges Catroux. Proponents of a fully independent, territorially circumscribed Syria faced competition not only from advocates of a more gradual disassociation from France but also from former supporters of 'Abd al-Rahman Shahbandar, who openly called for Amir 'Abdullah of Transjordan to be crowned king of Syria.[210] In addition, prominent merchants based in Aleppo harbored a long-standing interest in forging closer links to Turkey.[211] In the end, the National Bloc managed to win a majority of seats in the new assembly by mobilizing urban tradespeople to turn out to vote.[212] It accomplished this by pledging to "1. Revive and organize [Syria's] internal affairs, create new projects, laws, [promote] economic order, social reform, [and] exploit and protect the country's resources. 2. Exercise full political rights and take measures to achieve full practical independence and sovereignty."[213]

Immediately after assuming office, the National Bloc government launched a campaign to take full control of the armed forces. French officers had tried to influence the electoral campaign by means of the Troupes Speciales, particularly in the countryside.[214] It therefore came as no surprise that the most outspoken representative of Syria's rural population in the new assembly, Akram al-Hawrani, emerged as the primary proponent of immediate transfer of the Troupes to Syrian command. Other delegates argued against such a move, on the grounds that the Troupes Speciales du Levant was an essentially imperialist institution and the central administration's scarce resources should be reserved for more pressing projects.[215] Such differences of opinion made it impossible for the government to bargain effectively with the Free French, who insisted on retaining responsibility for the country's external defense.

As a sop to the nationalists, the French did agree to relinquish their remaining hold over the gendarmerie, "as well as certain aspects of internal security."[216] The National Bloc government immediately deployed gendarmes under its command to the 'Alawi-dominated mountains south of Latakia, as a way of buttressing the position of the provincial governor vis-à-vis the region's powerful local chieftains.[217] More important, the government negotiated a series of agreements that transferred the customs administration, the finance office, the press office, and several other key agencies into Syrian hands.[218] The Constituent Assembly even allocated funds to recruit and supply a national armed forces in its draft budget for 1944.[219]

Rich merchants acquiesced in the steady expansion of state power during 1943–44 out of a fear that Syria's petite bourgeoisie might forge a united front with disaffected urban workers. Reports that just this sort of cross-class political organization was taking shape in Homs appeared at the beginning of January 1944.[220] Communist activists managed to coordinate a brief but violent uprising of rural laborers, disaffected notables, and the urban poor in Hamah a month later.[221] Rioting erupted in Damascus once again in mid-March, sparked by a minor altercation between a group of Syrian gendarmes and a noncommissioned officer of the Troupes Speciales. Among those injured in the melee that followed was the director of religious endowments (awqaf). Consequently, calls for the populace to retaliate against French installations emanated from mosques throughout the city, and shopkeepers closed their doors. Worried that the situation might spiral out of control, Prime Minister Sa'dallah al-Jabri hurried back to the capital from Hamah and "at once called the various shaikhs and leaders together, told them he was sending his gendarmes into the bazaars the next day to force the merchants to open, and if they (the shaikhs) desired to provide the French with the spectacle of Syrians fighting each other, they could do so by opposing the gendarmes."[222]

Another round of popular disorders occurred in mid-May, after religious notables in Damascus exhorted their followers to protest the public activities of a group of prominent women.[223] The unrest quickly spread to Homs,

Hamah, and Aleppo, and was only suppressed when "tanks and armored cars" moved into the streets of the larger cities "flying the Syrian flag," thereby creating the impression "that the army had been taken over by the Syrians."[224] Toward the end of the year, an unexpected jump in the cost of living precipitated a succession of strikes and demonstrations across the country. Textile workers, cement workers, typesetters, tram operators, electricians, and employees of the Commission on Wheat and Cereals all walked off their jobs in November to demand immediate pay raises to cover rising prices for food and fuel.[225]

Challenges such as these provided the context in which Westphalian sovereignty took shape in wartime Syria. The rich merchants who controlled the country's predominantly low-profit, high-volume commerce found their political position severely undermined as a result of recurrent disruptions in foreign trade during the early 1940s. At the same time, tradespeople in the cities threatened to ally with industrial workers and the urban and rural poor in demanding a fundamental transformation of the structure of domestic society. The National Bloc leadership parried this threat by adopting a package of administrative measures that greatly enhanced the state's capacity to monitor and regulate the internal economy, while stepping up its demands for complete independence from France. Attempts to block the emergence of Westphalian sovereignty, most notably on the part of the commercial elite of Aleppo, failed not so much due to the inherent strength of the central bureaucracy as to basic incompatibilities of interest among the heterogeneous coalition of forces that stood to lose as a result of the consolidation of a self-interested, territorially bounded polity governed from Damascus.

Conclusion

Heightened levels of state regulation and surveillance in domestic society accompanied the turn to Westphalian sovereignty throughout the Arab world. But government agencies did not simply infiltrate local society of their own accord. A potent conjunction of commercial difficulties and radical political challenges provided the stimulus for more active, extensive, and sustained intervention on the part of state officials. Rich merchants acquiesced in this development not so much due to an interest in reducing transaction costs as out of an aversion to widespread disorder and revolutionary change. Nationalist elites shared these concerns, and adopted platforms that emphasized the unity and distinctiveness of each individual country as a way to undercut radical movements and organizations, and to prevent small manufacturers and traders from joining them in a campaign to overturn the existing order.

Furthermore, the coming of Westphalian sovereignty reflected the importance of popular participation and electoral institutions in Arab politics during the first half of the twentieth century. The shift to a narrowly self-interested, territorially limited conception of the state was largely orchestrated by the leaders of political parties, who found themselves competing against rival organizations for public support. In this way, as in so many others, the history of the Arab countries conforms to broader historical patterns. An anarchic states-system characterized by the norm of Westphalian sovereignty emerged in Europe in the decades after the Napoleonic wars, as elite-based liberal movements and parties struggled against dynastic rulers and radical forces alike. K. J. Holsti reminds us that "as the republican form of government spread through the [European] continent, territory also became linked to political rights and security. The state [came to provide] political goods of increasing diversity (health, education, civil liberties, and the like), and also protection against neighboring predators. Most importantly, the organic connection between geography and a 'people' created a moral good in the sense that now the state and its defining territory belong to the people."[226] Liberal democratic institutions failed to survive the 1950s in the Arab world, but the principles of Westphalian sovereignty that they helped to engender turned out to be much more durable.

CONCLUSION

Pan-Arabism, Postimperial Orders, and International Norms

By the mid-1950s, nationalist leaderships throughout the Arab world had adopted foreign policy postures that were predicated on (1) the renunciation of any claim to rule territory located outside the generally recognized boundaries of their respective countries, (2) a refusal to countenance any attempt by surrounding states to say how they should manage their own country's internal affairs, and (3) intrinsic rivalry and antagonism toward their neighbors. In short, the Arab world came to constitute an anarchic states-system characterized by the norm of Westphalian sovereignty. Other principles, most notably a commitment to act in ways that furthered the collective interests of the Arab people as a whole, continued to exert substantial influence on regional diplomacy from time to time. But the general predisposition of the leadership in each Arab capital was clear: to increase the power, wealth, and status of its own particular state, rather than sacrificing significant amounts of leverage, treasure, or prestige in pursuit of broader, multilateralist projects.

In the vanguard of this profound transformation in the structure of regional affairs marched Egypt and Tunisia. Nationalist leaders in these two countries abandoned the effort to re-create the Ottoman Empire or replace it with some form of comprehensive Arab political entity immediately after the First World War. Syrian nationalists followed suit two decades later, during the course of the Second World War. Nationalist leaderships in Jordan and Iraq took a decade longer to fall in line, but by the mid-1950s they too had given up the ambition to forge a unified Arab polity. With the demise of the Greater Syria and Fertile Crescent Unity projects, a territorially based conception of external sovereignty came to prevail as the standard of proper interstate behavior in this part of the world.[1]

Things might well have transpired differently. The leaders of the Egyptian nationalist movement persistently championed the creation of an integrated Arab political entity, headquartered in Cairo, throughout the first decade of the twentieth century. Prominent Tunisian nationalists worked with their comrades in Algeria, Morocco, and Tripolitania to set up a unified North African polity during the years of the First World War. The National Bloc in Damascus expressed strong interest in amalgamating with Jordan and Iraq on several occasions as the 1930s went by. It is therefore conceivable that the Arab world might have coalesced into at most one or two, rather than a dozen, states following the collapse of the Ottoman Empire. Any such tendency was stifled with the coming of British and French rule in 1918–20.[2] Yet Europe's imperial moment in the Middle East might still have generated multilateralist, rather than discrete, responses on the part of local nationalists. Why it did not has been explored in detail in the preceding chapters.

It remains to spell out the most important implications of the analysis presented here. Three merit brief discussion. The first addresses the problematic relationship between Pan-Arabism and Westphalian sovereignty. The second concerns what this study can contribute to the growing international relations literature on the collapse of empires. And the third situates the argument presented here in the context of influential explanations for the appearance and diffusion of international norms.

Antinomies of Pan-Arabism

It is often said, particularly but not exclusively by those poorly versed in the history and politics of the Middle East, that Pan-Arabism is inherently incompatible with the existence of self-interested, territorially bounded states. Hendrik Spruyt, for instance, remarks that "nonterritorial forms of organization such as the city-league then or pan-Arabism today are logically at odds with sovereign statehood."[3] Stephen Krasner similarly asserts that Pan-Arabism and Westphalian sovereignty constitute "alternative structures" of international relations.[4] Such statements echo views that recognized specialists in Middle Eastern affairs have advanced. Fouad Ajami, for instance, calls Pan-Arabism a "universalist system" akin to "the universalism of the Ottoman Empire," which stands fundamentally opposed to the fragmented regional order of the 1970s.[5] Michael Barnett claims that "an Arab nationalism that demanded territorial unification represented a direct challenge to the sovereign authority and territorial basis of Arab states. In these and other ways," he continues, "although Arab states were formally sovereign, they had to work out the meaning of sovereignty in practice, in conflict, and in relationship to a (prior) set of claims that derived from Arab nationalism."[6] Raymond Hinnebusch likewise underscores the "enduring rivalry between the norms of sovereignty and Pan-Arabism," whose "bottom line is that the embedding of a states system in a supra-state community built an enduring tension into the Arab system between the logic of sovereignty, in which each separate state, insecure amidst the anarchy of a states system, pursues its own interests and security, often against its Arab neighbours, and the counter norm which expects states sharing an Arab identity to act together for common interests."[7]

More cynical observers argue instead that Pan-Arabism has proven to be no more than a package of stratagems deployed by ambitious regional actors to rally broad support for their self-interested political objectives. Tawfig Hasou, for example, avers that "it was during the presidency of [Egypt's Gamal 'Abd al-] Nasser [from 1952 to 1970] that pan-Arabism experienced perhaps its most dynamic phase in recent history. For it was Nasser who captured the imagination and admiration of Arab nationalists. In return, Nasser capitalized on this concept to further his own and Egypt's interests in the Arab world."[8] Michael Doran traces this tendency to the pre-Nasir era. "Behind the idea of the [1949] Arab League Collective Security Pact," he concludes, "stood a vision of a new regional order. Cairo imagined an Arab world completely independent of Great Britain, presenting a common face to the outside world, and led by Egypt."[9] Still, he goes on to concede that it was under 'Abd al-Nasir that Pan-Arabism and Egyptian interests merged most closely: "Since Arab nationalism was the primary ideological and emotional identification of every Arab, . . . according to Nasir, Egypt had not just the right, but the duty to intrude into the affairs of other countries that were not conducting themselves in accordance with Arab nationalist principles. Nasir's Egypt then had a dual role — that of a traditional state and that of the revolutionary entity serving the high interests of Arab nationalism."[10]

In fact, the relationship between Pan-Arabism and Westphalian sovereignty is even more subtle. President ʿAbd al-Nasir consistently affirmed that any meaningful step toward Arab unity must be predicated on the underlying principle of self-determination. He thus opposed Iraq's bid to seize control of Kuwait in the summer of 1961 on the grounds that it represented an illegitimate form of political amalgamation, which he called "annexation."[11] Two years later, Egypt's foreign minister drew up a provisional agreement with the Algerian government, whose terms stipulated that "Arab unity, which is based first on unity of purpose and rests on the national unity of every Arab country, is inevitable from the historical, revolutionary and evolutionary points of view."[12] Other influential proponents of Pan-Arabism advocated equally hybrid unity schemes: Satiʿ al-Husri championed the establishment of a federal regional order, along the lines of the United States of America; ʿAbd al-Rahman al-Bazzaz and ʿIzzat Darwazah suggested similarly nebulous kinds of federative arrangements as the appropriate institutional structure for Arab unity.[13] Even the National Command of the Baʿth Party, arguably the staunchest promoter of Pan-Arabism throughout the 1940s and 1950s, tended to favor the emergence of federated entities as a first step toward greater integration.[14]

All of these unity projects envisaged an integrated political entity in which the member-states retained sole responsibility for managing their own internal affairs. At most, amalgamation would entail a unified foreign policy, particularly vis-à-vis the State of Israel and the western industrial powers, along with close cooperation on economic matters. The vision is captured most eloquently by Philip Hitti: "By union here we mean a somewhat loose political association of independent states, a federation, or confederation, of sovereign Arab units similar to the British Commonwealth of Nations minus the crown. Within such a federation the nationalist plans envisage further sharing in a common type of educational program, removal of economic barriers involving tariffs and of such impediments to travel and free intercourse as visas, the institution of a unified currency and postal service, and the adoption of a policy of joint action in all problems of military and foreign affairs."[15] Greater harmonization among the political systems of the member-states was expected to come about through a gradual process whereby less advanced countries would learn from those that had succeeded in moving farther along, not through active interference on the part of stronger or better-endowed partners.

Pan-Arabism's intimate connection with Westphalian sovereignty is evident in the one episode that is most often invoked to demonstrate the fundamental incompatibility between these two sets of political principles — the formation and subsequent collapse of the United Arab Republic (UAR). As early as June 1956, influential figures in Damascus began to suggest that Syria and Egypt could advance their common foreign policy objectives by pursuing unity with one another.[16] In November 1957, the speaker of the Syrian parliament, Akram al-Hawrani, called for the creation of a Syrian-Egyptian federation as the first step toward a more "comprehensive Arab union."[17] This suggestion was reiterated by senior officials of the Ba'th Party and high-ranking military commanders over the ensuing three months. Growing enthusiasm for federation with Egypt led the government in Damascus to dispatch the country's Ba'thi foreign minister to Cairo in January 1958 to discuss the terms under which such an arrangement might be consummated. Despite intense pressure from influential Syrian army officers, who demanded the immediate formation of a fully integrated entity, the Syrian foreign minister and Egyptian president instead agreed to set up a federal union in which "both countries would have separate budgets and parliaments, with some sort of joint elective body."[18] Further negotiations resulted in a complicated institutional arrangement consisting of "one president, a central and two regional parliaments, as well as a central and two regional cabinets."[19] Even after the inauguration of the UAR in February 1958, there continued to be "no integration" in the crucial area of "monetary and fiscal policies, as each region continued to have its own currency, central bank, and fiscal system, as well as civil administration and security services."[20]

This sort of institutional structure was intended to ensure that Syria's domestic arena would be insulated against direct Egyptian interference. As Elie Podeh observes, "it is hardly conceivable that the Syrians, as much as they were committed to pan-Arabism, would have agreed to relegate their state to the status of a province by initiating a complete merger with Egypt. It is more reasonable to assume that external and internal factors drove Syria to seek a union with Egypt, but a union that would allow them a measure of autonomy in Syrian affairs."[21] There is strong evidence that Syrian officials indeed expected the UAR to operate along strictly federal lines, in much the same fashion as the United States or West Germany.[22] In other words, even the most fully articulated institutional expression of the broad doctrine of Pan-Arabism turns out to have been compatible with, if not in fact predicated on, the principles of Westphalian sovereignty.

By the same token, it was when it became clear that the Egyptian authorities were intent on systematically usurping the internal prerogatives of the Syrian government that the UAR splintered. Syrian officials initially resented and then actively resisted Cairo's repeated attempts to impose Egyptian bureaucratic procedures on state agencies inside Syria.[23] Just five weeks after a unified central administration joining the two countries was finally set up, the authorities in Damascus dissolved the union.[24] Mustapha Kamil al-Sayyid astutely concludes that the UAR collapsed largely because "Syrian politicians and senior army officers wanted to exchange their allegiance to Nasser's leadership for a free hand in their own country and Nasser's endorsement of a prominent position for the Ba'th Party in particular in Syria."[25] Thus Egypt's evident lack of respect for key precepts of Westphalian sovereignty with regard to the "northern region" of the UAR contributed directly to the failure of the most important experiment in extrapolating a concrete integration program from the subtle package of principles associated with Pan-Arabism.

End of Empire Redux

Existing analyses of the end of empire in the field of international relations suffer from the same problem that plagues most historical scholarship on European imperialism: they pay inordinate attention to political, economic, and social trends in the imperial center and ignore the potential for agency that exists in peripheral areas. This viewpoint suffuses the literature surveyed in the introduction to this study, which most often attempts to explain the emergence of anarchic states-systems in former imperial peripheries in terms of the costs and benefits to the former core of making a concerted effort to restore the empire. It is equally evident in more recent writing. Hendrik Spruyt, for example, has followed up his pathbreaking analysis of the emergence of autonomous, territorial states in early modern Europe with a comparative examination of the impact that the end of European empires had on territorial arrangements in the periphery during the course of the twentieth century. He argues that one can account for divergent territorial outcomes in the former colonies in terms of the dominant pattern of civilian-military relations, the institutional structure of government, and the degree of unity exhibited by political and economic elites, all situated in the metropole.[26]

By contrast, the account offered here argues that the emergence of anarchic states-systems following the collapse of imperial structures of governance is driven by political-economic developments that take place outside the former core. This view parallels a wide range of "ex-centric" perspectives on the origins, evolution, and decline of European imperialism, which have deepened our understanding of the global politics of empire during the long nineteenth century.[27] Interestingly, Spruyt himself recognizes the importance of supplementing (if not supplanting) conventional core-oriented accounts of the end of empire with studies that focus on the periphery. In a companion essay to his book on the end of empire, he proposes to explain the emergence of Westphalian international orders in former imperial domains by charting the growth of the norm of "sovereign territorial rule" among nationalist leaderships in formerly peripheral areas.[28]

So why might nationalist leaders in the periphery adopt the notion of a self-interested, territorially bounded state? Spruyt adduces two major reasons. In the first place, nationalists shared their imperial overlords' contempt for older, precolonial forms of governance. Second, taking on the institutional and discursive attributes of modern European polities made it easier for newly independent rulers to be recognized and accepted by the wider international community.[29] More specifically, "the international order empowered those individual political elites who were willing to play according to existing rules, while denying such status to others. Consequently, strategically motivated indigenes had incentives to adopt behaviors rewarded by the system."[30]

Such considerations — or, in Spruyt's terms, "utilitarian calculations" — no doubt played a part in convincing nationalist leaders to adopt the principles of Westphalian sovereignty. But this line of argument once again draws attention away from politics in the periphery and emphasizes the ways that actors in the core shape postimperial outcomes. Only in passing does Spruyt remark that "the reward for successful propagation of such norms [as

Westphalian sovereignty] would be political office."[31] Yet as this study has shown, it is precisely the struggle to retain office in the face of threats from domestic political challengers that prompts nationalist leaderships to set up innovative agencies that enhance the state's capacity to monitor and regulate society, to raise the call for "complete independence," and to champion the strategic, diplomatic, and economic interests of a territorially bounded polity. Such steps set the stage for "the full extension of the Westphalian order" across the contemporary Arab world.[32]

Explaining International Norms

Standard accounts of the emergence, consolidation, and spread of international norms fall into three basic categories. One consists of analyses that are rooted in concepts borrowed from social psychology, such as identity formation, socialization, and learning. A second emphasizes the role of power politics in promoting general adherence to particular modes of state interaction. The third appropriates from the field of evolutionary biology the twin notions of adaptation and natural selection, and claims that once one country adopts a particularly advantageous foreign policy posture, such as Westphalian sovereignty, others must either follow suit or fall by the wayside.

Paradigmatic of the first, and at present most influential, line of argument is Alexander Wendt's discussion of the complicated process that accompanies structural change in the international arena. For Wendt, "because the structure of any internalized culture is associated with a collective identity, a change in that structure will involve a change in collective identity, involving the breakdown of an old identity and the emergence of a new [one]."[33] Novel identities tend to form through the workings of "reflected appraisals," in which "actors learn to see themselves as a reflection of how they are appraised by significant Others."[34] In international affairs, this dynamic tends to accelerate whenever states (1) stand highly dependent on one another, (2) seem likely to share a common fate, (3) closely resemble each other, and (4) find it hard to take advantage of one another.[35] Under these circumstances, leaders can be expected to abandon the "egoistic identities" that they have inherited from the past and start to "identify to varying degrees with others depending on who they are and what is at stake."[36]

Wendt recognizes that the argument he proposes suffers from two major shortcomings. First, it fails to address the crucial problem of how much "micro-level" identity change is necessary to produce "macro-level" alterations in international norms.[37] In the words of Martha Finnemore and Kathryn Sikkink, scholars "have not yet provided a theoretical account for why norm tipping occurs, nor criteria for specifying a priori where, when, and how we would expect it."[38] Second, his argument says little about what might produce crucial shifts in the four "master variables" that drive the process of collective identity formation. There is every reason to expect that changes in the degree of interdependence, the likelihood of sharing a common fate, systemic homogeneity, and levels of self-restraint arise from dynamics that are internal to the countries concerned. In Wendt's words, domestic factors "are likely to be crucial for any [specific developmental] pathway."[39] It is thus imperative to investigate the mechanisms through which domestic political conflicts generate foreign policies that lay the basis for such foundational norms as Westphalian sovereignty.

Moreover, Wendt's analysis of the emergence of international norms presumes that change takes place in one direction, with individual states gradually giving up their egoistic identities and interests and replacing them with more collectivist ones.[40] In his words, "I shall take a Lockean [international] culture as my starting point and focus on how it might be transformed into a Kantian culture."[41] Yet it is almost certainly a mistake to assume that norm transformation goes only one way.[42] The shift to Westphalian sovereignty represented every bit as crucial a transformation of the international culture of the mid-twentieth-century Middle East as any prospective turn to a Kantian world. States came to recognize and accept distinct limitations on their own actions and ambitions; each leadership defined its national interests in terms of the generally acknowledged values of the era; and regional institutions were set up to monitor and promote compliance with the established rules of the game. Wendt's four proposed "master variables" should therefore be able to explain the emergence of the norm that legitimated self-interested, territorially bounded polities, just as they might account for the appearance of other kinds of norms.

Taking each variable in turn: Levels of interdependence among Arab countries remained notoriously low during the era in which Westphalian sovereignty became established as a regional norm. Every Middle Eastern economy continued to be much more tightly connected to its former imperial power than it was to any of the surrounding countries. Furthermore, the slight but significant trend toward greater regional interdependence that accompanied the Second World War sharply reversed itself in the immediate postwar period.[43] There was thus little impetus for nationalist leaderships in the Arab world to adopt a broad conception of political identity. On the other hand, one might make a plausible case that the various Arab states confronted a common fate, particularly in the aftermath of the Second World War. The withdrawal of the imperial powers of Europe left them with the shared task of carving out a viable role for themselves in an increasingly bifurcated world, whose primary strategic focus lay elsewhere; with the important exception of petroleum, none of the goods that they produced elicited much demand on international markets; and the new State of Israel posed a severe challenge to regional stability that affected them all.

It is considerably harder to make a convincing case that the Arab states bore much resemblance to one another during the 1940s and 1950s. Even if the conventional distinction between radical and conservative regimes can no longer be sustained, there was little institutional affinity between the independent multiparty republic of Syria, the tutelary single-party republic of Tunisia, and the divergent constitutional monarchies of Egypt, Jordan, and Iraq. Finally, it might make sense to claim that all of the Arab states believed that they might take advantage of one another, and that they therefore accepted the constraints inherent in a regional order built on Westphalian sovereignty in order to protect themselves from being exploited. Nevertheless, such a statement verges on circularity and leaves unanswered the crucial question of why leaders developed such a high degree of mutual suspicion at this particular moment.

In light of these observations, and given the inability of Wendt's "state-centric" account to explain key aspects of the change from one international norm to another,[44] it is vital to supplement his argument by looking closely at the complex circumstances under which domestic social forces take actions that alter the institutional structure and corporate identities of individual polities. Over the long run, such dynamics seem to smooth out, along the lines of a Braudelian longue durée.[45] But in the pivotal medium term, internal political struggles and fluctuations in foreign trade produce a messier picture, with different states adopting innovative postures toward the outside world at various times and by divergent routes.

Perhaps the most cogent exposition of the argument that power politics induces the acceptance of international norms is Mark Zacher's analysis of the consolidation of the principle of territorial integrity during the course of the twentieth century. For Zacher, the sources of the presumption that a state's territory should remain intact have varied across different kinds of countries. The devastation of the two world wars, along with the subsequent appearance of nuclear weapons, convinced the leaders of "the Western industrial states" that territorial revisionism must be suppressed once and for all. "Western nations' concern was instrumental at its heart," Zacher asserts, "since states were concerned first and foremost with preventing the destruction of their own societies, though governments did share a certain moral concern for other societies as well."[46] "Non-Western or developing states," by contrast, gravitated toward an acceptance of the notion of territorial integrity as a result of three interrelated factors: (1) almost all of them held "ethnic groups that overlap borders and can provoke territorial irredentism"; and they remained comparatively weak in military terms not only (2) with regard to one another but also (3) "vis-à-vis Western supporters of the [territorial integrity] norm."[47] In addition, the steadily rising economic, strategic, and reputational cost of resorting to force to alter recognized territorial boundaries went a long way toward persuading leaders to accept the existing configuration of borders.[48] Most important, however, has been the role of the great powers in promoting and enforcing the rule that international boundaries should remain fixed: "If the Western states had not backed the territorial status quo in the developing world, a good number of territorial aggressions would have succeeded, and the commitment of the developing states to the territorial integrity norm would have probably declined markedly."[49]

Power politics can thus elucidate the emergence and consolidation of a key aspect of Westphalian sovereignty as a foundational norm of interaction among states. Yet besides the problematic nature of Zacher's proposed date for the appearance of this particular norm (viz., 1945), his argument implies that great powers possess the capacity to impose standards of international behavior of their own volition. This view ignores two basic features of norms. First, it dismisses the prescriptive, or normative, aspect of widely shared notions of appropriate behavior. Saying that a state's leaders act in accordance with some specific international norm due to outright coercion or a fear of punishment flies in the face of the usual meaning of the term.[50]

Second, Zacher's argument overlooks the pivotal role that subordinate actors play in making it possible for great powers to carry out the programs they envisage. In other words, it says nothing about why the most powerful states in the world, which evidently had a strong interest in establishing a global states-system rooted in Westphalian sovereignty, were able to accomplish this ambitious and complex project. It is of course possible that the norm of territorial integrity was engendered and maintained purely by force, but this seems unlikely. Local nationalists and state officials cannot simply be assumed to have been willing to go along with initiatives planned and undertaken by the great powers. At the very least, one must show that the leaders of less powerful states had an incentive to play along with stronger states. At most, one might argue that what looks like the result of initiative by the great powers turns out instead to be the product of local forces pursuing interests of their own, which simply turn out to be congruent with the preferences of the stronger states. Somewhere in between stands the Gramscian position that local nationalists tend to comply with the interests and demands of the great powers not because they are compelled to acquiesce but because they derive concrete benefits from doing so. In any case, explaining the emergence of international norms demands a close look at the interplay between domestic and international political dynamics.

The classical statement of the importance of adaptation and natural selection as an explanation for the consolidation of international norms is Hendrik Spruyt's work on the triumph of sovereign states in western Europe. Spruyt argues that political entities characterized by centralized administrations that exercised exclusive authority over well-defined territories enjoyed at least two strategic advantages compared to their rivals. In the first place, such polities "could credibly commit themselves and engage in long-run iterative relations," particularly with other sovereign states. Secondly, they "proved to be better at reducing transaction costs and providing for [sic] collective goods."[51] Consequently, economic and military elites in other kinds of political entities rushed to join forces with sovereign states. Those that could not form such an alliance did their best to mimic the institutions that gave states their strength and dynamism.[52] In this effort, they were assisted—sometimes consciously, sometimes inadvertently—by the rulers of sovereign states themselves, who tended to bestow a greater degree of recognition and legitimacy on those polities that most closely approximated their own systems of governance. Consequently, "the competitive nature of the system determined the nature of the constitutive units."[53]

Spruyt takes some pains to point out that explanations formulated in terms of natural selection should never be equated with simplistic teleological accounts, which assert that whatever entity ends up prevailing did so, or must have done so, because it was the one best suited to survive. Evolution does not occur as individuals take successive steps up a ladder. Instead, in Stephen Jay Gould's vivid metaphor, it takes place through sporadic bursts of discontinuous innovation, with only some of the new forms well enough adapted to their respective environments to flourish.[54] It is only in retrospect that we can trace a direct path from present entities to their predecessors. What drives the evolutionary process is therefore the sudden appearance of novel individuals, whose origins can seldom if ever be connected to changes in the surrounding environment. The potential for innovation inheres not in the structure of the situation, but rather in the makeup of the various units whose interaction constitutes the broader ecological system.

In the Middle East of the mid-twentieth century, nationalist leaders built new kinds of state institutions and mobilized popular sentiment on the basis of self-interested, territorially bounded polities as part of the struggle against radical challengers at home. These innovations may have accorded Egypt and Tunisia some sort of diplomatic or economic advantage, which may in part explain why it was the Egyptian nationalist leadership that took the initiative in organizing the Arab world's first regional organization, as well as why that organization was founded on the principles of Westphalian sovereignty. But this does not necessarily mean that the rival leaderships in Damascus, ʿAmman, and Baghdad purposely followed Cairo's example. Each of these regimes faced serious internal challenges, and it would require a good deal of historical spadework to determine whether they were consciously mimicking one another as they worked out ways to parry the domestic threat.

Types of Anarchic States-systems

International relations in the Middle East took three distinct forms during the course of the twentieth century. From 1900 to the end of the First World War, the nationalist leaderships of the Arab countries dealt with one another (as well as with outside actors) on the basis of four basic presumptions. First, they assumed that their respective states formed component parts of a more comprehensive political entity, whether the rapidly changing Ottoman

Empire, a nascent unified Arab polity, or some sort of subregional amalgam (for example, "le peuple algéro-tunisien" or Greater Syria). Second, they actively intervened in the domestic affairs of other countries, sometimes in support of their strategic allies and sometimes in an effort to hurt their adversaries. Third, they concentrated their primary antagonism against states located outside the region, most notably the imperial powers of Europe. And fourth, they each aspired to play the preeminent role in regional affairs, while expecting others to demur in the face of their evident supremacy. In other words, actors as diverse as Muhammad Farid, ʿAbdullah bin al-Husain and Nuri al-Saʿid all harbored the ambition of being recognized as the paramount leader of an integrated Arab world.

After the mid-1950s, the Middle Eastern states-system exhibited instead the features that are generally considered to be the defining characteristics of an anarchic international arena. Each set of Arab leaders acted to promote the narrow, short-term strategic interests of its own territorially bounded domain. Interfering in the internal politics of other countries was generally regarded as fundamentally illegitimate, and was for the most part abjured. Antagonism and rivalry among Arab states became the major focus of regional affairs, at times eclipsing deep-seated animosities and conflicts with Europe, the United States, Turkey, Iran, and Israel. Finally, the leaderships of the Arab states on the whole recognized one another as equals, and no longer expected any one of their number to emerge as the head of an amalgamated Arab polity.

Between the First World War and the mid-1950s, however, a composite states-system existed in the Middle East. Different Arab leaderships held sharply divergent conceptions of just what constituted their respective national interests: some concerned themselves primarily with threats to the security of the territory located inside the boundaries that their countries had inherited from the imperial era, whereas others conceived of the "national interest" in terms of threats and dangers common to the Arab world as a whole. No accepted norm existed that prohibited overt intervention in the domestic affairs of neighboring countries: some leaders engaged in such activities, while others refrained from doing so. Most Arab governments focused their antagonism on the imperial powers of Europe and the new State of Israel, although intra-Arab disputes played an increasingly prominent part in regional affairs as well. And there was substantial disagreement over just what might constitute leadership of the Arab world. Egyptian nationalists asserted that regional leadership could best be exerted through institutions like the Arab League, which recognized and codified the Westphalian sovereignty of each member-state. Their rivals in 'Amman and Baghdad held the sharply contrasting view that effective leadership was inseparable from actual suzerainty, and so the various Arab countries had to become fully amalgamated in order to achieve their overriding common objectives.

All three of these states-systems were anarchic in nature. No overarching authority structure existed that might have placed constraints on the actions of individual states or forced them to do things they did not want to do. Mainstream scholarship posits that the anarchic character of these three international arenas can be expected to have had a number of important implications: it compelled each state to give highest priority to policies that maximized its own individual security; it tempted leaders to put the most hostile interpretation possible on the actions of others; it heightened the importance of relative gains, while diminishing the value of absolute gains; and it tended to generate balancing behavior among states, while suppressing the urge to bandwagon with the strongest regional actor. Most scholars would go on to claim that the anarchic character of the regional order gave each Arab state a strong incentive to take advantage of every opportunity to improve its own position relative to that of others, that is, to seize the strategic initiative whenever possible.

Critics have disputed almost every one of these assertions. Perhaps the most intense recent debates among students of international relations involve whether relative gains are more prevalent than absolute gains, how likely it is that balancing will win out over bandwagoning, and whether it is more useful to assume that states are offensive opportunists or to conceive of them instead as defensive positionalists.[55] Each of these debates has progressed beyond claims and counterclaims on the part of the protagonists, and gravitated toward an acknowledgment that one outcome or the other is more likely to obtain depending on the circumstances that are present at any given time. Robert Powell, for example, argues that states tend to value relative gains more highly whenever the potential for warfare with adversaries is high, but give greater weight to absolute gains if the likelihood of war remains low.[56] Similarly, Stephen Van Evera asserts that balancing will be more frequent and effective whenever defensive weapons and strategies enjoy a clear advantage compared to offensive ones.[57]

Systematic investigation of analytically distinct types of anarchic states-systems can play a crucial role in resolving such conceptual puzzles. There is every reason to think that anarchic regional orders that consist exclusively of self-interested, territorially bounded, mutually antagonistic states will exhibit a preference for one kind of gains, whereas anarchic states-systems made up of actors who reject Westphalian sovereignty will be characterized by a quite different preference. It seems equally plausible to hypothesize that composite international arenas will demonstrate one way of responding to aggressors, while states-systems in which all actors share a predisposition toward Westphalian sovereignty will be characterized by another kind of response. Thinking carefully about the dynamics that are associated with various types of anarchic arenas is sure to shed light on a wide range of debates that will advance our understanding of international relations, both inside and outside the Middle East.

Notes

INTRODUCTION

1. Alan R. Taylor, *The Arab Balance of Power* (Syracuse: Syracuse University Press, 1982), 13–14.

2. Michael Barnett, "Sovereignty, Nationalism and Regional Order in the Arab States System," in Thomas J. Biersteker and Cynthia Weber, eds. *State Sovereignty as Social Construct* (Cambridge: Cambridge University Press, 1996), 161. See also M. E. Yapp, *The Near East since the First World War* (London: Longman, 1991), 35–46; Bahgat Korany, "Alien and Besieged Yet Here to Stay," in Ghassan Salamé, ed. *The Foundations of the Arab State* (London: Croom Helm, 1987), 74; Aviel Roshwald, *Ethnic Nationalism and the Fall of Empires: Central Europe, Russia and the Middle East 1914–1923* (London: Routledge, 2001), chap. 6; Raymond Hinnebusch, *The International Politics of the Middle East* (Manchester: Manchester University Press, 2003), 18–19.

3. Gabriel Ben-Dor, *State and Conflict in the Middle East* (New York: Praeger, 1983); Michael Barnett, "Institutions, Roles and Disorder: The Case of the Arab States System," *International Studies Quarterly* 37(September 1993); Bernard Lewis, *The Shaping of the Modern Middle East* (New York: Oxford University Press, 1994), chap. 4; Avi Shlaim, *War and Peace in the Middle East* (Harmondsworth: Penguin, 1994), 16–17; Raymond Hinnebusch, "The Middle East Regional System," in Raymond Hinnebusch and Anoushiravan Ehteshami, eds. *The Foreign Policies of Middle East States* (Boulder, Colo.: Lynne Rienner, 2002); Efraim Karsh, *Rethinking the Middle East* (London: Frank Cass, 2003), chap. 1. Tareq Y. Ismael claims, to the contrary, that the lack of congruence between nationalism and sovereignty set the stage for extraordinary efforts toward regional unity: see his *International Relations of the Contemporary Middle East* (Syracuse: Syracuse University Press, 1986), 55.

4. Fred H. Lawson, *Social Origins of Egyptian Expansionism during the Muhammad 'Ali Period* (New York: Columbia University Press, 1992); Abdeljelil Temimi, "Problems of Interpretation of North African History: The Impact of Information on the Policies of Hammuda Pasha (1810–13)," in George Joffe, ed. *North Africa: Nation, State and Region* (London: Routledge, 1993); K. E. Fleming, *The Muslim Bonaparte: Diplomacy and Orientalism in Ali Pasha's Greece* (Princeton: Princeton University

Press, 1999); 'Abd al-'Aziz Sulaiman Nuwwar, *Da'ud Pasha: Wali Baghdad* (Cairo: al-Dar al-Qawmiyyah lil-Taba'ah wal-Nashr, 1968); Hala Fattah, *The Politics of Regional Trade in Iraq, Arabia and the Gulf 1745–1900* (Albany: State University of New York Press, 1997); Dick Douwes, *The Ottomans in Syria* (London: I. B. Tauris, 2000); Muhammed H. Kutluoglu, *The Egyptian Question (1831–1841)* (Istanbul: Eren, 1998); Abdel-Rahim Mustafa, "Some Aspects of Egypt's Foreign Relations under Abbas I," *Annals of the Faculty of Arts of 'Ain Shams University* 8(1963).

5. Bruce Cronin, *Community Under Anarchy* (New York: Columbia University Press, 1999), chap. 1.

6. Frederick Stanley Rodkey, *The Turco-Egyptian Question in the Relations of England, France and Russia, 1832–1841* (New York: Russell and Russell, 1972); M. S. Anderson, *The Eastern Question 1774–1923* (London: Macmillan, 1966); L. Carl Brown, *International Politics and the Middle East* (Princeton: Princeton University Press, 1984); F. A. K. Yasamee, *Ottoman Diplomacy: Abdulhamid II and the Great Powers 1878–1888* (Istanbul: Isis, 1996); Kutluoglu, *Egyptian Question*; Ian S. Lustick, "The Absence of Middle Eastern Great Powers," *International Organization* 51(Autumn 1997).

7. Hendrik Spruyt, "The Prospects for Neo-Imperial and Nonimperial Outcomes in the Former Soviet Space," in Karen Dawisha and Bruce Parrott, eds. *The End of Empire?* (Armonk, N.Y.: M. E. Sharpe, 1997). See also Jack Snyder, *Myths of Empire* (Ithaca, N.Y.: Cornell University Press, 1991).

8. David Lake, "The Rise, Fall and Future of the Russian Empire: A Theoretical Interpretation," in Dawisha and Parrott, eds. *End of Empire?* 36–44.

9. Alexander J. Motyl, *Imperial Ends* (New York: Columbia University Press, 2001), 89–91.

10. Mark R. Beissinger, "Demise of an Empire-State," in Crawford Young, ed. *The Rising Tide of Cultural Pluralism* (Madison: University of Wisconsin Press, 1993), 111.

11. Karen Barkey, "Thinking About Consequences of Empire," in Karen Barkey and Mark von Hagen, eds. *After Empire* (Boulder, Colo.: Westview, 1997), 102–108.

12. Charles Tilly, "How Empires End," in Barkey and von Hagen, eds. *After Empire*, 6.

13. Elie Kedourie, *England and the Middle East* (London: Bowes and Bowes, 1956); Howard M. Sachar, *The Emergence of the Middle East 1914–1924* (New York: Knopf, 1969); Briton Cooper Busch, *Mudros to Lausanne: Britain's Frontier in West Asia, 1918–1923* (Albany: State University of New York Press, 1976); William I. Shorrock, *French Imperialism in the Middle East* (Madison: University of Wisconsin Press, 1976); Christopher M. Andrew and A. S. Kanya-Forstner, *The Climax of French Imperial Expansion 1914–1924* (Stanford: Stanford University Press, 1981); David Fromkin, *A Peace to End All Peace* (New York: Henry Holt, 1989); A. L. Macfie, *The End of the Ottoman Empire 1908–1923* (London: Longman, 1998); Elizabeth Thompson, *Colonial Citizens* (New York: Columbia University Press, 2000).

14. Albert Hourani, *Arabic Thought in the Liberal Age* (London: Oxford University

Press, 1970); William L. Cleveland, *The Making of an Arab Nationalist* (Princeton: Princeton University Press, 1971); C. Ernest Dawn, *From Ottomanism to Arabism* (Urbana: University of Illinois Press, 1973); Antonino Pellitteri, *Il Riformismo Musulmano in Siria (1870–1920)* (Naples: Instituto Universitario Orientale, 1987); Muhammad Y. Muslih, *The Origins of Palestinian Nationalism* (New York: Columbia University Press, 1988); David Dean Commins, *Islamic Reform: Politics and Social Change in Late Ottoman Syria* (New York: Oxford University Press, 1990); Rashid Khalidi et al., eds. *The Origins of Arab Nationalism* (New York: Columbia University Press, 1991); Eliezer Tauber, *The Emergence of the Arab Movements* (London: Frank Cass, 1993); Rashid Khalidi, *Palestinian Identity* (New York: Columbia University Press, 1997).

15. James L. Gelvin, *Divided Loyalties: Nationalism and Mass Politics in Syria at the Close of Empire* (Berkeley: University of California Press, 1998); Edmund Burke III, "Theorizing the Histories of Colonialism and Nationalism in the Arab Maghrib," in Ali Abdullatif Ahmida, ed. *Beyond Colonialism and Nationalism in the Maghrib* (New York: Palgrave, 2000); Aziz al-Azmeh, "Nationalism and the Arabs," in Derek Hopwood, ed. *Arab Nation, Arab Nationalism* (New York: St. Martin's, 2000); Fred H. Lawson, "The Northern Syrian Revolts of 1919–1921 and the Sharifian Regime: Congruence or Conflict of Interests and Ideologies?" in Thomas Philipp and Christoph Schumann, eds. *From the Syrian Land to the States of Syria and Lebanon* (Beirut: Orient-Institut der DMG, 2004).

16. Hasan Kayali, *Arabs and Young Turks* (Berkeley: University of California Press, 1997); Sabine Prator, *Der Arabische Faktor in der Jungturkischen Politik* (Berlin: Klaus Schwarz, 1993).

17. Yosef Lapid and Friedrich Kratochwil, "Revisiting the 'National': Toward an Identity Agenda in Neorealism?" in Yosef Lapid and Friedrich Kratochwil, eds. *The Return of Culture and Identity in IR Theory* (Boulder, Colo.: Lynne Rienner, 1996); Yosef Lapid, "Theorizing the 'National' in International Relations Theory," in Friedrich Kratochwil and Edward D. Mansfield, eds. *International Organization* (New York: Longman, 1994); Ole Waever, "Identity, Communities and Foreign Policy," in Lene Hansen and Ole Waever, eds. *European Integration and National Identity* (London: Routledge, 2002); Lars-Erik Cederman and Christopher Daase, "Endogenizing Corporate Identities: The Next Step in Constructivist IR Theory," *European Journal of International Relations* 9(March 2003).

18. F. H. Hinsley, *Nationalism and the International System* (London: Hodder and Stoughton, 1973), chaps. 5–7. See also F. H. Hinsley, "The Development of the European States System Since the Eighteenth Century," *Transactions of the Royal Historical Society*, fifth series, vol. 2 (London: Royal Historical Society, 1961). A similar position is taken by Barry Buzan and Richard Little, *International Systems in World History* (Oxford: Oxford University Press, 2000), chap. 14.

19. James Mayall, *Nationalism and International Society* (Cambridge: Cambridge University Press, 1990), 26. See also James Mayall, "Nationalism and the International Order," *Millennium* 14(Summer 1985).

20. Anthony D. Smith, "States and Homelands: The Social and Geopolitical Implications of National Territory," *Millennium* 10(Autumn 1981), 187. See also Anthony D. Smith, "Ethnic Identity and World Order," *Millennium* 12(Summer 1983); Anthony D. Smith, "Ethnie and Nation in the Modern World," *Millennium* 14(Summer 1985).

21. Indications that it in fact did so can be discerned in Robert C. Binkley, *Realism and Nationalism 1852–1871* (New York: Harper, 1935). Unfortunately, the issue at hand largely postdates the developments covered in Paul W. Schroeder, *The Transformation of European Politics 1763–1848* (Oxford: Clarendon, 1994).

22. Rodney Bruce Hall, *National Collective Identity* (New York: Columbia University Press, 1999), 212. See also Rodney Bruce Hall, "Territorial and National Sovereigns: Sovereign Identity and Consequences for Security Policy," *Security Studies* 8(Winter 1998–99/Spring 1999), 149–151.

23. Hall, *National Collective Identity*, chap . 8.

24. Ibid., 169. It is entirely possible that these effects should be traced to the revolutionary nature of nineteenth-century nationalism, rather than to nationalism per se. See Kyung-Won Kim, *Revolution and International System* (New York: New York University Press, 1970); Stephen M. Walt, *Revolution and War* (Ithaca, N.Y.: Cornell University Press, 1996).

25. Hall, *National Collective Identity*, 169.

26. Ibid., chap. 9.

27. Daniele Conversi, "Reassessing Current Theories of Nationalism: Nationalism as Boundary Maintenance and Creation," *Nationalism and Ethnic Politics* 1(Spring 1995), 77. See also Daniele Conversi, "Nationalism, Boundaries and Violence," *Millennium* 28(1999). And in a similar vein, Anthony W. Marx, *Faith in Nation: Exclusionary Origins of Nationalism* (Oxford: Oxford University Press, 2003).

28. Conversi, "Reassessing Current Theories," 79.

29. Ibid., 80.

30. Ibid., 81.

31. Ibid. Similar arguments are proposed in Richard Mansbach and Franke Wilmer, "War, Violence and the Westphalian State System as a Moral Community," in Mathias Albert, David Jacobson, and Yosef Lapid, eds. *Identities, Borders, Orders: Rethinking International Relations Theory* (Minneapolis: University of Minnesota Press, 2001); Anthony D. Smith, "War and Ethnicity: The Role of Warfare in the Formation, Self-Image and Cohesion of Ethnic Communities," *Ethnic and Racial Studies* 4(1981); and Kjetil Tronvoll, "Borders of Violence — Boundaries of Identity: Demarcating the Eritrean Nation-State," *Ethnic and Racial Studies* 22(November 1999).

32. Henry R. Nau, *At Home Abroad: Identity and Power in American Foreign Policy* (Ithaca, N.Y.: Cornell University Press, 2002), 29–33.

33. See Emanuel Adler and Michael Barnett, eds. *Security Communities* (Cambridge: Cambridge University Press, 1998).

34. Khaldun S. al-Husry, *Three Reformers: A Study in Modern Arab Political Thought* (Beirut: Khayats, 1966); Albert Hourani, *Arabic Thought in the Liberal Age*

1798–1939 (London: Oxford University Press, 1970); Rashid Khalidi, "'Abd al-Ghani al-'Uraisi and *al-Mufid*: The Press and Arab Nationalism before 1914," in Marwan R. Buheiry, ed. *Intellectual Life in the Arab East 1890–1939* (Beirut: American University of Beirut Press, 1981). See also 'Imad 'Abd al-Salam Rauf, "al-Jam'iyyat al-'Arabiyyah wa-Fikruha al-Qawmi," in *Tatawwur al-Fikr al-Qawmi al-'Arabi* (Beirut: Markaz Dirasat al-Wahdah al-'Arabiyyah, 1986).

35. The idea of a broad community that is expressed by the Arabic word *qawmiyyah* has a religious analogue in the Islamic term *ummah*, which has occasionally been used as a kind of synonym for *qawm* by both Islamists and secular ideologues. See Said Bensaid, "Al-Watan and Al-Umma in Contemporary Arab Use," in Salamé, ed. *Foundations of the Arab State*; W. Montgomery Watt, *Islamic Political Thought* (Edinburgh: Edinburgh University Press, 1968), 9–14; Tariq al-Bishri, *al-'Arab fi Muwajahah al-Udwan* (Cairo: Dar al-Shuruq, 2002).

36. Cecil A. Hourani, "The Arab League in Perspective," *Middle East Journal* 1(April 1947); Robert W. MacDonald, *The League of Arab States: A Study in the Dynamics of Regional Organization* (Princeton: Princeton University Press, 1965); Fayez A. Sayegh, *Arab Unity: Hope and Fulfillment* (New York: Devin-Adair, 1958); Ahmed M. Gomaa, *The Foundations of the League of Arab States* (London: Croom Helm, 1977).

37. A. Demeerseman, "Formulations de l'idée de patrie en Tunisie (1837–1872)," *IBLA: Revue de L'Institut des Belles Lettres Arabes à Tunis* 29(1966); Charles Wendell, *The Evolution of the Egyptian National Image* (Berkeley: University of California Press, 1972); F. Robert Hunter, *Egypt Under the Khedives 1805–1879* (Pittsburgh: University of Pittsburgh Press, 1984), 136–137; 'Izzat al-Qirni, *Fi al-Fikr al-Misri al-Hadith* (Cairo: al-Hayah al-Misriyyah al-'Ammah lil-Kitab, 1995); Rashid Khalidi, "Ottomanism and Arabism in Syria before 1914: A Reassessment," in Khalidi et al., eds. *Origins of Arab Nationalism*; Dina Rizk Khoury, *State and Provincial Society in the Ottoman Empire: Mosul, 1540–1834* (Cambridge: Cambridge University Press, 1997).

38. Israel Gershoni, *The Emergence of Pan-Arabism in Egypt* (Tel Aviv: The Shiloah Center for Middle Eastern and African Studies, 1981), 32.

39. Ibid., 35.

40. Ibid., 36.

41. Israel Gershoni and James P. Jankowski, *Egypt, Islam and the Arabs* (New York: Oxford University Press, 1986), 15.

42. Israel Gershoni and James P. Jankowski, *Redefining the Egyptian Nation 1930–1945* (Cambridge: Cambridge University Press, 1995), 1.

43. Ibid., 79.

44. Ibid., 142.

45. Charles D. Smith, "Imagined Identities, Imagined Nationalisms: Print Culture and Egyptian Nationalism in Light of Recent Scholarship," *International Journal of Middle East Studies* 29(November 1997). See also Israel Gershoni and James Jankowski, "Print Culture, Social Change and the Process of Redefining Imagined

Communities in Egypt," *International Journal of Middle East Studies* 31(February 1999); Charles D. Smith, "'Cultural Constructs' and Other Fantasies: Imagined Narratives in Imagined Communities," ibid.

46. Fouad Ajami, "The End of Pan-Arabism," *Foreign Affairs* 57(Winter 1978–79); Nabil Khoury, "The Pragmatic Trend in Inter-Arab Politics," *Middle East Journal* 36(Summer 1982); Ghassan Salamé, "Inter-Arab Politics: The Return of Geography," in William B. Quandt, ed. *The Middle East: Ten Years after Camp David* (Washington, D.C.: Brookings, 1988).

47. Malcolm H. Kerr, *The Arab Cold War* (London: Oxford University Press, 1971); Patrick Seale, *The Struggle for Syria* (New Haven, Conn.: Yale University Press, 1987); Adeed I. Dawisha, *Egypt in the Arab World* (London: Macmillan, 1976); Elie Podeh, *The Decline of Arab Unity* (Brighton: Sussex Academic Press, 1999).

48. Tawfic E. Farah, ed. *Pan-Arabism and Arab Nationalism: The Continuing Debate* (Boulder, Colo.: Westview, 1987); Shibley Telhami, "Power, Legitimacy and Peace-Making in Arab Coalitions: The New Arabism," in Leonard Binder, ed. *Ethnic Conflict and International Politics in the Middle East* (Gainesville: University Press of Florida, 1999).

49. Michael N. Barnett, *Dialogues in Arab Politics* (New York: Columbia University Press, 1998), 15.

50. Eberhard Kienle, *Ba'th v. Ba'th: The Conflict between Syria and Iraq 1968–1989* (London: I. B. Tauris, 1990); Malik Mufti, *Sovereign Creations: Pan-Arabism and Political Order in Syria and Iraq* (Ithaca, N.Y.: Cornell University Press, 1996). See also Michael Eppel, "The Elite, the Effendiyya and the Growth of Nationalism and Pan-Arabism in Hashemite Iraq, 1921–1958," *International Journal of Middle East Studies* 30(May 1998); Amatzia Baram, "Qawmiyya and Wataniyya in Ba'thi Iraq," *Middle Eastern Studies* 19(April 1983); Eberhard Kienle, "Arab Unity Schemes Revisited," *International Journal of Middle East Studies* 27(February 1995).

51. Alfred Bonné, *State and Economics in the Middle East* (London: Kegan Paul, 1948), chap. 10; Nazih N. Ayubi, *Over-stating the Arab State* (London: I. B. Tauris, 1995), chap. 3; Roger Owen, *State, Power and Politics in the Making of the Modern Middle East* (London: Routledge, 2000), chap. 1. More nuanced treatments can be found in Iliya Harik, "The Origins of the Arab State System," in Salamé, ed. *Foundations of the Arab State;* Ghassan Salamah, *al-Mujtama' wal-Dawlah fil-Mashriq al-'Arabi* (Beirut: Markaz Dirasat al-Wahdah al-'Arabiyyah, 1987); Sa'd al-Din Ibrahim et al., *al-Mujtama' wal-Dawlah fil-Watan al-'Arabi* (Beirut: Markaz Dirasat al-Wahdah al-'Arabiyyah, 1988).

52. C. Ernest Dawn, "The Formation of Pan-Arab Ideology in the Interwar Years," *International Journal of Middle East Studies* 20(February 1988); N. Masalha, "Faisal's Pan-Arabism, 1921–33," *Middle Eastern Studies* 27(October 1991); Ralph M. Coury, *The Making of an Egyptian Arab Nationalist: The Early Years of Azzam Pasha, 1893–1936* (Reading, England: Ithaca Press, 1998).

53. Stephen D. Krasner, *Sovereignty: Organized Hypocrisy* (Princeton: Princeton University Press, 1999), 20.

54. Kerr, *Arab Cold War*; Taylor, *Arab Balance of Power*; Stephan M. Walt, *The Origins of Alliances* (Ithaca, N.Y.: Cornell University Press, 1987).

55. Elie Podeh, *The Quest for Hegemony in the Arab World* (Leiden: Brill, 1995).

56. John C. Wilkinson, *Arabia's Frontiers* (London: I. B. Tauris, 1991); Abdulrahman R. al-Shamlan, *The Evolution of National Boundaries in the Southeastern Arabian Peninsula 1934–1955*, unpublished Ph.D. dissertation, University of Michigan, 1987.

57. Barnett, *Dialogues in Arab Politics*, 72–82; Bruce Maddy-Weitzman, *The Crystallization of the Arab State System 1945–1954* (Syracuse: Syracuse University Press, 1993); Avraham Sela, *The Decline of the Arab-Israeli Conflict* (Albany: State University of New York Press, 1998), chaps. 2–3.

58. Elie Podeh, "The Emergence of the Arab State System Reconsidered," *Diplomacy and Statecraft* 9(November 1998), 50–87.

59. Krasner, *Sovereignty*, 68.

60. Stephen D. Krasner, "Explaining Variation: Defaults, Coercion, Commitments," in Krasner, ed. *Problematic Sovereignty* (New York: Columbia University Press, 2001), 342.

61. Michael Ross Fowler and Julie Marie Bunck, *Law, Power and the Sovereign State* (University Park: Pennsylvania State University Press, 1995), 57.

62. Friedrich Kratochwil, "Of Systems, Boundaries and Territoriality: An Inquiry into the Formation of the State System," *World Politics* 39(October 1986), 27. See also Friedrich Kratochwil, *Rules, Norms and Decisions* (Cambridge: Cambridge University Press, 1989).

63. Kratochwil, "Of Systems, Boundaries and Territoriality," 33.

64. Thomas J. Biersteker and Cynthia Weber, "The Social Construction of State Sovereignty," in Biersteker and Weber, eds. *State Sovereignty as Social Construct* (Cambridge: Cambridge University Press, 1996), 14.

65. Alexander B. Murphy, "The Sovereign State System as Political-Territorial Ideal," in Biersteker and Weber, eds. *State Sovereignty as Social Construct*, 89–91.

66. Benno Teschke, "Theorizing the Westphalian System of States: International Relations from Absolutism to Capitalism," *European Journal of International Relations* 8(2002), 6. See also Benno Teschke, *The Myth of 1648* (London: Verso, 2003).

67. Teschke, "Theorizing the Westphalian System," 32.

68. Ibid., 33–34.

69. Ibid., 37.

70. Similar, but less stimulating, just-so stories can be found in Charles Tilly, *Coercion, Capital and European States* (Oxford: Blackwell, 1990); J. Samuel Barkin and Bruce Cronin, "The State and the Nation: Changing Norms and the Rules of Sovereignty in International Relations," *International Organization* 48(Winter 1994); Justin Rosenberg, *The Empire of Civil Society* (London: Verso, 1994), chap. 5; Barry Buzan and Richard Little, "Reconceptualizing Anarchy: Structural Realism Meets World History," *European Journal of International Relations* 2(December 1996); and Walter C. Opello and Stephen J. Rosow, *The Nation-State and Global Order* (Boulder, Colo.: Lynne Rienner, 1999). See also Sidney Tarrow, "From Comparative Histori-

cal Analysis to 'Local Theory': The Italian City-state Route to the Modern State," *Theory and Society* 33(June 2004).

71. Daniel Philpott, "The Religious Roots of Modern International Relations," *World Politics* 52(January 2000), 206. See also Daniel Philpott, *Revolutions in Sovereignty* (Princeton: Princeton University Press, 2001).

72. Philpott, "Religious Roots," 214.

73. F. H. Hinsley, *Sovereignty*, second edition (Cambridge: Cambridge University Press, 1986), chap. 5; Stephen D. Krasner, "Westphalia and All That," in Judith Goldstein and Robert O. Keohane, eds. *Ideas and Foreign Policy* (Ithaca, N.Y.: Cornell University Press, 1993); Andreas Osiander, "Sovereignty, International Relations and the Westphalian Myth," *International Organization* 55(Spring 2001); Eric Helleiner, "Historicizing Territorial Currencies," *Political Geography* 18(1999); Derek Croxton, "The Peace of Westphalia of 1648 and the Origins of Sovereignty," *The International History Review* 21(1999).

74. Hinsley, "Development of the European States System"; F. H. Hinsley, "The Concept of Sovereignty and the Relations between States," *Journal of International Affairs* 21(1967).

75. Alfred Guillaume, *Islam* (London: Cassell, 1956), 138; Bernard Lewis, *What Went Wrong?* (New York: Oxford University Press, 2002), 103–104; Abdelwahab Meddeb, *The Malady of Islam* (New York: Basic Books, 2003).

76. Janice E. Thomson, "State Sovereignty in International Relations: Bridging the Gap Between Theory and Empirical Research," *International Studies Quarterly* 39(June 1995). See also Hendrik Spruyt, "Historical Sociology and Systems Theory in International Relations," *Review of International Political Economy* 5(Summer 1998); Barry Buzan, *From International to World Society?* (Cambridge: Cambridge University Press, 2004), 270.

77. In addition to Philpott's work, see Nicholas Greenwood Onuf, *World of Our Making: Rules and Rule in Social Theory and International Relations* (Columbia: University of South Carolina Press, 1989); Jens Bartelson, *A Genealogy of Sovereignty* (Cambridge: Cambridge University Press, 1995); Alexander Wendt, *Social Theory of International Politics* (Cambridge: Cambridge University Press, 1999). A compelling critique of idealist approaches can be found in Jonathan Mercer, "Anarchy and Identity," *International Organization* 49(Spring 1995).

CHAPTER ONE

1. Rodd to Salisbury, 25 August 1899, Foreign Office (FO) 78/5024, Public Record Office (PRO), Kew; James Jankowski, "Egypt and Early Arab Nationalism, 1908–1922," in Rashid Khalidi et al., eds. *The Origins of Arab Nationalism* (New York: Columbia University Press, 1991), 246; Donald M. McKale, *War by Revolution: Germany and Great Britain in the Middle East in the Era of World War I* (Kent, Ohio: Kent State University Press, 1998), 23. See also Jamal 'Abd al-Hadi Mas'ud, *Misr bain al-Khilafah al-'Uthmaniyyah wal-Ihtilal al-Injilizi* (Cairo: Dar al-Tawzi' wal-Nashr al-Islamiyyah,

1995), 149–164; Nasr al-Din 'Abd al-Hamid Nasr, *Misr wal-Harakah al-Jami'ah al-Islamiyyah 1882–1914* (Cairo: al-Hayah al-Misriyyah al-'Ammah lil-Kitab, 1984).

2. See, for example, Ahmad Shafiq, *Mudhakkirati fi Nisf Qarn* (Cairo: Matba'ah Misr, 1932), 2: 306; Rashid I. Khalidi, *The Development of British Policy towards Syria and Arab Nationalism 1906–1914* (London: Ithaca Press, 1973), 247; Lukasz Hirszowicz, "The Sultan and the Khedive 1892–1908," *Middle Eastern Studies* 8(October 1972); O'Conor to Salisbury, 30 March 1899, FO 78/4992, PRO; O'Conor to Foreign Office, 13 February 1900, FO 78/5067, PRO.

3. Israel Gershoni and James P. Jankowski, *Egypt, Islam and the Arabs* (New York: Oxford University Press, 1986), 6–7; Arthur Goldschmidt, Jr., *The Egyptian Nationalist Party*, unpublished Ph.D. dissertation, Harvard University, 1968, 87–90. See also Muhammad 'Amara, *al-Jami'ah al-Islamiyyah wal-Fikrah al-Qawmiyyah 'ind Mustafa Kamil* (Beirut: al-Muassasah al-'Arabiyyah lil-Dirasat wal-Nashr, 1976); Fritz Steppat, "Nationalismus und Islam bei Mustafa Kamil: Ein Beitrag zur Ideengeschichte der Agyptischen Nationalbewegung," *Die Welt des Islams*, new series 4(1956).

4. Dennis Walker, "Mustafa Kamil's Party: Islam, Pan-Islamism and Nationalism," *Islam and the Modern Age* 12(May 1981), 91–92; Jacques Berque, *Egypt: Imperialism and Revolution* (New York: Praeger, 1972), 272.

5. Lord Lloyd, *Egypt Since Cromer* (London: Macmillan, 1933), 1: 42; Cromer to Lansdowne, 9 December 1905, FO 78/5431, PRO. See also Stanford J. Shaw and Ezel Kural Shaw, *History of the Ottoman Empire and Modern Turkey* (Cambridge: Cambridge University Press, 1977), 2: 210–211.

6. Walker, "Mustafa Kamil's Party," 102; J. Alexander, *The Truth About Egypt* (London: Cassell, 1911), 121–123.

7. Walker, "Mustafa Kamil's Party," 107; Alexander, *Truth About Egypt*, 74–77. See also Afaf Lutfi al-Sayyid, *Egypt and Cromer* (London: John Murray, 1968), 184.

8. Jankowski, "Egypt and Early Arab Nationalism," 252.

9. Gabriel R. Warburg, "The Sinai Peninsula Borders, 1906–47," *Journal of Contemporary History* 14(October 1979), 679; A. L. Rizq, "Azmah al-'Aqabah al-Ma'rufah bi-Hadithah Taba 1906," *al-Majallah al-Tarikhiyyah al-Misriyyah* 13(1967), 247–305; al-Sayyid, *Egypt and Cromer*, 166–167; Ann Elizabeth Mayer, *'Abbas Hilmi II: The Khedive and Egypt's Struggle for Independence*, unpublished Ph.D. dissertation, University of Michigan, 1978, 392–400.

10. G. P. Gooch and H. Temperley, eds. *British Documents on the Origins of the War 1898–1914* (London: HMSO, 1928), 5: 190–191.

11. Gershoni and Jankowski, *Egypt, Islam and the Arabs*, 7; 'Abd al-Rahman al-Rifa'i, *Mustafa Kamil: Ba'ith al-Harakah al-Wataniyyah* (Cairo: Maktabah al-Nahdah al-Misriyyah, 1950), 195–196; al-Sayyid, *Egypt and Cromer*, 190; Alexander, *Truth About Egypt*, 23–27, 62, 121–123.

12. James Jankowski, "Ottomanism and Arabism in Egypt, 1860–1914," *The Muslim World* 70(July–October 1980), 238; Alexander, *Truth About Egypt*, 161.

13. Ralph M. Coury, *The Making of an Egyptian Arab Nationalist* (Reading, England: Ithaca Press, 1998), 91–92 note 86.

14. Arthur Goldschmidt, Jr., "The Egyptian Nationalist Party: 1892–1919," in P. M. Holt, ed. *Political and Social Change in Modern Egypt* (London: Oxford University Press, 1968), 324–325; Alexander, *Truth About Egypt*, 172; Graham to Grey, 17 September 1909, FO 371/448, PRO; al-Sayyid, *Egypt and Cromer*, 190–191.

15. Alexander, *Truth About Egypt*, 245–246; Jankowski, "Ottomanism and Arabism in Egypt," 254–255.

16. Alexander, *Truth About Egypt*, 173.

17. Edmund Burke III, "Pan-Islam and Moroccan Resistance to French Colonial Penetration, 1900–1912," *Journal of African History* 13(1972), 108–109.

18. *Egyptian Gazette*, 7 January 1911.

19. al-Sayyid, *Egypt and Cromer*, 203. See also Jamal Zakariya Qasim, "Mawqif Misr min al-Harb al-Tarabulusiyyah 1911–1914," *al-Majallah al-Tarikhiyyah al-Misriyyah* 13(1967); Muhammad al-Tayyib al-Ashhab, *Barqah al-'Arabiyyah: Ams wal-Yawm* (Cairo: Matba'ah al-Hawari, 1947), 345–349; Cheetham to Grey, 29 April 1911, FO 371/1113, PRO.

20. Burke, "Pan-Islam and Moroccan Resistance," 110.

21. Ibid., 111.

22. Cheetham to Mallet, 19 August 1912, FO 371/1363, PRO; Kitchener to Grey, 8 December 1912, FO 800/48, PRO.

23. Shafiq, *Mudakkirati*, 2: 288–289.

24. Muhammad Farid, *Awraq Muhammad Farid* (Cairo: al-Hayah al-Misriyyah al-'Ammah lil-Kitab, 1978), 1: 176–177.

25. Ronald Storrs, *The Memoirs of Sir Ronald Storrs* (New York: Putnam's Sons, 1937), 152; "Intelligence News," 22 September 1914, War Office (WO) 157/698, PRO.

26. Storrs, *Memoirs*, 153.

27. Ibid., 160.

28. Malak Badrawi, *Political Violence in Egypt 1910–1924* (London: Curzon, 2000), 117.

29. Jankowski, "Egypt and Early Arab Nationalism," 259.

30. Gershoni and Jankowski, *Egypt, Islam and the Arabs*, 26; al-Sayyid, *Egypt and Cromer*, 190–191; Paul Salem, *Bitter Legacy* (Syracuse: Syracuse University Press, 1994), 210–211.

31. Jankowski, "Ottomanism and Arabism in Egypt," 239.

32. Storrs, *Memoirs*, 178. See also Yunan Labib Rizq, "al-'Alaqat al-'Arabiyyah al-Turkiyyah bayna al-Harbain al-'Alamain," in Ekmeleddin Ihsanoglu and Muhammad Safi al-Din Abu al-'Izz, eds. *al-'Alaqat al-'Arabiyyah al-Turkiyyah* (Istanbul: Research Center for Islamic History, Art and Culture, 1991), 1: 214.

33. Quoted in Lloyd, *Egypt Since Cromer*, 1: 263.

34. Ahmad 'Izzat 'Abd al-Karim, ed. *Khamsin 'Aman 'ala Thawrah 1919* (Cairo: Muassasah al-Ahram, 1969), document 14.

35. Elie Kedourie, *The Chatham House Version and other Middle-Eastern Studies* (Hanover, N.H.: University Press of New England, 1984), 92.

36. Afaf Lutfi al-Sayyid-Marsot, *Egypt's Liberal Experiment: 1922–1936* (Berkeley: University of California Press, 1977), 48–49; 'Abd al-'Aziz Fahmi, *Hathihi Hayyati* (Cairo: Dar al-Hilal, 1963), 76–81; 'Abd al-Khaliq Lashin, *Sa'd Zaghlul wa Dawruhu fi al-Siyassah al-Misriyyah* (Beirut: Dar al-'Awdah, 1975), 143.

37. Lloyd, *Egypt Since Cromer*, 1: 293; Louis J. Cantori, *The Organizational Basis for an Elite Political Party: The Egyptian Wafd*, unpublished Ph.D. dissertation, University of Chicago, 1966, 221–228, 246–247.

38. Quoted in Anwar G. Chejne, "Egyptian Attitudes toward Pan-Arabism," *Middle East Journal* 11(Summer 1957), 253. See also Mahmud Abu al-Fath, *al-Masalah al-Misriyyah wal-Wafd* (Cairo: n.p., 1921), 199; Anis Sayigh, *al-Fikrah al-'Arabiyyah fi Misr* (Beirut: Matba'ah Haikal al-Gharib, 1959), 142.

39. Gershoni and Jankowski, *Egypt, Islam and the Arabs*, 45.

40. Ahmad Shafiq, *Hawliyyat Misr al-Siyassiyyah* (Cairo: Matba'ah Shafiq Pasha, 1926), 1: 154–156.

41. Kedourie, *Chatham House Version*, 133–134.

42. Ibid., 136.

43. *al-Ahram*, 4 November 1919.

44. Malak Badrawi, *Isam'il Sidqi (1875–1950): Pragmatism and Vision in Twentieth Century Egypt* (Richmond: Curzon, 1996), 27.

45. Kedourie, *Chatham House Version*, chap. 6. See also Marcel Colombe, *L'Evolution de l'Egypte* (Paris: G. P. Maisonneuve, 1951), 281–304.

46. Egypt's self-interested, conflictful relations with its Arab neighbors during the 1930s and 1940s are thoroughly documented. See Basheer M. Nafi, "King Faisal, The British and the Project for a Pan-Arab Congress, 1931–33," *Islamic Studies* 37(1998); Thomas Mayer, "Egypt and the General Islamic Conference of Jerusalem in 1931," *Middle Eastern Studies* 18(July 1982); Gabriel Sheffer, "The Involvement of Arab States in the Palestine Conflict and British-Arab Relationship before World War II," *Asian and African Studies* (Jerusalem) 10(1974); Thomas Mayer, "Egypt and the 1936 Arab Revolt in Palestine," *Journal of Contemporary History* 19(April 1984); James Jankowski, "The Government of Egypt and the Palestine Question, 1936–1939," *Middle Eastern Studies* 17(October 1981); Michael Doran, *Pan-Arabism Before Nasser* (New York: Oxford University Press, 1999).

47. Arnold H. Green, *The Tunisian Ulama 1873–1915* (Leiden: Brill, 1978), 146–147.

48. Nicola A. Ziadeh, *Origins of Nationalism in Tunisia* (Beirut: American University of Beirut Press, 1962), 61–62; Green, *Tunisian Ulama*, 147–148; Nikki R. Keddie, "Pan-Islam as Proto-Nationalism," *Journal of Modern History* 41(March 1969).

49. Ziadeh, *Origins*, 63; Green, *Tunisian Ulama*, 147; Moncef Chennoufi, "Les deux séjours de Muhammad 'Abduh en Tunisie," *Les cahiers de Tunisie* 16(1968).

50. Ziadeh, *Origins*, 64; Muhammad al-Fadil Bin 'Ashur, *al-Harakah al-Adabiyyah wal-Fikriyyah fi Tunis* (Cairo: Jami'ah al-Duwwal al-'Arabiyyah, 1956), 44.

51. Green, *Tunisian Ulama*, 149.

52. Ali Mahjoubi, *Les origines du mouvement national en Tunisie 1904–1934* (Tunis:

Publications de l'Université de Tunis, 1982), 111; Mohamed Salah Lejri, *L'évolution du mouvement national tunisien des origines à la deuxième guerre mondiale* (Tunis: Maison tunisienne de l'édition, 1974), 1: 106; 'Alal al-Fasi, *The Independence Movements in Arab North Africa* (New York: Octogon, 1970), 46; Carmel Sammut, "L'action des jeunes tunisiens: Réformisme d'assimilation ou nationalisme d'émancipation?" *Revue d'histoire maghrébine* nos.10–11 (January 1978), 83.

53. Byron D. Cannon, "La constitution ottomane dans la stratégie politique jeune tunisienne, 1908–1910," *Les cahiers de Tunisie* 29(1981), 296.

54. Mongi Sayadi, *La première association nationale moderne en Tunisie: al-Jam'iyya al-Khalduniyya (1896–1958)* (Tunis: MTE, 1974); Lejri, *L'évolution du mouvement*, 1: 107–109.

55. Zaideh, *Origins*, 73; Bechir Tlili, "Problématique des processus de formation des faits nationaux et des idéologies nationalistes dans le monde islamo-méditerranéen de l'entre-deux-guerres (1919–1930): L'exemple de la Tunisie," *Les cahiers de Tunisie* 21(1973), 202.

56. 'Ashur, *al-Harakah al-Adabiyyah*, 121–122. See also Bechir Tlili, "Socialistes et jeunes-Tunisiens à la Veille de la grande guerre (1911–1913)," *Les cahiers de Tunisie* 22(1974).

57. Ziadeh, *Origins*, 75; Mahjoubi, *Origines*, 127–128; Sammut, "Action," 95–97.

58. Taoufik Ayadi, *Mouvement réformiste et mouvements populaires à Tunis (1906–1912)* (Tunis: Publications de l'université de Tunis, 1986), 139–145; Cannon, "Constitution ottomane," 288–289; al-Fasi, *Independence Movements*, 48; Green, *Tunisian Ulama*, 203.

59. Quoted in Ziadeh, *Origins*, 80; Daniel Goldstein, *Libération ou annexion* (Tunis: Maison tunisienne de l'édition, 1978), 48; Sammut, "Action," 109.

60. Ziadeh, *Origins*, 82; Jalal Yahya, *al-Maghrib al-Kabir* (Cairo: al-Hayah al-Misriyyah al-'Ammah lil-Kitab, 1966), 3: 1073–1074; Bechir Tlili, "Au seuil du nationalisme tunisien: Documents inédits sur le panislamisme au Maghrib (1919–1923)," *Africa* (Rome) 28(June 1973), 222 note 5; Mahjoubi, *Origines*, 107–108; Rachel Simon, *Libya between Ottomanism and Nationalism* (Berlin: Klaus Schwarz, 1987), 117; Salvatore Bono, "La Libye dans la Revue du Maghreb (1916–1918)," *Revue d'histoire maghrébine* nos. 71–72(May 1993).

61. 'Ashur, *al-Harakah al-Adabiyyah*, 100; Sammut, "Action," 125; Ayadi, *Mouvement reformiste*, 146–147; Carmel Sammut, *L'impérialisme capitaliste français et le nationalisme tunisien (1881–1914)* (Paris: Publisud, 1983), 295; Lejri, *L'évolution du mouvement*, 1: 144.

62. Green, *Tunisian Ulama*, 223; al-Tahir Ahmad al-Zawi, *Jihad al-Abtal fi Tarabulus al-Gharb* (Beirut: Dar al-Fath, 1970), 315–316.

63. Simon, *Libya*, 357 note 33; McKale, *War by Revolution*, 50.

64. Ziadeh, *Origins*, 86.

65. Mahjoubi, *Origines*, 141–146; Bechir Tlili, "La grande guerre et les questions tunisiennes: Le groupement de la 'Revue du Maghreb' (1916–1918)," *Les cahiers de Tunisie* 26(1978); al-Fasi, *Independence Movements*, 51; Tlili, "Seuil," 227 note.

66. Mahjoubi, *Origines*, 140–141; Tlili, "Seuil," 231; Lejri, *Evolution*, 1: 161–163. See also Mustapha Kraeim, *Nationalisme et syndicalisme en Tunisie 1918–1929* (Tunis: UGTT, 1976), 125–127.

67. Peter Heine, "Salih ash-Sharif at-Tunisi: A North African Nationalist in Berlin during the First World War," *Revue de l'Occident Musulman et de la Mediterranée* 33(1982), 93.

68. Mohammed Bach-Hamba, *Le peuple algéro-tunisien et la France* (Carthage: Beit al-Hikma, 1991); Mahmoud Abdelmoula, *Le mouvement patriotique de libération en Tunisie et le panislamisme (1906–1920)* (Tunis: Editions MTM, 1999), 256–258; Mahjoubi, *Origines*, 145, 198–199; Green, *Tunisian Ulama*, 229 note 75.

69. al-Tahir Khumairi, *Muntakhabat min al-Amthal al-ʿAmmiyyah al-Tunisiyyah* (Tunis: al-Dar al-Tunisiyyah lil-Nashr, 1967), 6; Kraeim, *Nationalisme et syndicalisme*, 130–131.

70. Abdelmoula, *Le mouvement patriotique*, 257.

71. Ziadeh, *Origins*, 91–92; Lejri, *Evolution*, 1:180–187; Tlili, "Faits nationaux," 206–207; Lisa Anderson, *The State and Social Transformation in Tunisia and Libya, 1830–1980* (Princeton: Princeton University Press, 1986), 163.

72. Odile Moreau, "Echoes of National Liberation: Turkey Viewed from the Maghrib in the 1920s," *Journal of North African Studies* 8(2003), 62–63.

73. Ibid., 66.

74. Ibid., 67.

75. Ibid., 65.

76. Mahjoubi, *Origines*, 190–191.

77. Ibid., 191–193.

78. al-Fasi, *Independence Movements*, 55.

79. Quoted in Ziadeh, *Origins*, 94.

80. Lejri, *L'évolution du mouvement*, 1: 195; Arnold J. Toynbee, *Survey of International Affairs 1925: The Islamic World since the Peace Settlement* (London: Oxford University Press, 1927), 176–178.

81. Tlili, "Faits nationaux," 209; M. Kraiem, "Le Parti Réformiste Tunisien (1920–1926)," *Revue d'histoire maghrébine* no. 4 (July 1975); Lejri, *Evolution*, 1: 209–210; Kraeim, *Nationalisme et syndicalisme*, 307–315.

82. Abdelmoula, *Le mouvement patriotique*, 260–261.

83. Anderson, *State and Social Transformation*, 163; Mahjoubi, *Origines*, 292.

84. Mahjoubi, *Origines*, 288; Tlili, "Faits nationaux," 212.

85. Anderson, *State and Social Transformation*, 163.

86. Abdelmoula, *Le mouvement patriotique*, 260; Tlili, "Au seuil du nationalisme tunisien," 230–235..

87. Tlili, "Faits Nationaux," 213.

88. Mahjoubi, *Origines*, 344–345, 360, 409; Anderson, *State and Social Transformation*, 165–166; Habib Bourgiba, *Muqaddamah al-Harakah al-Qawmiyyah* (Tunis: n.p., 1962), 55. See also Mohamed Chaabouni, "L'attitude des pays du Maghreb vis à vis du khalifa de 1914 a 1926," *Revue d'histoire maghrébine* nos. 69–70 (May 1993).

89. Walid Kazziha, "The Political Evolution of Transjordan," *Middle Eastern Studies* 15(May 1979), 239. See also Kamil Mahmud Khillah, *al-Tatawwur al-Siyassi li Sharq al-Urdun* (Tripoli, Libya: al-Munshaah al-'Ammah lil-Nashr wal-Tawzi' wal-I'lan, 1983), 346–428.

90. Yehoshua Porath, *In Search of Arab Unity 1930–1945* (London: Frank Cass, 1986), 84, 175; Itamar Rabinovich, "Inter-Arab Relations Foreshadowed: The Question of the Syrian Throne in the 1920s and 1930s," in *Festschrift in Honor of Dr. George S. Wise* (Tel Aviv: Tel Aviv University Press, 1981), 244.

91. Yehoshua Porath, "Abdallah's Greater Syria Programme," *Middle Eastern Studies* 20(April 1984), 177. See also Ron Pundik, *The Struggle for Sovereignty: Relations between Great Britain and Jordan, 1946–1951* (Oxford: Blackwell, 1994), 36–39.

92. Porath, "Abdallah's Greater Syria Programme," 180–181.

93. Mohammad Ibrahim Faddah, *The Middle East in Transition: A Study of Jordan's Foreign Policy* (London: Asia Publishing House, 1974), 144.

94. Benjamin Shwadran, *Jordan: A State of Tension* (New York: Council for Middle Eastern Affairs Press, 1959), 233.

95. Porath, "Abdallah's Greater Syria Programme," 182.

96. Muhammad Khalil, *The Arab States and the Arab League* (Beirut: Khayats, 1962), 2: 12–16.

97. George Kirk, *The Middle East in the War* (London: Oxford University Press, 1952), 336; Porath, *In Search of Arab Unity*, 183.

98. Porath, "Abdallah's Greater Syria Programme," 185.

99. Faddah, *Middle East in Transition*, 147.

100. Ibid., 149.

101. Ahmed M. Gomaa, *The Foundation of the League of Arab States* (London: Longman, 1977), 170–172.

102. Ibid., 219.

103. Aqil H. H. Abidi, *Jordan: A Political Study 1948–1957* (Bombay: Asia Publishing House, 1965), 22; Richard H. Pfaff, *Fertile Crescent Unity*, unpublished MA thesis, University of California, Berkeley, 1956, 20.

104. Gomaa, *Foundation of the League*, 221.

105. Ibid., 227.

106. Pfaff, *Fertile Crescent Unity*, 24.

107. Gomaa, *Foundation of the League*, 265.

108. Shwadran, *Jordan*, 238.

109. Ibid.

110. Faddah, *Middle East in Transition*, 150.

111. Ibid., 152.

112. George E. Kirk, "Cross-Currents Within the Arab League: The Greater Syria Plan," *The World Today* 4(January 1948), 19–20; Pfaff, *Fertile Crescent Unity*, 25–26.

113. Faddah, *Middle East in Transition*, 152.

114. Ibid., 151.

115. Shwadran, *Jordan*, 239.

116. Kirk, "Cross-Currents," 20.

117. Faddah, *Middle East in Transition*, 152.

118. Shwadran, *Jordan*, 239; Abidi, *Jordan*, 22; Mary C. Wilson, *King Abdullah, Britain and the Making of Jordan* (Cambridge: Cambridge University Press, 1987), 159.

119. Faddah, *Middle East in Transition*, 153.

120. Ibid., 155.

121. Avraham Sela, "Transjordan, Israel and the 1948 War," *Middle Eastern Studies* 28(October 1992), 631–632.

122. Thomas Mayer, "Arab Unity of Action and the Palestine Question, 1945–48," *Middle Eastern Studies* 22(July 1986), 345. See also Eugene L. Rogan, "Jordan and 1948: The Persistence of an Official History," in Eugene L. Rogan and Avi Shlaim, eds. *The War For Palestine* (Cambridge: Cambridge University Press, 2001).

123. Mayer, "Arab Unity of Action," 345.

124. Sela, "Transjordan," 637, 640–641.

125. Ibid., 667.

126. Faddah, *Middle East in Transition*, 158 note 58.

127. Shwadran, *Jordan*, 50; Benjamin Shwadran, "Jordan Annexes Arab Palestine," *Middle Eastern Affairs* 1(April 1950).

128. Shwadran, *Jordan*, 296.

129. Robert B. Satloff, *From Abdullah to Hussein* (New York: Oxford University Press, 1994), 19.

130. Shwadran, *Jordan*, 298; Bruce Maddy-Weitzman, *The Crystallization of the Arab State System 1945–1954* (Syracuse: Syracuse University Press, 1993), 147.

131. Bruce Maddy-Weitzman, "Jordan and Iraq: Efforts at Intra-Hashimite Unity," *Middle Eastern Studies* 26(January 1990), 66.

132. Abidi, *Jordan*, 81.

133. Satloff, *From Abdullah to Hussein*, 20; Abidi, *Jordan*, 81–82.

134. Kirkbride to Rapp, 2 August 1951, FO 371/91839, PRO; Abidi, *Jordan*, 88; Naseer H. Aruri, *Jordan: A Study in Political Development* (The Hague: Martinus Nijhoff, 1972), 90.

135. "Annual Report on the Hashemite Kingdom of the Jordan for 1951," 26 January 1952, FO 371/98856, PRO; Satloff, *From Abdullah to Hussein*, 26–29.

136. Ibid., 34; Raphael Patai, *The Kingdom of Jordan* (Princeton: Princeton University Press, 1958), 54.

137. Abidi, *Jordan*, 91.

138. Ibid., 95.

139. "Jordan-Iraq Union," *Middle Eastern Affairs* 3(February 1952), 53–54.

140. Satloff, *From Abdullah to Hussein*, 47.

141. Abidi, *Jordan*, 105; Satloff, *From Abdullah to Hussein*, 54.

142. Abidi, *Jordan*, 112.

143. Maddy-Weitzman, *Crystallization*, 169.

144. Khaldun S. Husry, "King Faisal I and Arab Unity, 1930–33," *Journal of Contemporary History* 10(April 1975); A. Shikara, "Faisal's Ambitions of Leadership in the Fertile Crescent," in Abbas Kelidar, ed. *The Integration of Modern Iraq* (New York: St. Martin's, 1979); Yehoshua Porath, "Iraq, King Faysal the First and Arab Unity," in M. Sharon, ed. *Studies in Islamic History and Civilization in Honour of Professor David Ayalon* (Leiden: Brill, 1986); Elie Podeh, "The Emergence of the Arab State System Reconsidered," *Diplomacy and Statecraft* 9(November 1998), 68–69.

145. Yehoshua Porath, "Nuri al-Sa'id's Arab Unity Programme," *Middle Eastern Studies* 20(October 1984), 78.

146. Ibid., 79–80.

147. Ibid., 80–81.

148. Ibid., 82.

149. Porath, *In Search of Arab Unity*, 45.

150. Ibid., 46.

151. Salah al-'Aqqad, *al-'Arab wal-Harb al-'Alamiyyah al-Thaniyyah* (Cairo: Jami'ah al-Duwwal al-'Arabiyyah, 1970), 94–95.

152. George Kirk, *The Middle East in the War* (London: Oxford University Press, 1952), 67–69; Porath, *In Search of Arab Unity*, 193.

153. Mamduh Rusan, *al-'Iraq wa Qadaya al-Sharq al-'Arabi al-Qawmiyyah, 1941–1958* (Beirut: al-Muassasah al-'Arabiyyah lil-Dirasah wal-Nashr, 1979), 34.

154. Ibid., 36.

155. Majid Khadduri, "The Scheme of Fertile Crescent Unity," in Richard N. Frye, ed. *The Near East and the Great Powers* (Cambridge, Mass.: Harvard University Press, 1951), 139–140; Porath, "Nuri al-Sa'id's Arab Unity Programme," 89–91; Su'ad Rauf Muhammad, *Nuri al-Sa'id wa Dawruhu fi al-Siyassah al-'Iraqiyyah 1932–1945* (Baghdad: Maktabah al-Yaqdha al-'Arabiyyah, 1988), 250–262.

156. Porath, *In Search of Arab Unity*, 55–56.

157. Rusan, *al-'Iraq wa Qadaya al-Sharq*, 39.

158. Porath, *In Search of Arab Unity*, 267.

159. Maddy-Weitzman, *Crystallization*, 19.

160. *al-Akhbar* (Baghdad), 23 March 1946.

161. Patrick Seale, *The Struggle for Syria* (New Haven, Conn.: Yale University Press, 1987), 51.

162. *Arab News Bulletin*, 1 March 1946; Majid Khadduri, *Independent Iraq* (London: Oxford University Press, 1951), 260.

163. Mayer, "Arab Unity of Action," 343.

164. Michael Eppel, *The Palestine Conflict in the History of Modern Iraq* (London: Frank Cass, 1994), 186.

165. Charles Tripp, "Iraq and the 1948 War," in Eugene L. Rogan and Avi Shlaim, eds. *The War for Palestine* (Cambridge: Cambridge University Press, 2001), 137.

166. Maddy-Weitzman, *Crystallization*, 95.

167. Phebe Marr, *The Modern History of Iraq* (Boulder, Colo.: Westview, 1985), 109.

168. Seale, *Struggle for Syria*, 50.
169. Maddy-Weitzman, *Crystallization*, 108.
170. Rusan, *al-'Iraq wa Qadaya al-Sharq*, 122; Seale, *Struggle for Syria*, 55–56.
171. Maddy-Weitzman, *Crystallization*, 110.
172. Ibid., 118; Pfaff, *Fertile Crescent Unity*, 37.
173. Maddy-Weitzman, *Crystallization*, 119–120.
174. Ibid., 122–123; Seale, *Struggle for Syria*, 83.
175. Maddy-Weitzman, *Crystallization*, 124.
176. Ibid., 146.
177. Ibid., 161–165.
178. Abubaker M. Saad, *Iraq and Arab Politics: The Nuri as-Said Era, 1941–1958*, unpublished Ph.D. dissertation, University of Washington, 1978, 237–238.
179. Seale, *Struggle for Syria*, 90.
180. Reeva Simon, "The Hashemite 'Conspiracy': Hashemite Unity Attempts, 1921–1958," *International Journal of Middle East Studies* 5(June 1974), 320.
181. Marr, *Modern History of Iraq*, 114; Michael Eppel, "The Fadhil al-Jamali Government in Iraq, 1953–54," *Journal of Contemporary History* 34(July 1999), 433–437.
182. Malik Mufti, *Sovereign Creations* (Ithaca, N.Y.: Cornell University Press, 1996), 38.
183. Bruce Maddy-Weitzman, "Jordan and Iraq: Efforts at Intra-Hashimite Unity," *Middle Eastern Studies* 76(January 1990), 67; Morrison to Troutbeck, 14 August 1951, FO 371/91703, PRO.
184. Saad, *Iraq and Arab Politics*, 184; Damascus to Foreign Office, 30 July 1951, FO 371/91851A, PRO; Troutbeck to Foreign Office, 3 August 1951, FO 371/91797, PRO.
185. Maddy-Weitzman, "Jordan and Iraq," 70.
186. "Iraqi Foreign Policy," 27 October 1953, WO 32/14869, PRO.
187. Porath, *In Search of Arab Unity*, 14.
188. Ibid., 161; Philip K. Hitti, "The Possibility of Union among the Arab States," *American Historical Review* 48(July 1943), 732; Philip S. Khoury, *Syria and the French Mandate* (Princeton: Princeton University Press, 1987), chap. 15.
189. Porath, "Abdallah's Greater Syria Programme," 83.
190. Daniel Pipes, *Greater Syria* (New York: Oxford University Press, 1990), 59.
191. Salma Mardam Bey, *Syria's Quest for Independence* (Reading, England: Ithaca Press, 1994), 28.
192. Ibid., 56–58.
193. Porath, *In Search of Arab Unity*, 194–195.
194. Ibid., 262.
195. Peter A. Shambrook, *French Imperialism in Syria 1927–1936* (Reading, England: Ithaca Press, 1998), 112.
196. Engert to Secretary of State, 8 October 1941, 890d.00/883, Record Group (RG) 59, United States National Archives (USNA), College Park.

197. Gwynn to Secretary of State, 26 October 1942, 890d.00/918, RG59, USNA.
198. Porath, *In Search of Arab Unity*, 263.
199. Freya Stark, *East Is West* (London: John Murray, 1945), 125.
200. Mardam Bey, *Syria's Quest*, 79.
201. Ibid., 86.
202. Ibid., 91–92.
203. Ibid., 114–115; Ahmed M. Gomaa, *The Foundation of the League of Arab States* (London: Croom Helm, 1977), 179–183.
204. Mardam Bey, *Syria's Quest*, 127.
205. Ibid., 138; James A. Melki, "Syria and the State Department 1937–47," *Middle Eastern Studies* 33(January 1997), 96–97.
206. Pipes, *Greater Syria*, 58; Porath, *In Search of Arab Unity*, 280.
207. Porath, *In Search of Arab Unity*, 278.
208. Gomaa, *Foundation of the League*, 218.
209. Ibid., 219.
210. Ibid., 220.
211. Ibid., 221–222.
212. Ibid., 236.
213. Maddy-Weitzman, *Crystallization*, 29–30.
214. Ibid., 31.
215. Mufti, *Sovereign Creations*, 47.
216. Maddy-Weitzman, *Crystallization*, 39.
217. *Arab News Bulletin*, 1 February 1947.
218. Maddy-Weitzman, *Crystallization*, 41.
219. Barry Rubin, *The Arab States and the Palestine Conflict* (Syracuse: Syracuse University Press, 1981), 171.
220. Joshua Landis, "Syria and the Palestine War: Fighting King 'Abdullah's 'Greater Syria Plan,' " in Rogan and Shlaim, eds. *War For Palestine*, 193–195; Mayer, "Arab Unity of Action," 344.
221. Rubin, *Arab States*, 187; Khoury, *Syria*, 622.
222. Hedley Bull and Adam Watson, eds. *The Expansion of International Society* (Oxford: Clarendon, 1984); Robert Jackson, The Global Covenant (Oxford: Oxford University Press, 2000); Yongjin Zhang, "China's Entry into International Society," *Review of International Studies* 17(1991); Shogo Suzuki, "Japan's Socialization into Janus-Faced European International Society," *European Journal of International Relations* 11(March 2005).
223. Yasuaki Onuma, "When Was the Law of International Society Born?" *Journal of the History of International Law* 2(2000); Robert H. Jackson and Carl G. Rosberg, "Why Africa's Weak States Persist: The Empirical and the Juridical in Statehood," *World Politics* 35(October 1982); Robert H. Jackson, *Quasi-States: Sovereignty, International Relations and the Third World* (Cambridge: Cambridge University Press, 1990); Jeffrey Herbst, *States and Power in Africa* (Princeton: Princeton University Press, 2000), chap. 4. It is wrongheaded, however, to claim that Westphalian sover-

eignty characterized relations between the European powers and their colonial possessions; see Edward Keene, *Beyond the Anarchical Society* (Cambridge: Cambridge University Press, 2002).

224. Benedict Anderson, *Imagined Communities* (London: Verso, 1983), 50–65. See also Basil Davidson, *The Black Man's Burden: Africa and the Curse of the Nation-State* (New York: Times Books, 1992).

CHAPTER TWO

1. Michael Mann, *The Sources of Social Power*, vol. 2 (Cambridge: Cambridge University Press, 1993), 69.

2. Ibid., 61. See also John A. Hall, *Powers and Liberties* (Oxford: Blackwell, 1986); Clive Ashworth and Christopher Dandeker, "Warfare, Social Theory and West European Development," *The Sociological Review* 35(February 1987); Anthony Jarvis, "Societies, States and Geopolitics: Challenges from Historical Sociology," *Review of International Studies* 15(July 1989).

3. Anthony Giddens, *The Nation-State and Violence* (Berkeley: University of California Press, 1985), chap. 3.

4. Ibid., 50.

5. Ibid., 95.

6. Christopher Dandeker, "The Nation-State and the Modern World System," in Jon Clark, Celia Modgil, and Sohan Modgil, eds. *Anthony Giddens: Consensus and Controversy* (London: Falmer, 1990), 265.

7. Giddens, *Nation-State and Violence*, 192; Dandeker, "Nation-State and the Modern World System," 263.

8. Justin Rosenberg, "A Non-Realist Theory of Sovereignty?: Giddens' *The Nation-State and Violence*," *Millennium* 19(Summer 1990), 251.

9. Giddens, *Nation-State and Violence*, 120. See also Peter J. Taylor, "The State as Container: Territoriality in the Modern World-system," *Progress in Human Geography* 18(June 1994); Martin Shaw, "War and the Nation-State in Social Theory," in David Held and John B. Thompson, eds. *Social Theory of Modern Societies: Anthony Giddens and his Critics* (Cambridge: Cambridge University Press, 1989); John Breuilly, "The Nation-State and Violence: A Critique of Giddens," in Clark, Modgil, and Modgil, eds. *Anthony Giddens*. A promising extension of this general approach can be found in Ann Firth, "State Form, Social Order and the Social Sciences: Urban Space and Politico-Economic Systems 1760–1850," *Journal of Historical Sociology* 16(March 2003).

10. Raouf Abbas Hamed, "The Siyasatname and the Institutionalization of Central Administration under Muhammad 'Ali" and Pascale Ghazaleh, "The Guilds: Between Tradition and Modernity," both in Nelly Hanna, ed. *The State and Its Servants* (Cairo: American University in Cairo Press, 1995); Kenneth M. Cuno, *The Pasha's Peasants* (Cambridge: Cambridge University Press, 1992); Roger Owen, *The Middle East in the World Economy 1800–1914* (London: Methuen, 1981), 150–151;

Laverne Kuhnke, *Lives at Risk: Public Health in Nineteenth-Century Egypt* (Cairo: American University in Cairo Press, 1990); Juan R. I. Cole, *Colonialism and Revolution in the Middle East* (Cairo: American University in Cairo Press, 1999), chaps. 1–3; Mine Ener, "At the Crossroads of Empires: Policies toward the Poor in Early- to Mid-nineteenth-Century Egypt," *Social Science History* 26(Summer 2002).

11. F. Robert Hunter, *Egypt under the Khedives, 1805–1879: From Household Government to Modern Bureaucracy* (Pittsburgh: University of Pittsburgh Press, 1984); F. Robert Hunter, "State-Society Relations in Nineteenth-Century Egypt: The Years of Transition, 1848–79," *Middle Eastern Studies* 36(July 2000).

12. Lord Lloyd, *Egypt Since Cromer* (London: Macmillan, 1933), 1: 16–17. See also Robert L. Tignor, "The 'Indianization' of the Egyptian Administration under British Rule," *American Historical Review* 68(April 1963); Robert L. Tignor, *Modernization and British Colonial Rule in Egypt 1882–1914* (Princeton: Princeton University Press, 1966); Owen, *Middle East in the World Economy*, 220–223; Roger Owen, "The Population Census of 1917 and Its Relationship to Egypt's Three 19th Century Statistical Regimes," *Journal of Historical Sociology* 9(December 1996).

13. Owen, *Middle East in the World Economy*, 223.

14. David S. Landes, *Bankers and Pashas* (Cambridge, Mass.: Harvard University Press, 1958); Abdel Maksud Hamza, *The Public Debt of Egypt* (Cairo: Government Press, 1944).

15. Tignor, *Modernization and British Colonial Rule*, 76–83, 363–364; Robert L. Tignor, "The Egyptian Revolution of 1919: New Directions in the Egyptian Economy," *Middle Eastern Studies* 12(October 1976), 47; Owen, *Middle East in the World Economy*, 224–225; Bent Hansen, *Egypt and Turkey* (Washington, D.C.: World Bank, 1991), 52.

16. Jacques Berque, *Egypt: Imperialism and Revolution* (New York: Praeger, 1972), 245–247; Robert L. Tignor, *State, Private Enterprise, and Economic Change in Egypt, 1918–1952* (Princeton: Princeton University Press, 1984), 15.

17. Lloyd, *Egypt Since Cromer*, 1: 147–150; E. R. J. Owen, "The Attitudes of British Officials to the Development of the Egyptian Economy, 1882–1922," in M. A. Cook, ed. *Studies in the Economic History of the Middle East* (London: Oxford University Press, 1970), 494.

18. Owen, *Middle East in the World Economy*, 224–225.

19. Tignor, *State, Private Enterprise and Economic Change*, 27.

20. Lloyd, *Egypt Since Cromer*, 1: 77–78.

21. Ibid., 1: 152.

22. Ibid., 1: 213.

23. See Jaspar Yeates Brinton, *The Mixed Courts of Egypt* (New Haven, Conn.: Yale University Press, 1930); Byron Cannon, *Politics of Law and the Courts in Nineteenth-Century Egypt* (Salt Lake City: University of Utah Press, 1988).

24. Tignor, *Modernization and British Colonial Rule*, 138–139. See also J. Morton Howell, *Egypt's Past, Present and Future* (Dayton, Ohio: Service Publishing, 1929),

chap. 22; Lloyd, *Egypt Since Cromer*, 1: 134–139, 208–272. Gorst's own assessment of the courts can be found in Lloyd, *Egypt Since Cromer*, 1: 13 note 1. Nathan Brown suggests that this situation opened a crucial space in which the nationalist movement could take shape: Nathan J. Brown, "Law and Imperialism: Egypt in Comparative Perspective," *Law and Society Review* 29(January 1995).

25. Clayton memorandum, 17 February 1920, Foreign Office (FO) 141/793, Public Record Office (PRO), Kew. See also Harold Tollefson, *Policing Islam: The British Occupation of Egypt and the Anglo-Egyptian Struggle over Control of the Police, 1882–1914* (Westport, Conn.: Greenwood, 1999).

26. *Egyptian Gazette*, 20 July 1934.

27. Lloyd, *Egypt Since Cromer*, 1: 271–272.

28. John Chalcraft, *The Striking Cabbies of Cairo and Other Stories: Crafts and Guilds in Egypt, 1863–1914*, unpublished Ph.D. dissertation, New York University, 2001, 206–207.

29. Jacques Berque, *Egypt: Imperialism and Revolution* (New York: Praeger, 1972), 129–130; Timothy Mitchell, *Rule of Experts* (Berkeley: University of California Press, 2002), 63–65.

30. J. Alexander, *The Truth About Egypt* (London: Cassell, 1911), 17.

31. Berque, *Egypt*, 285.

32. Lloyd, *Egypt Since Cromer*, 2: 70.

33. See Muhammad Mahmud al-Suruji, *al-Jaish al-Misri fi al-Qarn al-Tisa 'Ashr* (Cairo: Dar al-Ma'arif, 1967), 425–443; 'Abd al-'Azim Ramadan, *al-Jaish al-Misri fi al-Siyyasah* (Cairo: al-Hayah al-Misriyyah al-'Ammah al-Kitab, 1977), 73–90; Ahmad Shafiq, *Mudhakkirati fi Nisf Qarn* (Cairo: Matba'ah Misr, 1932), 2: 37–38.

34. Lloyd, *Egypt Since Cromer*, 2: 80.

35. L. Hirszowicz, "The Sultan and the Khedive, 1892–1908," *Middle Eastern Studies* 8(October 1972), 298; Shafiq, *Mudhakkirati*, 2: 58.

36. Arnold J. Toynbee, *Survey of International Affairs 1925: The Islamic World since the Peace Settlement* (London: Oxford University Press, 1927), 184–188; Yunan Labib Rizk, "A Deal That Was Never Ratified," *al-Ahram Weekly*, 30 November–6 December 2000.

37. Richard L. Hill, *Egypt in the Sudan* (London: Oxford University Press, 1959); Eve M. Troutt Powell, *A Different Shade of Colonialism: Egypt, Great Britain and the Mastery of the Sudan* (Berkeley: University of California Press, 2003); Ghada Hashem Talhami, *Egypt's 'Civilizing Mission': Khedive Isma'il's Red Sea Province, 1865–1885*, unpublished Ph.D. dissertation, University of Illinois, Chicago, 1975, xiii–xiv.

38. Talhami, *Egypt's "Civilizing Mission,"* xix.

39. Muddathir 'Abd al-Rahim, *Imperialism and Nationalism in the Sudan* (Oxford: Clarendon, 1969), 24–28.

40. Gabriel Warburg, *The Sudan under Wingate* (London: Frank Cass, 1971), 14; M. W. Daly, "The Development of the Governor-Generalship of the Sudan, 1899–1934," *Sudan Notes and Records* 61(1980), 29–30.

41. Gabriel Warburg, "The Governor-General of the Sudan and his Relations with the British Consuls-General in Egypt, 1899–1916," *Asian and African Studies* 5(1969), 102.

42. Warburg, *Sudan under Wingate*, 17.

43. Ibid., 36–42; M. W. Daly, *Empire on the Nile* (Cambridge: Cambridge University Press, 1986), 48–54.

44. Warburg, "Governor-General of the Sudan," 124–132; Daly, *Empire on the Nile*, chaps. 4 and 7; M. W. Daly, *Imperial Sudan* (Cambridge: Cambridge University Press, 1991), 1–7. See also Heather J. Sharkey, *Living with Colonialism: Nationalism and Culture in the Anglo-Egyptian Sudan* (Berkeley: University of California Press, 2003), chap. 4.

45. Lloyd, *Egypt Since Cromer*, 1: 218; Robert L. Tignor, "The Egyptian Revolution of 1919: New Directions in the Egyptian Economy," *Middle Eastern Studies* 12(October 1976), 43.

46. Lloyd, *Egypt Since Cromer*, 1: 245.

47. Tignor, "Egyptian Revolution of 1919," 44.

48. *Egyptian Gazette*, 5 February 1918.

49. P. G. Elgood, *Egypt and the Army* (London: Oxford University Press, 1924), 333–334.

50. *Egyptian Gazette*, 10 and 24 January 1918.

51. Tignor, *State, Private Enterprise, and Economic Change*, 92–93.

52. Ibid., 97–100.

53. Ibid., 70.

54. Joel Beinin and Zachary Lockman, *Workers on the Nile* (Princeton: Princeton University Press, 1987), 116.

55. Lloyd, *Egypt Since Cromer*, 2: 72.

56. Lucette Valensi, *Tunisian Peasants in the Eighteenth and Nineteenth Centuries* (Cambridge: Cambridge University Press, 1985); Abdelhamid Henia, *Le Grid: ses rapports avec le Beylik de Tunis, 1676–1840* (Tunis: University of Tunis, 1980), 212–222.

57. L. Carl Brown, *The Tunisia of Ahmed Bey* (Princeton: Princeton University Press, 1974).

58. Mustapha Kraiem, *La Tunisie précoloniale* (Tunis: Societé tunisienne de diffusion, 1973), 2: 15–18; Jamil M. Abun-Nasr, *A History of the Maghrib in the Islamic Period* (Cambridge: Cambridge University Press, 1987), 274–275.

59. F. Robert Hunter, "Farewell to the Tribes of Tunisia: Khayr al-Din and the Recovery of 1869–77," *Maghreb Review* 26(2001); Lisa Anderson, *The State and Social Transformation in Tunisia and Libya, 1830–1980* (Princeton: Princeton University Press, 1986), 85–87; Elbaki Hermassi, *Leadership and National Development in North Africa* (Berkeley: University of California Press, 1972), 51–53; A. Demeerseman, "Formulations de l'idée de patrie en Tunisie (1837–1872)," *IBLA: Revue de L'Institut des Belles Lettres Arabes à Tunis* 29(1966), 35–71 and 109–142; Charles Combs Harber, *Reforms in Tunisia 1855–1878*, unpublished Ph.D. dissertation, Ohio State University, 1970.

60. Anderson, *State and Social Transformation*, chap. 7; Asma Larif-Beatrix, *Edification étatique et environnement culturel* (Paris: Publisud, 1988); Ali Mahjoubi, *L'établissement du protectorat francais en Tunisie* (Tunis: Publications de l'Université de Tunis, 1977), 271–281; Jurgen Rosenbaum, *Frankreich in Tunisien: Die Anfange des Protektorates 1881–1886* (Zurich: Atlantis, 1971).

61. Mounira M. Charrad, *States and Women's Rights* (Berkeley: University of California Press, 2001), 91. For a contrasting view, see Hermassi, *Leadership*, 51.

62. Elie Fitoussi and Aristide Benazet, *L'état tunisien et le protectorat francais* (Paris: Rousseau, 1931), 1: 223–230; Andre Martel, "Le Makhzen du Sud tunisien (1881–1910)," *Les cahiers de Tunisie* 14(1966).

63. Julia A. Clancy-Smith, *Rebel and Saint* (Berkeley: University of California Press, 1994); Mahmoud Abdelmoula, *Jihad et colonialisme: La Tunisie et la Tripolitaine (1914–1918)* (Tunis: Editions Tiers-Monde, 1987); Salim Labid, "al-Qabilah wal-Isti'mar Malahizat hawl Thawrah al-Junub al-Tunisi 1915–1918," *Revue d'histoire maghrébine* nos. 77–78(May 1995).

64. Fathi Lissir, *Les tribus de l'extreme sud tunisien sous administration militaire française: Cas de la confédération Ourghemma (1881–1939)* (Zaghouan: Fondation Temimi, 1998), part 3; Daniel Goldstein, *Libération ou annexion* (Tunis: Maison tunisienne de l'édition, 1978), 146–154.

65. Carmel Sammut, *L'imperialisme capitaliste français et le nationalisme tunisien (1881–1914)* (Paris: Publisud, 1983), 135–137; Mohamed Salah Lejri, *L'évolution du mouvement national tunisien des origines a la deuxième guerre mondiale* (Tunis: Maison tunisienne de l'édition, 1974), 1: 73–74; Mahfoud Bennoune, "Primary Capital Accumulation in Colonial Tunisia," *Dialectical Anthropology* 4(July 1979), 94–95.

66. Noureddine Dougui, "Monographie d'une grande entreprise coloniale: la Compagnie des Phosphates et du Chemin de Fer de Gafsa 1897–1930," *Correspondances de l'IRMC*, 3.

67. Fitoussi and Benazet, *L'état tunisien*, 2: 633–636.

68. Ibid., 640.

69. Rene Gallissot, *L'économie de l'Afrique du Nord* (Paris: Presses Universitaires de France, 1961), 58.

70. Fitoussi and Benazet, *L'état tunisien*, 2: 674–676.

71. Ibid., 679–670.

72. Sammut, *L'imperialisme capitaliste français*, 109.

73. Fitoussi and Benazet, *L'état tunisien*, 2: 683–684; Abdelaziz Thaalbi, *La Tunisie martyre* (Beirut: Dar al-Gharb al-Islami, 1985), 132–133.

74. Goldstein, *Libération*, 29.

75. Charrad, *States and Women's Rights*, 117; Thaalbi, *La Tunisie martyre*, 37–38.

76. Lejri, *L'évolution du mouvement*, 1: 62–63; Elisabeth de Mouilleau, *Fonctionnaires de la République et artisans de l'Empire: Le cas des controleurs civils en Tunisie* (Paris: L'Harmattan, 2000).

77. Anderson, *State and Social Transformation*, 145–146.

78. Ibid., 147–148; Barbour, 298–299.

79. Fitoussi and Benazet, *L'état tunisien*, 2: 393–395.

80. Carmel Sammut, "L'action des jeunes Tunisiens: Réformisme d'assimilation ou nationalisme d'émancipation?" *Revue d'histoire maghrébine* nos. 10–11 (January 1978), 97; Bennoune, "Primary Capital Accumulation," 91.

81. Fitoussi and Benazet, *L'état tunisien*, 2: 403–404; Lejri, *L'évolution du mouvement*, 1: 68–69. See also Byron D. Cannon, "The Beylical Habus Council and Suburban Development: Tunis, 1881–1914," *The Maghreb Review* 7(January–April 1982); Byron D. Cannon, "Entrepreneurial Management of Tunisia's Private Habous Patrimony, 1902–1914," *The Maghreb Review* 10(March–June 1985); Byron D. Cannon, "Le marché de location des Habous en Tunisie: Dialectique de développement agricole, 1875–1902," in Cannon, ed. *Terroirs et sociétés au Maghreb et au Moyen Orient* (Lyon: IRMAC, 1983–84).

82. Fitoussi and Benazet, *L'état tunisien*, 1: 286, 311.

83. Ibid., 308–309.

84. Ibid., 343.

85. Ibid., 301.

86. Goldstein, *Libération*, 58–59.

87. James Raider Mood, *Tunis: Its Resources, Industries, and Commerce with Reference to United States Trade* (Washington, D.C.: Government Printing Office, 1923), 38–39.

88. Ali Mahjoubi, *Les origines du mouvement national en Tunisie 1904–1934* (Tunis: Publications de l'Université de Tunis, 1982), 184–185.

89. Mahjoubi, *Origines*, 155.

90. Mahjoubi, *Origines*, 162; Kraeim, *Nationalisme et Syndicalisme*, 69, 73–78.

91. Goldstein, *Libération*, 208.

92. Ibid., 60–61.

93. Mahjoubi, *Origines*, 167; Lejri, *L'évolution du mouvement*, 1: 69–70.

94. Goldstein, *Libération*, 249–251; Mahjoubi, *Origines*, 168–169.

95. Anderson, *State and Social Transformation*, 164.

96. Byron D. Cannon, "Socio-Governmental Intermediaries in Tunisia under the Early Protectorate: A Case Study of the Amin al-Suq," *Revue d'histoire maghrébine* nos. 7–8 (January 1977); Mahjoubi, *Origines*, 187.

97. Mahjoubi, *Origines*, 175–179.

98. Ibid., 171–172.

99. Kraeim, *Nationalisme et syndicalisme*, 106–116.

100. Cookingham to Secretary, 25 January 1924, vol. 94, Record Group (RG) 84, United States National Archives (USNA), College Park.

101. Smith to Secretary, 7 November 1925, 851s.01/2, RG 57, USNA.

102. George Grassmuck, "Selected Materials on Iraq and Jordan: The Development of Political Documentation," *American Political Science Review* 51(December 1957), 1081.

103. Mustafa Hamarneh, *Social and Economic Transformation of Trans-Jordan, 1921–1946*, unpublished Ph.D. dissertation, Georgetown University, 1985, 215.

104. Nazih N. Ayubi, *Over-Stating the Arab State* (London: I. B. Tauris, 1995), 114.

105. P. J. Vatikiotis, *Politics and the Military in Jordan* (New York: Praeger, 1967), 44; Ma'an Abu Nowar, *The History of the Hashemite Kingdom of Jordan*, vol. 1 (Oxford: Ithaca Press, 1989), 44; Eugene L. Rogan, *Frontiers of the State in the Late Ottoman Empire* (Cambridge: Cambridge University Press, 1999), chap. 9; Joseph A. Massad, *Colonial Effects: The Making of National Identity in Jordan* (New York: Columbia University Press, 2001), 28–29.

106. F. G. Peake, "Trans-Jordan," *Journal of the Royal Central Asian Society* 26(July 1939), 384–388; Hamarneh, *Social and Economic Transformation*, 139–142.

107. Aqil H. H. Abidi, *Jordan: A Political Study 1948–1957* (Bombay: Asia Publishing House, 1965), 15; Mary C. Wilson, *King Abdullah, Britain and the Making of Jordan* (Cambridge: Cambridge University Press, 1987), 78–79; Massad, *Colonial Effects*, 24–25.

108. Hani Hurani, *al-Tarkib al-Iqtisadi al-Ijtima'i li-Sharq al-Urdun* (Beirut: Markaz al-Abhath li Munazzamah al-Tahrir al-Filastiniyyah, 1978), 69.

109. Abla M. Amawi, *State and Class in Transjordan: A Study of State Autonomy*, unpublished Ph.D. dissertation, Georgetown University, 1993, 390–392.

110. Ibid., 401.

111. Ibid., 409.

112. Eugene L. Rogan, "The Making of a Capital: Amman, 1918–1928," in Jean Hannoyer and Seteney Shami, eds. *Amman* (Amman: Centre d'Etudes et de Recherches sur le Moyen-Orient Contemporain, 1996).

113. V. M. Amadouny, "The Formation of the Transjordan-Syria Boundary, 1915–32," *Middle Eastern Studies* 31(July 1995).

114. Wilson, *King Abdullah*, 100.

115. Nowar, *History of the Hashemite Kingdom of Jordan*, 77.

116. Wilson, *King Abdullah*, 73–74.

117. Hamarneh, *Social and Economic Transformation*, 137–138.

118. Rogan, "Making of a Capital," 101.

119. Hamarneh, *Social and Economic Transformation*, 144; Jeffery A. Rudd, "Origins of the Transjordan Frontier Force," *Middle Eastern Studies* 26(April 1990).

120. Wilson, *King Abdullah*, 99.

121. Hamarneh, *Social and Economic Transformation*, 147; Riccardo Bocco and Tariq M. Tell, "Pax Britannica in the Steppe: British Policy and the Transjordan Bedouin," in Eugene L. Rogan and Tariq Tell, eds. *Village, Steppe and State: The Social Origins of Modern Jordan* (London: British Academic Press, 1994), 116.

122. Wilson, *King Abdullah*, 99; Bocco and Tell, "Pax Britannica," 119; Massad, *Colonial Effects*, 58–59 and chap. 3.

123. A. Konikoff, *Trans-Jordan: An Economic Survey* (Jerusalem: Jewish Agency for Palestine, 1943), 112.

124. Amawi, *State and Class*, 386–387.

125. Michael R. Fischbach, "British Land Policy in Transjordan," in Rogan and Tell, eds. *Village, State and Steppe*, 91–92.

126. Konikoff, *Trans-Jordan*, 93.

127. Ibid., 101.

128. Alfred G. Musrey, *An Arab Common Market: A Study of Inter-Arab Trade Relations, 1920–67* (New York: Praeger, 1969), 19.

129. Ibid., 26.

130. Ibid., 58.

131. Michael Mann, *The Sources of Social Power: The Rise of Classes and Nation-States, 1760–1914* (Cambridge: Cambridge University Press, 1993), 59–61.

132. Hamarneh, *Social and Economic Transformation*, 165; Amawi, *State and Class*, 527–528.

133. Hamarneh, *Social and Economic Transformation*, 186; Bocco and Tell, "Pax Britannica," 125.

134. Fischbach, "British Land Policy," 106–107.

135. Abla M. Amawi, "The Consolidation of the Merchant Class in Transjordan during the Second World War," in Rogan and Tell, eds. *Village, State and Steppe*, 180–181.

136. Amawi, *State and Class*, chap. 6.

137. Roger Owen, "Class and Class Politics in Iraq before 1958," in Robert A. Fernea and William Roger Louis, eds. *The Iraqi Revolution of 1958* (London: I. B. Tauris, 1991), 155; Charles Tripp, *A History of Iraq* (Cambridge: Cambridge University Press, 2000), 51. A somewhat different picture of Iraq between 1920 and 1932 is presented in Toby Dodge, *Inventing Iraq* (New York: Columbia University Press, 2003).

138. Hanna Batatu, *The Old Social Classes and the Revolutionary Movements of Iraq* (Princeton: Princeton University Press, 1978), 23.

139. 10 November 1918, FO 371/4148, PRO. See also Anthony B. Toth, "Raiding and the Twilight of Bedouin Power: British Tribal Policy and the Camel Nomads of Iraq, 1921–1930," paper presented to the annual convention of the Middle East Studies Association, Washington, D.C., November 2000.

140. Kathleen M. Langley, *The Industrialization of Iraq* (Cambridge, Mass.: Harvard University Press, 1967), chap. 4; Batatu, *Old Social Classes*, 33.

141. Pierre Marthelot, "Bagdad: notes de Geographie Urbaine," *Annales de Geographie* no. 401 (January–February 1965).

142. Batatu, *Old Social Classes*, 469.

143. Joseph Sassoon, *Economic Policy in Iraq 1932–1950* (London: Frank Cass, 1987), 45. See also Ilyahu Dankur, ed. *Dalil al-Mamlakah al-ʿIraqiyyah* (Baghdad: Dar al-Mustaqbal 1936), 251.

144. Langley, *Industrialization of Iraq*, 65–66.

145. Sassoon, *Economic Policy*, 152–153.

146. Marr, *Modern History of Iraq*, 49; Guzine A. K. Rasheed, "Development of

Agricultural Land Taxation in Modern Iraq," *Bulletin of the School of Oriental and African Studies* 25(1962).

147. Sassoon, *Economic Policy*, 80–81.

148. Tripp, *History of Iraq*, 73.

149. Paul P. J. Hemphill, "The Formation of the Iraqi Army, 1921–33," in Abbas Kelidar, ed. *The Integration of Modern Iraq* (New York: St. Martin's, 1979); Khaled Salih, *State-Making, Nation-Building and the Military: Iraq, 1941–1958* (Goteborg: Goteborg University, 1996), chap. 3; Raja' al-Khattab, *Tasis al-Jaish al-'Iraqi* (Baghdad: Maktabah al-Hurriyyah, 1979). On the Assyrian revolt, see Sami Zubaida, "Contested Nations: Iraq and the Assyrians," *Nations and Nationalism* 6(Summer 2000).

150. Mohammad A. Tarbush, *The Role of the Military in Politics: As Case Study of Iraq to 1941* (London: Kegan Paul International, 1982), 94.

151. 'Abd al-Razzaq al-Hassani, *Tarikh al-Wizarat al-'Iraqiyyah* (Sidon: Matba'ah al-'Irfan, 1953), 4: 117–121; Ibrahim Muhammad al-Aqidi, *The Iraqi Army and Politics 1941–1953*, unpublished Ph.D. dissertation, University of Exeter, 1989, 48–55.

152. Tripp, *History of Iraq*, 96; Fadil al-Barak, *Dawr al-Jaish al-'Iraqi fi Hukumah al-Difa' al-Watani wal-Harb ma'a Britainia sanah 1941* (Baghdad: al-Dar al-'Arabiyyah lil-Taba'ah, 1979), 54–56.

153. al-Aqidi, *Iraqi Army and Politics*, 119–136.

154. Muhammad Salman Hasan, *al-Tatawwur al-Iqtisadi fi al-'Iraq* (Saidah: al-Maktabah al-'Asriyyah, 1956), 78–79.

155. Sassoon, *Economic Policy*, 51.

156. Langley, *Industrialization of Iraq*, 57; Carl Iversen, *A Report on Monetary Policy in Iraq* (Baghdad: National Bank of Iraq, 1954), 31.

157. Sassoon, *Economic Policy*, 62; Edith Penrose and E. F. Penrose, *Iraq* (London: Benn, 1978), 150.

158. Daniel Silverfarb, *Britain's Informal Empire in the Middle East* (New York: Oxford University Press, 1986), chap. 7.

159. *Report by His Majesty's Government . . . on the Administration of 'Iraq for the period January to October, 1932* (London: HMSO, 1933), 483–485.

160. Khadduri, *Independent Iraq*, 143.

161. Marr, *Modern History of Iraq*, 91–92.

162. Daniel Silverfarb, *The Twilight of British Ascendancy in the Middle East* (New York: St. Martin's, 1994), 34.

163. Samira Haj, *The Making of Iraq* (Albany: State University of New York Press, 1997), 99.

164. Sassoon, *Economic Policy*, 126.

165. 12 January 1944, FO 371/40041, PRO.

166. Philip S. Khoury, *Syria and the French Mandate* (Princeton: Princeton University Press, 1987), 440–441, 623.

167. Ibid., 470.

168. Ibid., 518–519.

169. Joshua M. Landis, *Nationalism and the Politics of Za'ama*, unpublished Ph.D. dissertation, Princeton University, 1997, chaps. 1–2.
170. Khoury, *Syria*, 528.
171. Ibid., 534.
172. Ibid., 441 note 29.
173. Ibid., 467–468.
174. Ibid., chap. 19.
175. Nacklie E. Bou-Nacklie, *Les Troupes Speciales du Levant*, unpublished Ph.D. dissertation, University of Utah, 1989, 308–310.
176. Ibid., 329–331.
177. Ibid., 331.
178. Ibid., 332.
179. Ibid., 333.
180. Ibid., 354–355.
181. Ibid., 357.
182. Ibid., 358.
183. Ibid., 369; Stephen H. Longrigg, *Syria and Lebanon under French Mandate* (London: Oxford University Press, 1958), 349.
184. James A. Melki, "Syria and the State Department 1937–47," *Middle Eastern Studies* 33(January 1997), 102.
185. Ibid., 103.
186. Ibid., 103–104.
187. Albert H. Hourani, *Syria and Lebanon* (London: Oxford University Press, 1946), 171.
188. Ibid., 289; Longrigg, *Syria and Lebanon*, 341.
189. Hourani, *Syria and Lebanon*, 290.
190. Patrick Seale, *The Struggle for Syria* (New Haven, Conn.: Yale University Press, 1987), 94.
191. Longrigg, *Syria and Lebanon*, 294.
192. Ibid., 301.
193. Ibid., 302.
194. Ibid., 303.
195. Ibid., 337; Spears to Cairo, 24 September 1942, Special Operations Executive (HS) 3/212, PRO.
196. Gordon H. Torrey, *Syrian Politics and the Military 1945–1958* (Columbus: Ohio State University Press, 1964), 77.
197. Ibid., 78.
198. Ibid., 79.

CHAPTER THREE

1. Hendrik Spruyt, *The Sovereign State and Its Competitors* (Princeton: Princeton University Press, 1994), 64–65.

2. Spruyt, *Sovereign State*, 66.
3. Roger Owen, *The Middle East in the World Economy 1800–1914* (London: Methuen, 1981), 219.
4. John Chalcraft, *The Striking Cabbies of Cairo and Other Stories: Crafts and Guilds in Egypt, 1863–1914*, unpublished Ph.D. dissertation, New York University, 2001, 257, 270, 297–298.
5. Owen, *Middle East in the World Economy*, 241. See also Samir Radwan, *Capital Formation in Egyptian Industry and Agriculture 1882–1967* (London: Ithaca Press, 1974), 169.
6. Bent Hansen and Edward F. Lucas, "Egyptian Foreign Trade, 1885–1961: A New Set of Trade Indices," *The Journal of European Economic History* 7(Fall and Winter 1978), 435.
7. Ibid., 437.
8. Ibid., 439.
9. Radwan, *Capital Formation*, 129.
10. Ibid., 118–119.
11. Ibid., 170.
12. Chalcraft, *Striking Cabbies of Cairo*, 199.
13. Ibid., 200 note 27.
14. Pierre Arminjon, *La situation économique et financière de l'Egypte* (Paris: Librairie Generale de Droit et de Jurisprudence, 1911), 343; I. G. Levi, "Le commerce et l'industrie," in *L'égypte: Aperçu historique et géographique* (Cairo: Institut Francais d'Archéologie Orientale, 1926), 285.
15. Chalcraft, *Striking Cabbies of Cairo*, 202.
16. Ibid., 237.
17. Ibid., 251–252.
18. See Edwin Levy, "Les événements de 1907 et la Situation Actuelle de l'Egypte," *L'Egypte contemporaine* 3(1911).
19. Owen, *Middle East in the World Economy*, 224.
20. Eric Davis, *Challenging Colonialism* (Princeton: Princeton University Press, 1983), 118–119.
21. Ibid., 122.
22. Owen, *Middle East in the World Economy*, 238.
23. Davis, *Challenging Colonialism*, 76.
24. Joel Beinin and Zachary Lockman, *Workers on the Nile* (Princeton: Princeton University Press, 1987), 67–69; Amin 'Izz al-Din, *Tarikh al-Tabaqah al-'Amilah al-Misriyyah munthu Nashatiha hatta Thawrah 1919* (Cairo: Dar al-Katib al-'Arabi lil-Taba'ah wal-Nashr, 1967), 124–131.
25. Beinin and Lockman, *Workers on the Nile*, 70.
26. Ibid., 119; Robert L. Tignor, "The Egyptian Revolution of 1919: New Directions in the Egyptian Economy," *Middle Eastern Studies* 12(October 1976), 59–61.
27. Davis, *Challenging Colonialism*, 120.

28. Mahmud Zayid, "Nashat Hizb al-Ahrar al-Dusturiyyin fi Misr, 1922–24," *al-Abhath* 16(March 1963).

29. Owen, *Middle East in the World Economy*, 227.

30. Hansen and Lucas, "Egyptian Foreign Trade," 439.

31. Davis, *Challenging Colonialism*, 130; Tignor, "Egyptian Revolution of 1919," 61–63.

32. Hansen and Lucas, "Egyptian Foreign Trade," 440.

33. Tarik M. Yousef, *Egypt's Growth Performance under Economic Liberalism: A Reassessment with New GDP Estimates, 1885–1945*, Working Paper 0211, Economic Research Forum, Cairo, 2002.

34. Daniel Goldstein, *Libération ou annexion* (Tunis: Maison Tunisienne de l'édition, 1978), 56, 65 note 7; James Raider Mood, *Tunis: Its Resources, Industries, and Commerce with Reference to United States Trade* (Washington, D.C.: Government Printing Office, 1923), 48–49.

35. Cookingham to Rhodes and Co., 17 November 1922, vol. 90, Record Group (RG) 84, United States National Archives (USNA), College Park.

36. Mahfoud Bennoune, "Primary Capital Accumulation in Colonial Tunisia," *Dialectical Anthropology* 4(July 1979), 95.

37. Naval Intelligence Division, *Tunisia* (Oxford: Oxford University Press, 1945), 312; Mood, *Tunis*, 48–49; Mustapha Kraeim, *Nationalisme et Syndicalisme en Tunisie 1918–1929* (Tunis: UGTT, 1976), 54. See also "Zinc in Tunisia," 5 July 1925, 851s.6355, RG 57, USNA; Beylard to Cookingham, 1 June 1922, vol. 90, RG 84, USNA.

38. Naval Intelligence Division, *Tunisia*, 285; Andre Nouschi, "La colonisation de la Tunisie: Des terres ou des capitaux," *Les cahiers de Tunisie* 14(1966), 182; Rodd Balek, *La Tunisie après la guerre* (Paris: Comité de l'Afrique Francaise, 1920–21), 322–325.

39. Naval Intelligence Division, *Tunisia*, 269.

40. Résidence Générale de la République Française, *Notice générale sur la Tunisie: 1881–1921* (Toulouse: Imprimerie du Centre, 1922), 339. Somewhat different figures are presented in Ali Mahjoubi, *Les origines du mouvement national en Tunisie 1904–1934* (Tunis: Publications de l'Université de Tunis, 1982), 157.

41. Goldstein, *Libération*, 61–62; Mahjoubi, *Origines*, 160–161.

42. Goldstein, *Libération*, 69 note 53.

43. Mahjoubi, *Origines*, 344; Jacques Berque, *French North Africa* (London: Faber and Faber, 1967), 158.

44. Kenneth Brown, "Muhammad Ameur: A Tunisian Comrade," in Edmund Burke III, ed. *Struggle and Survival in the Modern Middle East* (Berkeley: University of California Press, 1993), 257.

45. Ibid., 254; Berque, *French North Africa*, 147–148; "Le nationalisme musulman en Tunisie," *L'Afrique francaise*, July 1931, 438.

46. Abdelaziz Thaalbi, *La Tunisie martyre* (Beirut: Dar al-Gharb al-Islami, 1985), 132–133; Paul Sebag, *La Tunisie* (Paris: Editions Sociales, 1951), 127.

47. Carmel Sammut, "L'Action des jeunes Tunisiens: Reformisme d'assimilation ou nationalisme d'émancipation?" *Revue d'histoire maghrébine* nos. 10–11(January 1978), 73.

48. Mahjoubi, *Origines*, 176–179; Mood, *Tunis*, 38–39.

49. Mahjoubi, *Origines*, 171.

50. Mahmoud Abdelmoula, *Le mouvement patriotique de libération en Tunisie et le panislamisme (1906–1920)* (Tunis: Editions MTM, 1999), 78–79.

51. Ibid., 201.

52. Balek, *La Tunisie après la Guerre*, 14. See also Cookingham to Sec. of State, 19 August 1919, 851s.6158, RG 57, USNA.

53. Mood, *Tunis*, 49.

54. Mahjoubi, *Origines*, 326–327.

55. Ibid., 353–356.

56. Ibid., 438; Paul Sebag, *Tunis: Histoire d'une ville* (Paris: L'Harmattan, 1998), 400–401.

57. Mustafa Hamarneh, *Social and Economic Transformation of Trans-Jordan 1921–1946*, unpublished Ph.D. dissertation, Georgetown University, 1985, 183–184; Abla M. Amawi, *State and Class in Transjordan: A Study of State Autonomy*, unpublished Ph.D. dissertation, Georgetown University, 1993, 430–450.

58. Abla M. Amawi, "The Consolidation of the Merchant Class in Transjordan during the Second World War," in Rogan and Tell, eds. *Village, Steppe and State*, 177.

59. Ibid., 515–516.

60. British report quoted in ibid., 518.

61. Amawi, *State and Class*, 520.

62. Ibid., 522.

63. Alfred G. Musrey, *An Arab Common Market* (New York: Praeger, 1969), 59.

64. Amawi, "Consolidation of the Merchant Class," 182; Naseer H. Aruri, *Jordan: A Study in Political Development* (The Hague: Martinus Nijhoff, 1972), 93; Aqil H. H. Abidi, *Jordan: A Political Study 1948–1957* (Bombay: Asia Publishing House, 1965), 200.

65. Hamarneh, *Social and Economic Transformation*, 189.

66. Amnon Cohen, *Political Parties in the West Bank under the Jordanian Regime 1949–1967* (Ithaca, N.Y.: Cornell University Press, 1982), 144–145, 164–166; Marion Boulby, *The Muslim Brotherhood and the Kings of Jordan 1945–1993* (Atlanta: Scholars Press, 1999), 50–52; Peter Gubser, *Politics and Change in al-Karak, Jordan* (London: Oxford University Press, 1973), 135–136.

67. Ibrahim Gharayibah, *Jama'ah al-Ikhwan al-Muslimin fil-Urdun 1946–1996* ('Amman: Dar Sindibad lil-Nashr, 1996).

68. "Monthly Situation Report for the Jordan for the Month of October 1949," 7 November 1949, Foreign Office (FO) 371/75273, Public Record Office (PRO), Kew.

69. 'Isam Sakhnini, "Damm Filastin al-Wusta ila Sharqi al-Urdun," *Shu'un Filastiniyyah* no. 40(December 1974).

70. "Monthly Situation Report for the Jordan for the Month of March 1950," 1 April 1950, FO 371/82703, PRO.

71. Shaul Mishal, *West Bank/East Bank: The Palestinians in Jordan 1949–1967* (New Haven, Conn.: Yale University Press, 1978), 21 note 9.

72. Gad C. Gilbar, "The Economy of Nablus and the Hashemites: The Early Years, 1949–56," *Middle Eastern Studies* 25(January 1989), 52.

73. Abidi, *Jordan: A Political Study*, 199.

74. 'Amman Chancery to Eastern Department, 27 August 1951, FO 371/91789, PRO.

75. Musrey, *Arab Common Market*, 34–35.

76. Ibid., 71–72; Aruri, *Jordan*, 64.

77. Musrey, *Arab Common Market*, 59–60.

78. Raphael Patai, *The Kingdom of Jordan* (Princeton: Princeton University Press, 1958), 106.

79. Musrey, *Arab Common Market*, 83–87.

80. James Baster, "The Economic Problems of Jordan," *International Affairs* (January 1955).

81. Abidi, *Jordan: A Political Study*, 102 note 44.

82. Kingston, "Breaking the Patterns," 190.

83. Ibid., 196–197.

84. Ibid., 198–200.

85. Ibid., 188.

86. Ibid., 200.

87. Mudhaffar Husain Jamil, *Siyassah al-'Iraq al-Tijariyyah* (Cairo: Matba'ah al-Nahdah, 1949), 540–541.

88. Muhammad Salman Hasan, *al-Tatawwur al-Iqtisadi fil-'Iraq* (Beirut: al-Maktabah al-'Asriyyah, 1965), 289.

89. Joseph Sassoon, *Economic Policy in Iraq 1932–1950* (London: Frank Cass, 1987), 204; *Report by His Majesty's Government . . . on the Administration of 'Iraq for the Period January to October, 1932* (London: His Majesty's Stationery Office, 1933), 503.

90. Sassoon, *Economic Policy*, 195; *Report by His Majesty's Government*, 503.

91. Charles Tripp, *A History of Iraq*, new edition (Cambridge: Cambridge University Press, 2002), 114; Phebe Marr, *The Modern History of Iraq*, second edition (Boulder, Colo.: Westview, 2004), 63; Hanna Batatu, *The Old Social Classes and the Revolutionary Movements of Iraq* (Princeton: Princeton University Press, 1978), 299–300. Greater detail can be found in 'Abd al-Amir al-Akam, *Tarikh Hizb al-Istiqlal al-'Iraqi 1946–1958* (Baghdad: Wizarah al-Thaqafah wal-I'lam, 1980).

92. Batatu, *Old Social Classes*, 306.

93. Marr, *Modern History of Iraq*, 63; Batatu, *Old Social Classes*, 305. See also Fadil Husain, *Tarikh al-Hizb al-Watani al-Dimuqrati* (Baghdad: Matba'ah al-Sha'b, 1963).

94. Hadi Husain 'Ulaiwi, *al-Ahzab al-Siyassiyyah fil-'Iraq* (Beirut: Riad el-Rayyes, 2001), 119–121.

95. Daniel Silberfarb, "Britain and Iraqi Barley during the Second World War," *Middle Eastern Studies* 31(July 1995), 526.

96. Sassoon, *Economic Policy*, 139.

97. Ribhi Abu El-Haj, "Capital Formation in Iraq, 1922–1957," *Economic Development and Cultural Change* 9(1961), 611–612.

98. International Bank for Reconstruction and Development, *The Economic Development of Iraq* (Baltimore: Johns Hopkins University Press, 1952), 2; Doris Goodrich Adams, *Iraq's People and Resources* (Berkeley: University of California Press, 1958), 100–101.

99. Kathleen M. Langley, *The Industrialization of Iraq* (Cambridge, Mass.: Harvard University Press, 1967), 58–59.

100. Ibid., 74.

101. Ibid., 85–86.

102. Abdul Ghani Al Dalli, "Problems of Industrial Enterprise in Iraq," *Middle East Economic Papers 1954* (Beirut: Economic Research Institute of the American University of Beirut, 1954), 44.

103. Ibid., 89–90.

104. See, for example, "Basra Consulate-General Monthly Summary March 1951," in Robert L. Jarman, ed. *Political Diaries of the Arab World: Iraq*, vol. 7: 1948–1958 (London: Archive Editions, 1998), 181.

105. Troutbeck to Eden, 23 January 1953, in ibid., 250–254.

106. Norman Burns and Allen D. Edwards, "Foreign Trade," in S. Himadeh, ed. *Economic Organization of Syria* (Beirut: American University of Beirut Press, 1936), 237.

107. Ibid., 238–239.

108. Ibid., 236.

109. Doreen Warriner, *Land Reform and Development in the Middle East* (London: Oxford University Press, 1962), 73; International Bank for Reconstruction and Development, *The Economic Development of Syria* (Baltimore: Johns Hopkins University Press, 1955), 323.

110. Alfred G. Musrey, *An Arab Common Market* (New York: Praeger, 1969), 35.

111. Warriner, *Land Reform*, 74.

112. Ibid., 76.

113. Ibid., 77.

114. *al-Majmu'ah al-Iqtisadiyyah al-Sanawiyyah li Ghurfah Tijarah Halab 1947* (Aleppo: Aleppo Chamber of Commerce, 1947), 9–10.

115. "Review of the Lebanese and Syrian Press," 15 May 1943, 890d.9111/198, RG 59, USNA.

116. Musrey, *Arab Common Market*, 36.

117. Eugen Wirth, *Syrien: Eine Geographische Landeskunde* (Darmstadt: Wissenschaftliche Buchgesellschaft, 1971), 316.

118. Geoffrey D. Schad, "Class and Nationalism during the Mandate: The Development of the Aleppine Industrial Bourgeoisie, 1920–1946," paper presented

to the annual convention of the Middle East Studies Association, Chicago, 1998; "Working Conditions in Handicrafts and Modern Industry in Syria," *International Labour Review* 39(1934).

119. *al-Majmu'ah al-Iqtisadiyyah*, 9–10.

120. Wadsworth to Merriam, 10 May 1944, 890e.659/1, RG 59, USNA.

121. Edmund Y. Asfour, *Syria: Development and Monetary Policy* (Cambridge, Mass.: Harvard University Press, 1967), 30–31.

122. Ibid., 31.

123. Engert to Secretary of State, 20 August 1941, 890d.00/873, RG 59, USNA.

124. "Review of the Lebanese and Syrian Press," 15 May 1943, 890d.9111/198, RG 59, USNA.

125. "Review of the Lebanese and Syrian Press," 29 May 1943, 890d.9111/199, RG 59, USNA.

126. "Review of the Syrian Press," 12 July 1943, 890d.9111/203, RG 59, USNA.

127. Umar F. Abd-Allah, *The Islamic Struggle in Syria* (Berkeley: Mizan, 1983), 92–94.

128. Ishak Musa Husaini, *The Moslem Brethren* (Beirut: Khayats, 1956), 76.

129. James C. Drewry, *An Analysis of the 1949 Coups d'Etat in Syria in Light of Fertile Crescent Unity*, unpublished MA thesis, American University of Beirut, 1960, 155.

130. Batatu, *Old Social Classes*, 728.

131. Gordon H. Torrey, *Syrian Politics and the Military 1945–1958* (Columbus: Ohio State University Press, 1964), 157; Majid Khadduri, "The Scheme of Fertile Crescent Unity," in Richard N. Frye, ed. *The Near East and the Great Powers* (Cambridge, Mass.: Harvard University Press, 1951), 163.

132. Khadduri, "Fertile Crescent Unity," 163.

133. Torrey, *Syrian Politics*, 158 note 31.

134. Ibid., 60.

135. Khoury, *Syria*, 606–607.

136. Farrell to Secretary of State, 7 August 1943, 890d.00/969, RG 59, USNA.

137. Khoury, *Syria*, 607.

138. "The Greater Syria Movement," 10 January 1948, FO 371/61497, PRO.

139. Noureddine Bouchair, *The Merchant and Moneylending Class of Syria under the French Mandate, 1920–1946*, unpublished Ph.D. dissertation, Georgetown University, 1986, 136–137.

140. Khoury, *Syria*, 601.

141. Farrell to Secretary of State, 7 July 1943, 890d.00/961, RG 59, USNA.

142. "Greater Syria Movement," 10 January 1948, FO 371/61497, PRO.

143. Ibid.

144. Engert to Secretary of State, 20 August 1941, 890d.00/873, RG 59, USNA.

145. Longrigg, *Syria and Lebanon*, 337.

146. Ibid., 336 note 1.

147. Wasserman to McGuire, 29 September 1944, 890d.24/9-2944, RG 59, USNA.

148. Steven Heydemann, *Authoritarianism in Syria: Institutions and Social Conflict 1946–1970* (Ithaca, N.Y.: Cornell University Press, 1999), 70–71.

149. Ronald Rogowski, *Commerce and Coalitions* (Princeton: Princeton University Press, 1989).

CHAPTER FOUR

1. Fred H. Lawson, "Domestic Conflict and Foreign Policy: The Contribution of Some Undeservedly Neglected Historical Studies," *Review of International Studies* 11(October 1985); Peter Gourevitch, *Politics in Hard Times* (Ithaca, N.Y.: Cornell University Press, 1986); Jack Snyder, *Myths of Empire: Domestic Politics and International Ambition* (Ithaca, N.Y.: Cornell University Press, 1991); Charles A. Kupchan, *The Vulnerability of Empire* (Ithaca, N.Y.: Cornell University Press, 1994).

2. Robert L. Tignor, *State, Private Property, and Economic Change in Egypt, 1918–1952* (Princeton: Princeton University Press, 1984), 33.

3. Samir Radwan, *Capital Formation in Egyptian Industry and Agriculture 1882–1967* (London: Ithaca Press, 1974), 102.

4. Pierre Arminjon, *La situation économique et financière de l'Egypte* (Paris: Librairie Generale de Droit et de Jurisprudence, 1911), 247–249. See also C. Artaud, "L'Industrie sucriere et la culture de la canne a sucre en Egypte," *L'Egypte contemporaine* 1(1910).

5. As reported by John Chalcraft, *The Striking Cabbies of Cairo and Other Stories*, unpublished Ph.D. dissertation, New York University, 2001, 187.

6. Roger Owen, "The Study of Middle Eastern Industrial History: Notes on the Interrelationship between Factories and Small-Scale Manufacturing with Special References to Lebanese Silk and Egyptian Sugar, 1900–1930," *International Journal of Middle East Studies* 16(November 1984), 480.

7. Tignor, *State, Private Property, and Economic Change*, 53.

8. *Egyptian Gazette*, 17 January 1918.

9. Ibid., 26 and 28 January 1918.

10. Ibid., 4 February 1918. See also ibid., 7 February 1918.

11. Ibid., 14 and 16 February 1918.

12. Tignor, *State, Private Property, and Economic Change*, 51.

13. Chalcraft, *Striking Cabbies of Cairo*, 250 note 21.

14. Ibid., 285.

15. Ibid., 277.

16. Ibid., 294.

17. Ibid., 299–300.

18. Tignor, *State, Private Property, and Economic Change*, 56–57.

19. P. G. Elgood, *Egypt and the Army* (London: Oxford University Press, 1924, 333–334.

20. *Egyptian Gazette*, 5 February 1919.

21. Ibid., 4 February 1919.

22. Tignor, *State, Private Property, and Economic Change*, 51–54.

23. Chalcraft, *Striking Cabbies of Cairo*, 202.

24. Ibid., 200.

25. Elgood, *Egypt and the Army*, 324 note 1.

26. Robert L. Tignor, "The Egyptian Revolution of 1919: New Directions in the Egyptian Economy," *Middle Eastern Studies* 12(October 1976), 61–62.

27. See *Egyptian Gazette*, 25 and 28 April 1919.

28. Marius Deeb, *Party Politics in Egypt: The Wafd and Its Rivals 1919–1939* (London: Ithaca Press, 1979), 33.

29. Ibid.

30. Rauf ʿAbbas Hamid, *al-Harakah al-ʿUmmaliyyah fi Misr 1899–1952* (Cairo: Dar al-Katib al-ʿArabi lil-Tabaʿah wal-Nashr, 1967); Amin ʿIzz al-Din, *Tarikh al-Tabaqah al-ʿAmilah al-Misriyyah munthu Nashatiha hatta Thawrah 1919* (Cairo: Dar al-Katib al-ʿArabi lil-Tabaʿah wal-Nashr, 1967), chap. 2; Zachary Lockman, "'Worker' and 'Working Class' in pre-1914 Egypt: A Rereading," in Zachary Lockman, ed. *Workers and Working Classes in the Middle East* (Albany: State University of New York Press, 1994), 88–90; Joel Beinin and Zachary Lockman, *Workers on the Nile* (Princeton: Princeton University Press, 1987), chap. 3.

31. Beinin and Lockman, *Workers on the Nile*, 63–64 and 74–75.

32. Ibid., 79.

33. Ibid., 85.

34. *Egyptian Gazette*, 6 February 1918.

35. Beinin and Lockman, *Workers on the Nile*, 91.

36. Zachary Lockman, "The Social Roots of Nationalism: Workers and the National Movement in Egypt, 1908–19," *Middle Eastern Studies* 24(October 1988), 455.

37. Tuck to Secretary of State, 28 April 1919, 883.00/151, Record Group (RG) 59, United States National Archives (USNA), College Park.

38. Gary to Secretary of State, 11 November 1919, 883.504/1, RG 59, USNA.

39. *Egyptian Gazette*, 15 and 26 May 1919.

40. Beinin and Lockman, *Workers on the Nile*, 111.

41. Ibid., 126.

42. Gary to Secretary of State, 1 September 1919, 883.00/195, RG 59, USNA.

43. Cairo Agency to Secretary of State, 28 November 1919, 883.00/233, RG 59, USNA.

44. De Bilkin to Secretary of State, 1 March 1920, 883.00/270, RG 59, USNA.

45. Beinin and Lockman, *Workers on the Nile*, 116; Marius Deeb, "Labour and Politics in Egypt, 1919–1939," *International Journal of Middle East Studies* 10(May 1979), 187.

46. Younan Labib Rizk, "The Development of the Ministerial System in Egypt: 1878–1923," in Nelly Hanna, ed. *The State and its Servants* (Cairo: American University in Cairo Press, 1995), 93.

47. Tignor, "Egyptian Revolution of 1919," 59–60 and 64.

48. Tignor, *State, Private Property and Economic Change*, 92–94.

49. ʻAbd al-Rahman al-Rafiʻi, *Muhammad Farid* (Cairo: Maktabah al-Nahdah al-Misriyyah, 1961), 91.

50. Zaheer Masood Quraishi, *Liberal Nationalism in Egypt* (Allahabad: Kitab Mahal, 1967), 27.

51. Mahmud Kamil, *Ashhar al-Qadaya al-Misriyyah* (Cairo: Dar al-Maʻarif, 1946), 130. See also Jacob M. Landau, "Prolegomena to a Study of Secret Societies in Modern Egypt," *Middle Eastern Studies* 1(January 1965).

52. Quraishi, *Liberal Nationalism in Egypt*, 38; L. N. Vatolina, *Sovremennii Yegipet* (Moscow: USSR Academy of Sciences, 1949), 71.

53. Mahmud Y. Zayid, "Nashat Hizb al-Wafd al-Misri, 1918–1924," *al-Abhath* no. 16 (June 1962); Louis J. Cantori, *The Organizational Basis of an Elite Political Party: The Egyptian Wafd*, unpublished Ph.D. dissertation, University of Chicago, 1966, 152–163; Erez Manela, "The Wilsonian Moment and the Rise of Anticolonial Nationalism: The Case of Egypt," *Diplomacy and Statecraft* 12(December 2001).

54. Mahmud Y. Zayid, *Egypt's Struggle for Independence* (Beirut: Khayats, 1965), 80.

55. Muhammad Husain Haikal, *Mudhakkirat fi al-Siyassah al-Misriyyah* (Cairo: Maktabah al-Nahdah al-Misriyyah, 1951), 1: 82.

56. ʻAbd al-Rahman al-Rafiʻi, *Thawrah Sanah 1919* (Cairo: Maktabah al-Nahdah al-Misriyyah, 1955), 1: 101–104; P. G. Elgood, *The Transit of Egypt* (London: Edward Arnold, 1928), 222–223; Quraishi, *Liberal Nationalism in Egypt*, 47; Cantori, *Organizational Basis*, 176.

57. Zayid, *Egypt's Struggle for Independence*, 80.

58. al-Rafiʻi, *Muhammad Farid*, 94.

59. Ibid., 95.

60. Mustapha Kraeim, *Nationalisme et syndicalisme en Tunisie 1918–1929* (Tunis: UGTT, 1976), 54–55; Smith to Sec., 12 April 1927, 851s.6377/3, RG 57, USNA. On the parallel trend for zinc, see Smith to Sec., 10 September 1925, 851s.6355, RG 57, USNA.

61. Eqbal Ahmad and Stuart Schaar, "M'hamed Ali: Tunisian Labor Organizer," in Edmund Burke III, ed. *Struggle and Survival in the Modern Middle East* (Berkeley: University of California Press, 1993), 199.

62. Kraeim, *Nationalisme et syndicalisme*, 389–390.

63. Ibid., 86.

64. Ibid., 390–392; Claude Liauzu, "Mouvement ouvrier, mouvement national, mouvements sociaux dans la Tunisie Coloniale," *Pluriel* no. 15 (1978), 75.

65. Kraeim, *Nationalisme et syndicalisme*, 73–74.

66. Ibid., 77.

67. Daniel Goldstein, *Libération ou annexion* (Tunis: Maison tunisienne de l'édition, 1978), 61.

68. Goldstein, *Libération*, 219.

69. Ibid., 126.

70. Ibid., 218.

71. Ibid., 228; Eqbal Ahmad, *Politics and Labor in Tunisia*, unpublished Ph.D. dissertation, Princeton University, 1967, 55.

72. Goldstein, *Libération*, 229; Jacques Berque, *French North Africa: The Maghrib Between Two World Wars* (New York: Praeger, 1967), 24.

73. Ahmad, *Politics and Labor in Tunisia*, 54.

74. Mustapha Kraiem, *Le Parti Communiste Tunisien pendant la période coloniale* (Tunis: Institut Supérieur d'Histoire du Mouvement National, 1997), chap. 2.

75. Liauzu, "Mouvement ouvrier," 81–82; Ahmad, *Politics and Labor in Tunisia*, 61; Abdelbaki Hermassi, *Mouvement ouvrier en société coloniale la Tunisie entre les deux guerres*, unpublished Ph.D. dissertation, Ecole Pratique des Hautes Etudes, Paris, 1966, 28–36.

76. Ahmad, *Politics and Labor in Tunisia*, 62.

77. Smith to Sec., 10 September 1925, 851s.6355, RG 57, USNA.

78. Ahmad, *Politics and Labor in Tunisia*, 62–63.

79. Kraeim, *Nationalisme et syndicalisme*, 543.

80. Ibid., 579–580.

81. Ibid., 582.

82. Ahmad, *Politics and Labor in Tunisia*, 64–65; Abdesslem Ben Hamida, *Le syndicalisme tunisien de la deuxième guerre mondiale à l'autonomie interne* (Tunis: Publications de l'Université de Tunis, 1989), 76–77.

83. M. Kraiem, "La question du droit syndical en Tunisie (1882–1932)," *Revue d'histoire maghrébine* no. 3 (January 1975), 35.

84. Ibid., 39.

85. Ibid., 36–37.

86. Kraeim, *Nationalisme et syndicalisme*, 601.

87. Ibid., 600.

88. Ibid., 602.

89. *Tunis socialiste*, 15 December 1924.

90. Kraeim, *Nationalisme et syndicalisme*, 602.

91. "Review of the Press," n.d. [fall 1924], Box 1647, RG 165, USNA.

92. Berque, *French North Africa*, 82.

93. "Monthly Situation Report on Transjordan for the Month of June 1949," 12 June 1949, Foreign Office (FO) 371/75273, Public Record Office (PRO), Kew.

94. "The Jordan Economic Report, 1 July–31 December 1951," FO 371/98871, PRO.

95. Shaul Mishal, *West Bank/East Bank: The Palestinians in Jordan, 1949–1967* (New Haven, Conn.: Yale University Press, 1978), 21; Gad Gilbar, "The Economy of Nablus and the Hashemites: The Early Years, 1949–56," *Middle Eastern Studies* 25(January 1989), 52.

96. Gilbar, "Economy of Nablus," 53.

97. "Weekly Summary of the Jordanian Press," n.d. [July 1951], 16/942, RG 226, USNA.

98. Aqil H. H. Abidi, *Jordan: A Political Study 1948–1957* (Bombay: Asia Publishing House, 1965), 102 note 44.

99. Marion Boulby, *The Muslim Brotherhood and the Kings of Jordan 1945–1993* (Atlanta: Scholars Press, 1999), 53.

100. "Monthly Situation Report on Transjordan for the Month of April 1948," 4 May 1948, FO 371/68845, PRO.

101. "Monthly Situation Report on Transjordan for the Month of May 1948," 2 June 1948, FO 371/68845, PRO.

102. "Jordan: Annual Review for 1950," 13 January 1951, FO 371/98857, PRO; Amnon Cohen, *Political Parties in the West Bank under the Jordanian Regime, 1949–1967* (Ithaca, N.Y.: Cornell University Press, 1982), 28.

103. Cohen, *Political Parties*, 29.

104. Ibid., 30.

105. Ibid., 31.

106. Ibid., 32–33.

107. Ibid., 69.

108. Ibid., 100; Paul W. T. Kingston, "Breaking the Patterns of Mandate: Economic Nationalism and State Formation in Jordan, 1951–57," in Rogan and Tell, eds. *Village, Steppe and State*, 195.

109. "Resumé of Statement of Policy of Tewfiq Pasha Abul Huda to Parliament on September 18th, 1951," FO 371/91789, PRO.

110. Ibid.

111. "Record of Conversation with Tewfiq Abul Huda," 8 October 1952, FO 816/177, PRO.

112. "Monthly Situation Report for the Jordan for the Month of November 1949," FO 371/75273, PRO; John B. Glubb, *A Soldier with the Arabs* (London: Hodder and Stoughton, 1957), 289.

113. Glubb, *Soldier with the Arabs*, 290.

114. Avi Plascov, *The Palestinian Refugees in Jordan 1948–1957* (London: Frank Cass, 1981), 94.

115. Cohen, *Political Parties*, 163.

116. P. J. Vatikiotis, *Politics and the Military in Jordan* (New York: Praeger, 1967), 80.

117. "Jordan: Annual Review for 1949," FO 371/82702, PRO.

118. "Jordan: Annual Review for 1950," FO 371/91788, PRO.

119. Carl Iversen, *A Report on Monetary Policy in Iraq* (Baghdad: National Bank of Iraq, 1954), 73–74.

120. Hanna Batatu, *The Old Social Classes and the Revolutionary Movements of Iraq* (Princeton: Princeton University Press, 1978), 264.

121. Samira Haj, *The Making of Iraq* (Albany: State University of New York Press, 1997), 51–52.

122. Batatu, *Old Social Classes*, 312–318.

123. Ibid., 305.

124. Ibid., 306. See also Ja'far 'Abbas Humaidi, *al-Tatawwurat al-Siyassiyyah fil-'Iraq 1941–1953* (al-Najaf: Matba'ah al-Nu'man, 1976), 194–210.

125. Ibid., 586–587; "Basra Consulate-General Monthly Summary November 1951," in Robert L. Jarman, ed. *Political Diaries of the Arab World: Iraq*, vol. 7: 1948–1958 (London: Archive Editions, 1998), 218.

126. Batatu, *Old Social Classes*, 551; Khaled Salih, *State-Making, Nation-Building and the Military: Iraq, 1941–1958* (Goteborg: Goteborg University, 1996), 113–115.

127. Majid Khadduri, *Independent Iraq* (London: Oxford University Press, 1951), 272.

128. Batatu, *Old Social Classes*, 565.

129. Mahmud Shabib, *Wathbah fi al-'Iraq wa Suqut Salih al-Jabr* (Baghdad: Dar al-Thaqafah, 1988), 8.

130. Salih, *State-Making, Nation-Building and the Military*, 115–117.

131. Labor Adviser to Embassy, 14 May 1948, FO 371/68479, PRO.

132. Matthew Elliot, "*Independent Iraq*" (London: Tauris Academic, 1996), 81.

133. Daniel Silverfarb, *The Twilight of British Ascendancy in the Middle East* (New York: St. Martin's), 191.

134. Ibid., 194.

135. Ibid., 197.

136. Beeley to Cairo, 22 March 1951, FO 371/91674, PRO; Troutbeck to Eden, 18 September 1952, FO 371/91676, PRO; Phebe Marr, *The Modern History of Iraq* (Boulder, Colo.: Westview, 1985), 111.

137. Batatu, *Old Social Classes*, 664.

138. Ibid., 476.

139. Ibid., 668; Salih, *State-Making, Nation-Building and the Military*, 119; "Disturbances in Bagdad," 3 December 1952, FO 371/98736, PRO.

140. Joseph D. Coppock, *Foreign Trade of the Middle East: Instability and Growth, 1946–1962* (Beirut: American University of Beirut Press, 1966), 59; Alfred Michaelis, "Economic Recovery and Development of Iraq," *Middle Eastern Affairs* 3(April 1952), 102; Iversen, *Report on Monetary Policy*, 74.

141. U. Zaher, "The Opposition," in CARDRI, *Saddam's Iraq* (London: Zed, 1986), 169; Charles Tripp, *A History of Iraq*, revised edition (Cambridge: Cambridge University Press, 2002), 130–131; Batatu, *Old Social Classes*, 666–667.

142. Marr, *Modern History of Iraq*, 112.

143. "Disturbances in Bagdad," 5.

144. Troutbeck to Eden, 23 January 1953, in Jarman, ed. *Political Diaries*, 253–254.

145. Ibid., 94.

146. Elliot, "*Independent Iraq*," 103–104.

147. Bromley to Eden, 21 March 1953, FO 371/104665, PRO; Troutbeck to Churchill, 22 June 1953, FO 371/104665, PRO.

148. Michael Eppel, "The Fadhil al-Jamali Government in Iraq, 1953–54," *Journal of Contemporary History* 34(July 1999), 427–428; Guzine A. K. Rasheed, "Devel-

opment of Agricultural Land Taxation in Modern Iraq," *Bulletin of the School of Oriental and African Studies* 25(1962), 267; Troutbeck to Eden, 11 January 1954, in Jarman, ed. *Political Diaries*, 281–282.

149. Ferhang Jalal, *The Role of Government in the Industrialization of Iraq 1950–1965* (London: Frank Cass, 1972),17; Tripp, *History of Iraq*, 138.

150. Jalal, *Role of Government*, 43.

151. Ibid., 63.

152. Stephen Hemsley Longrigg and Frank Stoakes, *Iraq* (London: Benn, 1958), 78.

153. Tripp, *History of Iraq*, 135.

154. Elliot, "*Independent Iraq*," 110.

155. See Baqir Muhammad Jawwad al-Zujaji, *al-Ruwaya al-ʿIraqiyyah wa Qadayah al-Rif* (Baghdad: Dar al-Rashid lil-Nashr, 1983), 13.

156. Marion Farouk-Sluglett and Peter Sluglett, "The Social Classes and the Origins of the Revolution," in Robert A. Fernea and Wm. Roger Louis, eds. *The Iraqi Revolution of 1958: The Old Social Classes Revisited* (London: I. B. Tauris, 1991), 126–127.

157. Tripp, *History of Iraq*, 130; Batatu, *Old Social Classes*, 671–672.

158. Marr, *Modern History of Iraq*, 112.

159. Eppel, "The Fadhil al-Jamali Government," 436.

160. Philip S. Khoury, *Syria and the French Mandate* (Princeton: Princeton University Press, 1987), chap. 22.

161. Ibid., 577–578.

162. Ibid., 578; Noureddine Bouchair, *The Merchant and Moneylending Class of Syria under the French Mandate, 1920–1946*, unpublished Ph.D. dissertation, Georgetown University, 1986, 140.

163. Ellen Lust-Okar, "The Emergence of Opposition Movements: Syrian Nationalists' Activities in 1941," unpublished ms., 20.

164. Engert to Secretary of State, 7 February 1941, 890d.00/809, RG 59, USNA.

165. Elisabeth Longuenesse, "Labor in Syria," in Ellis Goldberg, ed. *The Social History of Labor in the Middle East* (Boulder, Colo.: Westview, 1996), 106.

166. Khoury, *Syria*, 590–591; Engert to Secretary of State, 24 April 1941, 890d.00/822, RG 59, USNA; *New York Times*, 26 March 1941.

167. Khoury, *Syria*, 591; Aviel Roshwald, *Estranged Bedfellows: Britain and France in the Middle East during the Second World War* (New York: Oxford University Press, 1990), 54.

168. *New York Times*, 30 March 1941.

169. "Disturbances in Syria," 28 March 1941, 890d.00/814, RG 59, USNA.

170. Lust-Okar, "Opposition Movements," 38.

171. *New York Times*, 28 April 1941.

172. Engert to Secretary of State, 24 April 1941, 890d.00/822, RG 59, USNA.

173. Khoury, *Syria*, 591; Naval Intelligence Division, *Syria* (London: Oxford University Press, 1943), 151 and 149.

174. *New York Times*, 6 March 1941.

175. A. B. Gaunson, *The Anglo-French Clash in Lebanon and Syria, 1940–45* (New York: St. Martin's, 1987), 28.

176. Lust-Okar, "Opposition Movements," 38.

177. Hourani, *Syria and Lebanon*, 236.

178. Engert to Secretary of State, 31 October 1941, 890d.00/871, RG 59, USNA.

179. Engert to Secretary of State, 29 September 1941, 890d.00/886, RG 59, USNA.

180. Ibid.

181. Quoted in ibid.

182. Khoury, *Syria*, 595; Spears Mission Beirut to Commander-in-Chief Middle East, 25 February 1942, FO 371/31471, PRO.

183. Cairo to Foreign Office, 27 February 1942, FO 371/31471, PRO.

184. "Quarterly Intelligence Report," April–June 1942, FO 406/80, PRO.

185. "Weekly Political Summary," 30 April 1942, FO 371/31472, PRO.

186. Engert to Secretary of State, 27 May 1942, 890d.50/31, RG 59, USNA.

187. Gwynn to Secretary of State, 24 October 1942, 890d.5123/8, RG 59, USNA.

188. A. Aziz Allouni, "The Labor Movement in Syria," *Middle East Journal* 13(Winter 1959), 66.

189. Ibid.

190. "Weekly Political Summary," 11 June 1942, FO 371/31473, PRO; "Quarterly Intelligence Report," July–September 1942, FO 406/80, PRO. On women's participation in these demonstrations, see Elizabeth Thompson, *Colonial Citizens: Republican Rights, Paternal Privilege and Gender in French Syria and Lebanon* (New York: Columbia University Press, 2000), 233–234.

191. "Weekly Political Summary," 15 July 1942, Special Operations Executive (HS) 3/212, PRO.

192. "Weekly Political Summary," 30 July 1942, HS 3/212, PRO.

193. "Quarterly Intelligence Report," July–September 1942, FO 406/80, PRO.

194. "Weekly Political Summary," 5 August 1942, FO 371/31474, PRO.

195. "Weekly Political Summary," 18 September 1942, HS 3/212, PRO; "Weekly Political Summary," 23 November 1942, HS 3/212, PRO; "Weekly Political Summary," 7 October 1942, FO 371/31478, PRO.

196. "Quarterly Intelligence Report," October–December 1942, FO 406/80, PRO.

197. Wadsworth to Secretary of State, 30 December 1942, 890d.00/928, RG 59, USNA; "Weekly Political Summary," 30 December 1942, FO 371/35174, PRO.

198. Wadsworth to Secretary of State, 4 January 1942 [sic: 1943], 890d.00/929, RG 59, USNA.

199. "Weekly Political Summary," 6 January 1943, FO 371/35174, PRO.

200. "Weekly Political Summary," 20 January 1943, FO 371/35174, PRO.

201. "Review of the Lebanese and Syrian Press," 20 February 1943,

890d.9111/191, RG 59, USNA; "Weekly Political Summary," 10 February 1943, HS 3/212, PRO; Beirut to Cairo, 10 February 1943, FO 371/35174, PRO; Khoury, *Syria*, 599.

202. "Review of the Lebanese and Syrian Press," 6 March 1943, 890d.9111/193, RG 59, USNA; "Weekly Political Summary," 17 February 1943, HS 3/212, PRO; "Weekly Political Summary," 3 March 1943, HS 3/212, PRO.

203. Wadsworth to Secretary of State, 24 March 1943, 890d.00/949, RG 59, USNA; Khoury, *Syria*, 600.

204. "Review of the Lebanese and Syrian Press," 15 May 1943, 890d.9111/198, RG 59, USNA.

205. "Review of the Lebanese and Syrian Press," 20 February 1943, 890d.9111/191, RG 59, USNA.

206. "Review of the Lebanese and Syrian Press," 1 May 1943, 890d.9111/197, RG 59, USNA; "Review of the Lebanese and Syrian Press," 15 May 1943, 890d.9111/198, RG 59, USNA.

207. "Review of the Lebanese and Syrian Press," 15 May 1943, 890d.9111/198, RG 59, USNA.

208. "New Measures to Check Speculation," 16 July 1943, 890d.51/80, RG 59, USNA.

209. "Review of the Lebanese and Syrian Press," 12 June 1943, 890d.9111/200, RG 59, USNA; "Weekly Political Summary," 9 August 1943, FO 371/35210, PRO.

210. Khoury, *Syria*, 599.

211. Farrell to Secretary of State, 7 July 1943, 890d.00/961, RG 59, USNA; "Review of the Lebanese and Syrian Press," 29 May 1943, 890d.9111/199, RG 59, USNA; Khoury, *Syria*, 601.

212. Khoury, *Syria*, 601–602.

213. Farrell to Secretary of State, 7 August 1943, 890d.00/969, RG 59, USNA.

214. Farrell to Secretary of State, 7 July 1943, 890d.00/961, RG 59, USNA.

215. Nacklie E. Bou-Nacklie, *Les Troupes Speciales du Levant*, unpublished Ph.D. dissertation, University of Utah, 1989, 354–355.

216. Roshwald, *Estranged Bedfellows*, 170.

217. Joshua M. Landis, *Nationalism and the Politics of Za'ama*, unpublished Ph.D. dissertation, Princeton University, 1997, 141.

218. Albert K. Hourani, *Syria and Lebanon* (London: Oxford University Press, 1946), 289; Salma Mardam Bey, *Syria's Quest for Independence* (Reading, England: Ithaca Press, 1994), 116.

219. Hourani, *Syria and Lebanon*, 292.

220. "The Opposition in Homs," 8 January 1944, 16/695, RG 226, USNA.

221. "Communists and the Hama Incident," 20 February 1944, 16/857, RG 226, USNA.

222. "Monthly Political Review—Syria," February–April 1944, 890d.00/982, RG 59, USNA.

223. Satterthwaite to Secretary of State, 23 May 1944, 890d.00/983, RG 59,

USNA; "Monthly Political Review—Syria," 25 May 1944, 890d.00/984, RG 59, USNA; Thompson, *Colonial Citizens*, 261–264.

224. "Causes and Effects of the Riots in Damascus on 20 May," 26 May 1944, 16/913, RG 226, USNA.

225. "Monthly Political Review—Syria," November 1944, 890d.00/12–244, RG 59, USNA; "Weekly Political Summary," 14 November 1944, FO 371/40306, PRO.

226. K. J. Holsti, *Taming the Sovereigns: Institutional Change in International Politics* (Cambridge: Cambridge University Press, 2004), 85.

CONCLUSION

1. On international norms, see Jeffrey W. Legro, "Which Norms Matter?" *International Organization* 51(Winter 1997); Martha Finnemore and Kathryn Sikkink, "International Norm Dynamics and Political Change," *International Organization* 52(Autumn 1998); Andrew Hurrell, "Norms and Ethics in International Relations," in Walter Carlsnaes, Thomas Risse, and Beth A. Simmons, eds. *Handbook of International Relations* (London: Sage, 2002).

2. Edward Keene, *Beyond the Anarchical Society* (Cambridge: Cambridge University Press, 2002), 126–135; Elie Kedourie, *England and the Middle East* (London: Bowes and Bowes, 1956); Elizabeth Monroe, *Britain's Moment in the Middle East 1914–71* (London: Chatto and Windus, 1981); Christopher M. Andrew and A. S. Kanya-Forstner, *The Climax of French Imperial Expansion 1914–1924* (Stanford: Stanford University Press, 1981); William I. Shorrock, *French Imperialism in the Middle East* (Madison: University of Wisconsin Press, 1976).

3. Hendrik Spruyt, "Institutional Selection in International Relations: State Anarchy as Order," *International Organization* 48(Autumn 1994), 555.

4. Stephen D. Krasner, "Explaining Variation: Defaults, Coercion, Commitments," in Stephen D. Krasner, ed. *Problematic Sovereignty* (New York: Columbia University Press, 2001), 328. See also Alexander Wendt, "Anarchy Is What States Make of It," *International Organization* 46(Spring 1992), 414.

5. Fouad Ajami, "The End of Pan-Arabism," in Tawfic E. Farah, ed. *Pan-Arabism and Arab Nationalism* (Boulder, Colo.: Westview, 1987), 106.

6. Michael Barnett, *Dialogues in Arab Politics* (New York: Columbia University Press, 1998), 32.

7. Raymond Hinnebusch, *The International Politics of the Middle East* (Manchester: Manchester University Press, 2003), 64.

8. Tawfig Y. Hasou, *The Struggle for the Arab World* (London: KPI, 1985), 54.

9. Michael Doran, *Pan-Arabism Before Nasser* (New York: Oxford University Press, 1999), 195.

10. Adeed Dawisha, *Arab Nationalism in the Twentieth Century* (Princeton: Princeton University Press, 2003), 152.

11. Malcolm H. Kerr, *The Arab Cold War* (London: Oxford University Press, 1971), 20.

12. Quoted in Elie Podeh, "To Unite or Not to Unite—That is Not the Question," *Middle Eastern Studies* 39(January 2003), 166.

13. Elie Podeh, *The Decline of Arab Unity* (Brighton: Sussex Academic Press, 1999), 26.

14. Salah al-Din Bitar, *al-Siyassah al-'Arabiyyah bain al-Mabda' wal-Tatbiq* (Beirut: Dar al-Tali'ah, 1960), 43–48.

15. Philip K. Hitti, "The Possibility of Union among the Arab States," *The American Historical Review* 48(July 1943), 729.

16. Podeh, *Decline of Arab Unity*, 31; Nizar 'Urabi, *Matha Yajri fi Suriya?* (Damascus: Manshurat Dar al-Fikr, 1962); Salah Nasr, *'Abd al-Nasir wa Tajrubah al-Wahdah* (Cairo: al-Watan al-'Arabi, 1976); 'Awni Farsakh, *al-Wahdah fi al-Tajrubah* (Beirut: Dar al-Masirah, 1980).

17. Podeh, *Decline of Arab Unity*, 36; Mustapha Kamil al-Sayyid, "The Rise and Fall of the United Arab Republic," in Michael C. Hudson, ed. *Middle East Dilemma* (New York: Columbia University Press, 1999), 116; James Jankowski, *Nasser's Egypt, Arab Nationalism and the United Arab Republic* (Boulder, Colo.: Lynne Rienner, 2002), 101–103.

18. Podeh, *Decline of Arab Unity*, 44.

19. Ibid., 45.

20. al-Sayyid, "Rise and Fall of the United Arab Republic," 118.

21. Podeh, *Decline of Arab Unity*, 45.

22. Ibid., 46.

23. al-Sayyid, "Rise and Fall of the United Arab Republic," 118.

24. Jankowski, *Nasser's Egypt*, 163–164.

25. al-Sayyid, "Rise and Fall of the United Arab Republic," 124.

26. Hendrik Spruyt, *Ending Empire: Contested Sovereignty and Territorial Partition* (Ithaca, N.Y.: Cornell University Press, 2005), chap.1.

27. Ronald E. Robinson, "Non-European Foundations of European Imperialism," in Roger Owen and Bob Sutcliffe, eds. *Studies in the Theory of Imperialism* (London: Longman, 1972); John Gallagher, "Nationalisms and the Crisis of Empire, 1919–1922," *Modern Asian Studies* 15(1981); C. A. Bayly, *Imperial Meridien* (London: Longman, 1989).

28. Hendrik Spruyt, "The End of Empire and the Extension of the Westphalian System," *International Studies Review* 2(Summer 2000), 77–80.

29. David Strang, "Anomaly and Commonplace in European Political Expansion," *International Organization* 45(Spring 1991); Connie L. McNeely, *Constructing the Nation-State* (Westport, Conn.: Greenwood, 1995).

30. Spruyt, "End of Empire," 80.

31. Ibid., 86.

32. Ibid., 88.

33. Alexander Wendt, *Social Theory of International Politics* (Cambridge: Cambridge University Press, 1999), 338. See also Petr Drulak, "The Problem of Struc-

tural Change in Alexander Wendt's Social Theory of International Politics," *Journal of International Relations and Development* 4(December 2001).

34. Wendt, *Social Theory*, 341.

35. Ibid., 343–363.

36. Ibid., 364.

37. Ibid., 365–366.

38. Finnemore and Sikkink, "International Norm Dynamics," 901. See also Annika Bjorkdahl, "Norms in International Relations: Some Conceptual and Methodological Reflections," *Cambridge Review of International Affairs* 15(April 2002), 18–19.

39. Wendt, *Social Theory*, 364. See also Stephen D. Krasner, "Explaining Variation: Defaults, Coercion, Commitments," in Stephen D. Krasner, ed. *Problematic Sovereignty* (New York: Columbia University Press, 2001), 342; J. Samuel Barkin and Bruce Cronin, "The State and the Nation: Changing Norms and the Rules of Sovereignty in International Relations," *International Organization* 48(Winter 1994), 130; Gregory A. Raymond, "Problems and Prospects in the Study of International Norms," *Mershon International Studies Review* 41(November 1997), 232.

40. Wendt, *Social Theory*, 314.

41. Ibid., 338. See Hidemi Suganami, "Alexander Wendt and the English School," *Journal of International Relations and Development* 4(December 2001).

42. See Katalin Sarvary, "Devaluing Diplomacy? A Critique of Alexander Wendt's Conception of Progress and Politics," *Journal of International Relations and Development* 4(December 2001).

43. Alfred G. Musrey, *An Arab Common Market* (New York: Praeger, 1969), chaps. 1–4; Roger Owen and Sevket Pamuk, *A History of Middle East Economies in the Twentieth Century* (London: I. B. Tauris, 1998).

44. Brulak, "Problem of Structural Change," 373–376.

45. Ibid., 370–371; John G. Ruggie, "What Makes the World Hang Together? Neo-utilitarianism and the Social Constructivist Challenge," *International Organization* 52(Autumn 1998), 875.

46. Mark W. Zacher, "The Territorial Integrity Norm: International Boundaries and the Use of Force," *International Organization* 55(Spring 2001), 238.

47. Ibid., 242.

48. Ibid., 243–244.

49. Ibid., 245. See also Tanisha Fazal, "The Origins and Implications of the Territorial Sovereignty Norm," paper presented at the annual convention of the American Political Science Association, 2001.

50. Finnemore and Sikkink, "International Norm Dynamics," 891–892. See also Barry Buzan, *From International to World Society?* (Cambridge: Cambridge University Press, 2004), 22.

51. Hendrik Spruyt, *The Sovereign State and Its Competitors* (Princeton: Princeton University Press, 1994), 171–172.

52. Ibid., 176–177; Spruyt, "Institutional Selection in International Relations," 550.

53. Spruyt, *Sovereign State and Its Competitors*, 180. See also Ann Florini, "The Evolution of International Norms," *International Studies Quarterly* 40(September 1996).

54. Stephen Jay Gould, *The Structure of Evolutionary Theory* (Cambridge, Mass.: Harvard University Press, 2001).

55. Joseph M. Grieco, "Anarchy and the Limits of Cooperation," *International Organization* 42(August 1988); Duncan Snidal, "Relative Gains and the Pattern of International Cooperation," *American Political Science Review* 85(September 1991); Robert Powell, "Absolute and Relative Gains in International Relations Theory," *American Political Science Review* 85(December 1991); Randall L. Schweller, "Neorealism's Status Quo Bias: What Security Dilemma?" *Security Studies* 5(Spring 1996); Eric J. Labs, "Beyond Victory: Offensive Realism and the Expansion of War Aims," *Security Studies* 6(Summer 1997); Andrew Kydd, "Sheep in Sheep's Clothing: Why Security Seekers Do Not Fight Each Other," *Security Studies* 7 (Autumn 1997); Jeffrey W. Taliaferro, "Security Seeking under Anarchy: Defensive Realism Revisited," *International Security* 25(Winter 2000–01).

56. Powell, "Absolute and Relative Gains."

57. Stephen Van Evera, *The Causes of War* (Ithaca, N.Y.: Cornell University Press, 1999).

index